THE ORIGINS OF THE COLD WAR
AND CONTEMPORARY EUROPE

Modern Scholarship on European History

Henry A. Turner, Jr.
General Editor

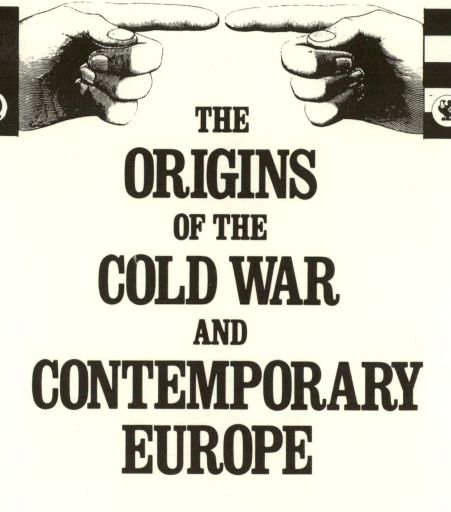

THE
ORIGINS
OF THE
COLD WAR
AND
CONTEMPORARY
EUROPE

EDITED WITH AN INTRODUCTION BY
CHARLES S. MAIER
Modern Scholarship on European History

New Viewpoints
A Division of Franklin Watts
New York | London | 1978

New Viewpoints
A Division of Franklin Watts
730 Fifth Avenue
New York, New York 10019

Library of Congress Cataloging in Publication Data
Main entry under title:

The Origins of the cold war and contemporary
Europe.

(Modern scholarship on European history)
Includes bibliographical references and index.
1. World politics—1945—   —Addresses, essays,
lectures. 2. Europe—Politics and government—
1945—   —Addresses, essays, lectures. 3. Economic assistance, American—Europe—Addresses, essays, lectures. I. Maier, Charles S.
D843.O65   327'.09'044   78–17915
ISBN 0–531–05397–0
ISBN 0–531–05607–4 pbk.

Acknowledgments

The author gratefully acknowledges the following authors and publishers: the Charles Warren Center for Studies in American History at Harvard University and the editors of *Perspectives in American History* for permission to reprint his own article "Revisionism and the Interpretation of Cold War Origins" from *Perspectives in American History*, IV (1970), pp. 313–347; Franz Schurmann and Pantheon Books division of Random House, Inc., for permission to reprint selections from pages 8–17, 46–53, 56–62, 64–68, 91–100, 105–107 of *The Logic of World Power: An Inquiry into the Origins, Currents and Contradictions of World Politics* (New York, 1974); Radomír Luža and Princeton University Press for permission to reprint "Czechoslovakia Between Democracy and Communism," from Luža and Victor S. Mamatey, eds., *A History of the Czechoslovak Republic, 1914–1948* (copyright [c] 1973 by Princeton University Press), pp. 387–415; Daniel Yergin and Houghton Mifflin Company, for permission to reprint chapter 12, "The Margin of Safety," from *Shattered Peace: The Origins of the Cold War and the National Security State* (Boston, 1977), pp. 303–335 with end notes, pp. 472–477; John Gimbel and Stanford University Press and the Board of Trustees of the Leland Stanford Junior University for permission to reproduce chapter 19 (pages 247–266) and pages 267–270, 274–279 of chapter 20 along with the end notes (pp. 325–331) from *The Origins of the Marshall Plan*, copyright (c), 1976; Hadley Arkes and Princeton University Press for permission to reprint chapter 14, "Theory and Coercion in the ECA," from *Bureaucracy, the Marshall Plan, and the National Interest* (copyright [c] 1972 by Princeton University Press), pp. 301–321; and to Lutz Niethammer and the Bund Verlag of Cologne, Germany for permission to reprint the major portion (pp. 313–354) of the essay "Strukturreform und Wachstumspakt," from Heinz Oskar Vetter, ed., *Vom Sozialîstengesetz zur Mitbestimmung. Zum 100. Geburtstag von Hans Böckler* (Cologne, 1975), pp. 303–358.

Contents

vii

Introduction

The selection of essays in this volume has a purpose different from most other Cold War anthologies. I have focused less on the question of responsibility for the Cold War than upon the relationship of the Soviet-American antagonism to national political and social developments after World War II. Thus this collection intentionally omits some articles that were central to historical debate five to ten years ago. At that time scholarship centered on the question of "revisionism," or the reassessment of the respective contributions of the United States and the Soviet Union to the bitter post-World War II military and ideological confrontation. That debate, in my view, has not been neatly resolved, although issues have been narrowed and language has become less stridently polemical. Non-revisionists recognize that imperial as well as idealistic impulses motivated the American conduct of world politics, while recent critics are less accusatory than their predecessors a decade back. But just as important, the question of guilt or innocence has become less preoccupying as scholars have turned toward exploring the effect of the Cold War upon individual societies.

This volume seeks to illuminate the interaction of the Cold War with domestic politics and social structures. The emphasis is suggested by the fact that the anthology forms part of a series on "Modern Scholarship on European History." It also derives from my own scholarly interests, since I am in the midst of research on the reorganization of the European political economy after the Second World War. One aspect of that investigation must be the influence of the Cold War: the impact of the United States and the Soviet Union on countries that had toppled from an earlier preeminence into disarray and exhaustion.

On the other hand, the Cold War was only one of several factors in the formation of contemporary Europe: the reaction to the mass unemployment of the 1930s, the rejection of fascist authoritarianism, the response to decolonization, growing wealth—all have helped create the political society we have today. This collection cannot illuminate all these aspects; it can only begin to reveal the interaction of the superpowers' rivalry and the shaping of contemporary European institutions. Nevertheless, these articles summon the historian of Europe to consider the bipolar conflict that overshadowed his countries of concern. And they call upon the American historian to move outside the usual studies of Washington's diplomacy to reflect on the effects it produced within other societies.

Unfortunately, the few essays chosen here can represent only the beginning of this dual enterprise. The size of the volume alone compels a narrow selection. But there are further difficulties as well. The archival sources that most historians of Europe can utilize are less available for the period after 1945, although they can draw upon the United States diplomatic records now open for research through 1950 and the British cabinet papers, which are sequentially released with a thirty-year delay, such that 1947's records thus opened on January 1, 1978. Many of the essays published on this period are thus based upon private holdings, on the press, official statements, congressional or parliamentary debates, and the like. In some cases, too, potentially valuable chapters from larger books lack a sufficient impact when extracted: they cannot be used alone effectively. Some of the European literature, moreover, goes into a level of detail on episodes whose intensive coverage cannot easily be justified in this collection. Thus many factors have constrained selection, and scholars in the field may miss articles here that they would have preferred to see.

The first two pieces are intended to provide overviews of Cold War issues and the sources of American policy; for without the background of United States choices, European results cannot properly be appreciated. I have led off with a historiographical résumé I wrote in 1970 designed to clarify the status of debate as it then existed. Some of the outstanding works since that date will be cited in the following pages. My own work criticized revisionist scholarship, and while I sought to be fair, readers may naturally dissent. Even as a critic, moreover, one must recognize that in historical writing the question of "fruitfulness" is a different one from that of being right or wrong. For example, the Beard thesis on the origins of the Constitution and the Turner thesis on the closing of the frontier set new questions and opened up new research hypotheses even if they were later modified. So, too, the major critical histories of American policy have forced debate and compelled an inquiry into aspects of our goals and strategies that were previously unquestioned.

The second selection, a patchwork extract from Franz Schurmann's book, *The Logic of World Power,* is more an essay than a monograph. In my judgment Schurmann has written a very suggestive discussion of American objectives, though it is one that is hard to confirm with documentation. But of all the works that try to plumb the relationship between American capitalism and United States foreign policy, his is one of the most subtle and interesting. It makes full allowance for the fact that business interests in the United States have generally fallen into at least two major groups that tend to encourage different foreign-policy orientations. It further stresses the natural connection between high-technology weaponry and the centralization of executive power.

The following selections concern the formation of American policies and their impact upon European societies. The harshest impact of the Cold War fell, of course, on Eastern Europe, and I have chosen for inclusion here an essay on the history of Czechoslovakia from 1945 until the communist take-over in 1948. The author is an experienced historian of international affairs, has a command of East European languages, and offers one of the few treatments in English that concentrates on the internal developments of an East European society from its own point of view. Luža's essay reveals how difficult the maintenance of a compromise course was for the Czech democracy. On the other hand, Daniel Yergin has suggested that, for all the ruthlessness of the Czech communists and the Soviet leadership, grave deficiencies in American diplomacy facilitated the communist take-over. In a chapter of his book—not the one included here—he argues that American policymakers by and large wrote off Czechoslovakia by the fall of 1947. If Yergin's interpretation is correct, then Washington's failure takes on tragic proportions and must be seen as reminiscent of the Anglo-French write-off of Czechoslovakia that had taken place at Munich a decade earlier. For more detail on the countries of Eastern Europe and their fate, the student can turn later to Hugh Seton-Watson's account or to François Fejtö's.[1] And for a radically different perspective, Gabriel Kolko's work remains problematic but an important component of the historical debate. According to Kolko, no real grounds for democratic reconstruction had existed in most countries of Eastern Europe. Prewar elites had generally been compromised by collaboration with the Germans or presented such an artificial and narrow social base in Bulgaria, Rumania, and even Poland, that only communist-sponsored ruling groups could effectively replace them.[2] Such an assessment, in my opinion, overlooks the fact that broad-based peasant parties with social-democratic preferences did get launched

after World War II, and their leadership was purposefully decimated—
exiled, imprisoned, executed—by Soviet-backed communists.

Surveying Eastern Europe, most Cold War historians have felt dismayed enough by the results that they have continually asked whether
American policy contributed to the outcome, either by not contesting
the area more forcefully, or by not ceding influence more gracefully
and thereby allowing the Soviets to feel secure without repressive measures. On this issue the recent argumentation of Lynn Etheridge Davis's
The Cold War Begins: Soviet-American Conflict Over Eastern Europe,
is challenging. Davis, currently serving as a deputy assistant secretary
of defense, has suggested that Washington followed an unfruitfully ambivalent policy toward Eastern Europe. By constant verbal refusal to accept the region's incorporation into a Soviet sphere of interest, Washington envenomed relations with Moscow. American policymakers, in
her critical view, indulged in a rhetorical demand for free elections and
liberal procedures in the area without serious reflection as to how to
press these aims. The United States did not use economic bargaining
concretely nor did Washington effectively encourage institutional bul-
warks for liberal government, and hardly thought out what democratic elections might have guaranteed.[3] This view tends to agree with
the arguments of anti-Soviet "realist" foreign policy advisers at the
time, preeminently George Kennan, who argued that a frank acceptance of spheres of influence would have kept the Soviet-American confrontation from heating up and certainly would have lost us no more
influence in Eastern Europe and sacrificed no more liberty for its in-
habitants than the "Wilsonian" insistence on self-determination. Before
the student accepts this powerful argumentation, however, he or she
should review the memoir of the then ambassador to the Soviet Union,
W. Averell Harriman. In his book, Harriman illuminates the persist-
ing and compelling hold that ideas of self-determination and democracy
exerted; his account suggests that for Americans to have sanctioned a
division of Europe after a war to liberate the continent was hardly
possible. Harriman's chapters on the Polish issue, as seen from his
Moscow vantage in 1944–45, are central narratives of the issue that
lay at the beginning of Cold War hostility.[4]

The evolution of American policy from the 1944–45 disputes over
Poland to the Czech coup and the Berlin Blockade of 1948–49 has
been presented and interpreted many times. While it is always partially misleading to select one moment or two in a chain of events as
the decisive turning point, nonetheless the period from early 1947 to
early 1948 did witness accelerated crises and responses. The Truman
Doctrine announced in March 1947, the communization of Hungary,
the exclusion of the Western communists from the Belgian, French, and

Italian governing coalitions, announcement of the Marshall Plan, decisive steps toward the permanent division of Germany, and the Czech
coup—all contributed to a qualitative escalation of the Cold War. To
convey the progress and flavor of events in that urgent year, I have
chosen Daniel Yergin's chapter on the origins of the Marshall Plan. As
is clear from Yergin, the Marshall Plan and the division of Germany
were inextricably linked. Indeed that is the argument of John Gimbel's
work, which follows Yergin's: namely, that the Marshall Plan represented a strategy for reviving the crippled German economy—as demanded by the American War Department and our Occupation authorities—without antagonizing would-be French allies. By fusing
German recovery funds into a European-wide scheme, Gimbel argues,
the incompatible objectives could be resolved on a higher level. Gimbel's work deserves attention, and it follows his revealing book on the
effects of the American occupation in Marburg and his more inclusive
*Politics and the Military: The American Occupation of Germany,
1945-1949.*[6] This thesis may be overstressed, however. A European-
wide concept of European aid arose from broader considerations than
just those of finessing French objections to aiding German recovery. It
accompanied a new global outlook toward the contest with the Soviet
Union. What in 1945 and 1946 could still appear as local trouble spots
in Eastern Europe or the Middle East now loomed as mere probes on
the part of a persistently expansionist and ideologically hostile power.
Even when George Kennan, writing as Mr. X, counseled that Soviet
aggressiveness was probably limited to contiguous regions, Americans read not what he said about the limits of Russian aims, but
about their continuity and pervasiveness.[7] Consequently, by 1947
Washington policymakers and the community of those concerned about
America's role, such as the leadership that periodically assembled at the
Council on Foreign Relations in New York, sought a unified coordination of foreign assistance. The Truman Doctrine of March 1947 already
signaled the United States determination to judge guerrilla movements
in peripheral noncommunist regimes as part of a unitary threat of subversion. By June, the Marshall Plan's stress on recovery as a problem
of the European core region responded to the forebodings of a vast
confrontation of blocs. Whether the United States had to enter a bitter
ideological conflict with the Soviets over Europe may remain debatable;
but given the premises of the conflict, the Marshall Plan represented a
creative policy vision. First of all, it finally specified a consistent
American need to help the reconstruction of European capital and
mixed economies if liberal democracy were to prove viable; second, it
charted a continental strategy that recognized the Atlantic political
economy as a coherent arena of struggle.

Unfortunately, scholarship on the workings of the Marshall Plan remains sparse. Except for explanatory material generated at the time of the European Recovery Program itself, there is little on how the program was run. Hadley Arkes's book, *Bureaucracy, the Marshall Plan, and the National Interest,* is an exception. Although it is aimed at the concerns of political scientists, I have included in this collection a useful chapter from his book on the impact of the Marshall Plan in Europe.

The announcement of the Truman Doctrine and the carrying through of the Marshall Plan from early 1947 to mid 1948 marked a year and a half of decisive political realignment in the West European nations. During the key months from the winter crisis of 1947 through the Berlin Blockade, European political leaders interpreted the American initiative as a clear signal to establish noncommunist coalitions. On the other side, communist leaders also made the Marshall Plan the touchstone of their political decisions. Once the Czechoslovak government reversed its plans under Soviet pressure to participate in the initial conference of European countries working out a response to the American aid offer, Western communists embarked upon a bitter opposition to the Marshall Plan as an instrument of United States hegemony. Their reaction proved almost self-fulfilling in that it confirmed the end of the united postwar labor movements and accelerated the unification of the Western zones of Germany. Doubtless a whole set of issues separated communists from social democrats: memories of old post-World War I schisms, fear on the part of social democrats that communist domination of the union federations would mean loss of any autonomy, and apprehension on the part of the communists that realization of the Marshall Plan would subordinate Western societies to an American political vision. Thus the American initiative provided a year-long theme for ideological conflict, punctuated by great strikes in Italy and France from the autumn of 1947 through the summer of 1948 that consummated the division of the labor movement. For a discussion of this schism I have included here a translation of a synthetic essay by the German scholar Lutz Niethammer that examines the international breakdown of the post-1944 effort at united trade unions.

The political developments during the same years are as crucial as those in the union movement, but suitable scholarly essays are difficult to find. Increasingly the Italians are publishing significant material about the transition from the Resistance coalition comprising Communists, Socialists, Liberals, and Christian Democrats to a noncommunist Christian Democratic-dominated phalanx. Likewise, they have contributed close studies of labor-union development, but the detail involved makes selection difficult.[8] Scholarship on postwar French history is sparse and is composed predominantly of quasi-journalistic accounts, such as those by Alexander Werth, Jacques Fauvet, and Georgette Elgey, although scholarly treatments of special subjects exist.[9] I have not attempted to survey the material that might illuminate the trends in the smaller countries of Europe.

In summary, two tasks confront the historical investigator of this period. The first is simply to establish what happened, to reconstruct a narrative on the basis of documentation that, while huge, is still very incomplete. Second, the historian must try to discern in the welter of recent events relationships that future historians will see more easily—although always, of course, according to their own generation's preoccupations.

The more recent the period, the more difficult is this second task. I do not think it unfair to judge that by and large Cold War history has so far been disappointing in this regard. Too often it has become ensnared in polemics and fixed upon blame. In a search for the liveliness and excitement of journalism, some authors have tended to muster picturesque quotations—e.g., Truman's telling off Molotov—but have sometimes neglected to recreate the context of documents or the social and institutional milieu in which national policy emerged by fits and starts. The researchers who have ferreted out new documentation have often failed to achieve that sense of sovereign synthesis that good history attains, while those writers who like to convey the impression of impartially mastering the era often decline to confront uncomfortable evidence.

Yet only insofar as historians both plunge into the documents and derive underlying configurations can they go beyond just a more inclusive reportage. Only in the search for at least partial coherence can they test the given patterns that they will otherwise impose willy-nilly merely because they have grown up on the ideological concepts suggested by Cold War conflict. The historian's task involves not merely fighting the controversies of the day or even of the decade. It demands making contemporary history an object of perspective and reflection to at least the same order of relative dispassion that would be sought in judging earlier epochs. For the era of the Cold War, this scientific task remains to be accomplished. The essays here are meant as an invitation to students to participate in that intellectual enterprise.

Notes

1. Hugh Seton-Watson, *The East European Revolution,* 3rd ed. (New York: Praeger, 1956); François Fejtö, *Histoire des démocraties populaires,* 2 vols. (Paris: Editions du Seuil, 1952, 1969).
2. Gabriel Kolko, *The Politics of War: The World and United States*

Foreign Policy, 1943–1945 (New York: Random House, 1968). See also Gabriel and Joyce Kolko, *The Limits of Power: The World and United States Foreign Policy, 1945–54* (New York: Harper & Row, 1972).

3. Lynn Etheridge Davis, *The Cold War Begins: Soviet-American Conflict over Eastern Europe* (Princeton, N.J.: Princeton University Press, 1974).

4. W. Averell Harriman and Elie Abel, *Special Envoy to Churchill and Stalin, 1941–1946* (New York: Random House, 1975), especially chapters 14–15. See also Ito Takayuki, "The Genesis of the Cold War: Confrontation over Poland, 1941–44," which draws upon Polish and Russian sources, in Yonusuke Nagai and Akira Iriye, eds., *The Origins of the Cold War in Asia* (New York: Columbia University Press and University of Tokyo Press, 1977), pp. 147–202.

5. Daniel Yergin, *Shattered Peace: The Origins of the Cold War and the National Security State* (Boston: Houghton Mifflin, 1977), pp. 346–350.

6. John N. Gimbel, *The Origins of the Marshall Plan* (Stanford: Stanford University Press, 1976); also *The American Occupation of Germany: Politics and the Military, 1945–1949* (Stanford: Stanford University Press, 1968); also, *A German Community under American Occupation: Marburg, 1945–52* (Stanford: Stanford University Press, 1961).

7. George F. Kennan, "The Sources of Soviet Conduct," *Foreign Affairs* (July 1947). The student should also read Kennan's *Memoirs 1925–50* and *Memoirs 1950–63* (Boston: Little, Brown & Co., 1969, 1972) to get an insight into Kennan's mode of analysis: subtle, minor-key, premised on long-term national psychological characteristics, profoundly repelled by Russia even when fascinated, constantly disillusioned about the possibilities for conducting diplomacy in a democracy with a strong legislative scrutiny over foreign affairs.

8. For English-language surveys, see H. Stuart Hughes, *The United States and Italy* (Cambridge, Mass.: Harvard University Press, 1965); Norman Kogan, *Italy and the Allies* (Cambridge, Mass.: Harvard University Press, 1962); and Giuseppe Mammarella, *Italy After Fascism: A Political History 1943–1965,* Elizabeth and Victor Velen, eds. (Notre Dame, Ind.: University of Notre Dame Press, 1966). In Italian, see on the political scene, Enzo Piscitelli, *Da Parri a De Gasperi, Storia del dopoguerra 1945/1948* (Milan: Feltrinelli, 1975); A. Gambino, *Storia del dopoguerra della Liberazione al potere DC* (Bari: Laterza, 1975); and for the social struggles, Fabio Levi, Paride Rugafiori, Salvatore Vento, *Il triangolo industriale tra ricostruzione e lotta di classe 1945/48* (Milan: Feltrinelli, 1974).

9. See Alexander Werth, *France, 1940–1955* (London: R. Hale, 1956); Georgette Elgey, *La république des illusions* (Paris: A. Fayard, 1965); also Jacques Fauvet, *Histoire de la IVe République* (Paris: A. Fayard, 1960). For an English-language survey, consult Phillip Williams, *Politics in Post-War France* (London: Longmans Green, 1954). For excellent bibliographical suggestions and a closely argued account of events in 1947, see Wilfried Loth, "Das Ausscheiden der französischen Kommunisten aus der Regierung 1947," *Vierteljahrshefte für die Zeitgeschichte,* vol. 26, nr. 1 (January 1978), pp. 9–65.

THE ORIGINS OF THE COLD WAR AND CONTEMPORARY EUROPE

1

Charles S. Maier

Revisionism and the Interpretation of Cold War Origins

This essay should serve to orient the reader in the "revisionist" controversy concerning the origins of the Cold War. It surveys most of the major literature up to 1970. Dissertations and books have continued in full spate during the present decade. In addition to those cited in the notes to the Introduction, the reader might also turn to the following: John Lewis Gaddis, The United States and the Origins of the Cold War *(New York: Columbia University Press, 1972)—a counter-revisionist statement that illuminates the domestic pressures in the making of United States foreign policy; Diane Shaver Clemens,* Yalta *(New York: Oxford University Press, 1970); Adam B. Ulam,* The Rivals *(New York: Viking, 1971); and the revised version of Walter LaFeber,* America, Russia and the Cold War, *3rd ed. (New York: John Wiley and Sons, 1976). The essays in the Nagai–Iriye volume,* The Origins of the Cold War in Asia *(full citation in Note 4 of the editor's introduction) are also very useful. For biographical treatments see Alonzo L. Hamby,* Beyond The New Deal: Harry S. Truman and American Liberalism *(New York: Columbia University Press, 1973)—a somewhat defensive defense; and two biographies of a major "cold warrior":* Gaddis Smith, Dean Acheson. The American Secretaries of State and their Diplomacy, *vol. 16. Robert H. Ferrell, ed. (New York: Cooper Square Publishers, 1972), and David S. McLellan,* Dean Acheson: The State Department Years *(New York: Dodd, Mead & Company, 1976). For a revisionist collective biography see Lloyd C. Gardner,* Architects of Illusion *(Chicago: Quadrangle, 1972). Townsend Hoopes'* The Devil and John Foster Dulles *(Boston: Atlantic-Little, Brown, 1973) concentrates on the 1950s, but is an exciting portrait of an ardent Cold War stalwart. Needless to say, these titles represent just a fragment of the continuing literature.*

In including my own essay in this collection, I have asked myself would I have written it differently today? I do not really think so. On the other hand, I might emphasize the transition from Roosevelt to Truman more strongly. While Soviet-American antagonism was emerging in any case, the tone of diplomacy matters almost as much as the substance; and through inexperience and distrust that tone on our side became suddenly harsher and cruder. It may seem curious to assert that Truman's bluntness should really influence the reaction of a dictator capable of murdering entire cohorts of his colleagues. Yet precisely because Stalin was so sensitive to the real and imagined fluctuations in his political environment, the Truman–Byrnes diplomacy may have contributed to defensiveness, insecurity and churlishness. Whether it basically affected the outcome in those states where Soviet power was decisive, however, still seems to me an open question. Second, the issue of German reparations appears more important to me now—not because ultimately the Soviets were morally entitled to a given quota of German industrial equipment beyond what they uprooted immediately as war booty or extracted thereafter, but because the reparation issue lay at the root of all the German problems and elevated what was originally an area of cooperation into the most refractory conflict of all. Finally, I would now stress the importance of the events from early 1947 through spring of 1948, not for the "origins" of the Cold War, which lay in the East European disputes of 1944–46, but for the decisive stages in the outcome of the Cold War and the division of Europe.

Few historical reappraisals have achieved such sudden popularity as the current revisionist critique of American foreign policy and the origins of the Cold War. Much of this impact is clearly due to Vietnam. Although the work of revision began before the United States became deeply involved in that country, the war has eroded so many national self-conceptions that many assumptions behind traditional Cold War history have been cast into doubt. For twenty years the Soviet-American conflict was attributed to Stalin's effort to expand Soviet control through revolutionary subversion,[1] or, as in a more recent formulation, to "the logic of his position as the ruler of a totalitarian society and as the supreme head of a movement that seeks security through constant expansion." [2] Revisionist assailants of this view have now found readers receptive to the contrary idea that the United States must bear the blame for the Cold War. The preoccupation with America's historical guilt distinguishes the new authors not only from anti-communist historians but from earlier writers who felt the question of blame was inappropriate. William McNeill, for example, in an outstanding account written at the height of the Cold War, stressed a nearly inevitable falling-out among allies who had never been united save to fight a common enemy.[3] This viewpoint has been preserved in some recent accounts; but since Denna Fleming's massive Cold War history of 1961, the revisionists have gone on to indict the United States for long-term antipathy to communism, insensitivity to legitimate Soviet security needs, and generally belligerent behavior after World War II.[4]

The revisionist version of Cold War history includes three major elements: an interpretation of Eastern European developments; an allegation of anti-Soviet motives in the Americans' use of the atomic bomb; and a general Marxian critique of the alleged American search for a world capitalist hegemony. Since these three elements comprise a detailed reassessment of the role of the United States in world politics they deserve to be discussed and evaluated in turn; but in the end one must consider the more fundamental question of the conceptual bases of revisionist history.

The revisionists are divided among themselves about the turning points and the causes of American aggressiveness, but all agree that the traditional description of the crucial events in Eastern Europe must be radically altered. The old version of the roots of the Cold War charged Soviet Russia with progressively tightening totalitarian control from mid-1944. In effect the earlier historians only confirmed the diagnosis of Ambassador Averell Harriman in Moscow, whose cables between late 1943 and early 1945 changed from emphasizing the needs of a functioning wartime alliance to stressing the difficulties of prolonging cooperation in the face of Soviet ambitions.[5] In this evolution of views, the Russian refusal to facilitate Anglo-American supply flights to the Warsaw uprising of August 1944 and Moscow's backing for its own Polish government later in that year provoked major western disillusionment. It was agreed after 1945 that the germs of the Cold War lay in Stalin's intransigence on the Polish issue.

In contrast to this interpretation, the revisionists charge that the United States forced Stalin into his stubborn Polish policy by backing the excessive aspirations of the exile Polish government in London. Revisionist accounts emphasize how antagonistic the State Department's refusal to sanction any territorial changes during the war must have appeared in Moscow. They point out that the territory that the Soviets had annexed in 1939, and which the Poles were contesting, had restored the 1919 Curzon line of mediation and merely reversed Poland's own acquisitions by war in 1920–1921. At the Teheran Conference in December 1943, Churchill and Roosevelt had loosely consented to Poland's borders being shifted westward. Even Harriman backed the British in counseling the London Poles to accept the terms the Soviets were offering in October 1944.[6] Only when the Russians produced their own so-called Lublin Committee and thereafter Polish government—allegedly out of frustration and bitterness at the unyielding stance of the London Poles—did the focus switch from the question of territory to that of regimes.[7] At the Yalta conference, Stalin agreed to add some Western Poles to the communist-based government and to move toward free elections; and if the United States had continued to accept the Yalta provisions in a generous spirit, the revisionists maintain, the earlier disputes might have been overcome. Gar Alperovitz argues in detail that after Yalta Roosevelt sought to persuade Churchill to move toward the Soviet position on the key question of who would determine which Western Polish leaders might be invited to join the expanded Warsaw government. But Roosevelt's successors, notably President Truman and Secretary of State James Byrnes, put up a harsh fight to reverse this supposed acquiescence in the creation of a basically communist-dominated government.[8]

This American attitude toward Polish issues, the revisionists claim, was typical of a wide range of Eastern European questions where the United States appeared to be set upon frustrating Russia's international security. From the summer of 1945 Truman and Byrnes, it is charged, sought to reverse the pro-Soviet governments in Rumania and Bulgaria by blustering with atomic weapons.[9] The American opposition to Soviet demands for territorial security and friendly neighboring states allegedly forced the Russians away from their minimal aims of 1943–1945, which envisaged United Front coalition regimes, to the ruthless communization they imposed by 1947–1948. Had the United States not demanded total openness to Western influence, the revisionists imply, Poland, Bulgaria, and Rumania might have survived as Hungary and Czechoslovakia did until 1947–1948 and Finland thereafter. But in fact, they argue, the parties and social groups that Washington desired to entrench could only intensify Stalin's mistrust. In revisionist eyes these groups were either unworthy or unviable: unworthy because they regrouped pre-war reactionary elements who had often been pro-German, unviable because even when democratic they were doomed to fall between the more intransigent right and the Russian-backed left.[10]

Even more fundamental from the revisionist point of view, there was no legitimacy for any American concern with affairs in that distant region. However ugly the results in Eastern Europe, they should not really have worried Washington. Russia should have been willingly accorded unchallenged primacy because of her massive wartime sacrifices, her need for territorial security, and the long history of the area's reactionary politics and bitter anti-bolshevism. Only when Moscow's deserved primacy was contested did Stalin embark upon a search for exclusive control.[11]

These revisionist assessments of the United States's political choices in Eastern Europe are valid in some respects, simplistic in others. It is true that American policymakers sought to establish agrarian democracies and based their hopes upon peasant proprietors and populist-like parties whose adherents had oscillated between left and right before the war. As revisionist accounts suggest, these occupied a precarious middle ground in Polish politics and an even narrower one in the former Axis satellites, Rumania and Bulgaria, where the Russians may have felt entitled to complete hegemony. Churchill for one felt that his "percentages" agreement of October 1944 had sanctioned Soviet control over these countries as a *quid pro quo* for the Russians' acceptance of British dominance in Greece. And whatever the effective status of that arrangement, Stalin might well have considered his domination of Rumania no more than the counterpart of Allied exclusion of the Soviets from any effective voice in Italy.[12]

But despite revisionist implications to the contrary, the major offense of the middle- and pro-Western groups in Soviet eyes was not really their collusion with rightists. The Russians themselves, after all, supported the far more fascist-tainted Marshall Badoglio as Italian premier. The major crime of the pro-Western elements seems really to have been the desire to stay independent of Soviet influence in a situation of Soviet-American polarization that made independence seem enmity. Perhaps the pro-Westerners acted imprudently by looking to Washington: Benes won three years of Czech democracy by collaboration with Moscow—but one might argue from his example that either the collaboration prolonged the Czech respite or that it helped contribute to the final undermining of Prague's independence. In any case the outcome throughout the area was communist dictatorship. Between 1945 and 1947 the peasant party and social democratic leaders were harassed in their assemblies and organizations, tried for treason by communist interior ministries, driven abroad or into silence, and finally, as with the case of Nikola Petkov, the Bulgarian agrarian party leader, executed.[13]

This bleak result naturally undercut those who advocated voluntarily relinquishing United States influence in the area. Opposing the official American rejection of spheres of influence, Henry Wallace on one side, and Henry Stimson and George Kennan on the other, counseled restraint and acceptance of the new status quo;[14] but few contemporary advocates could wholeheartedly celebrate a policy of spheres of influence. It was justified from expedience and as a second-best alternative. As a former advocate recalls, it had always to be advanced as a melancholy necessity, especially as the men for whom Western liberals felt most sympathy were liquidated.[15] To follow a policy of abnegation might indeed have allowed more openness in Eastern Europe; on the other hand, the Stalinist tendencies toward repression might well have followed their own Moscow-determined momentum.

If as a group the revisionists condemn the American role in Eastern Europe, they diverge beyond that point of criticism. One major area of debate among them concerns the use of the atomic bomb, which, while it must be weighed as an important issue in its own right, also signals a basic methodological division. Although the revisionist writing that often seems most hostile to received opinion is that of Gar Alperovitz, he is not the most radical of the dissenting historians. His writings involve a less thoroughgoing critique of United States institutions than the contributions of either William Appleman Williams or Gabriel Kolko. What has elevated Alperovitz to the role of the revisionist *enfant terrible* is his thesis that the United States used nuclear weapons against the Japanese largely to overawe the Soviets. Still, his version of events hinges less on structural elements in American life than on the contingent roles of personality and technological opportunity.

There are two aspects of Alperovitz's thesis: first, that before Hiroshima, expectation of the bomb's availability caused decisive tactical changes in American diplomacy; second, that the weapon was used wantonly when it became available, in part to limit Soviet penetration into the Far East, and more generally because only a combat demonstration would create a sufficient impression to prevent absolute Soviet control over Eastern Europe. Only the desire to have the atomic bomb in hand, Alperovitz argues, led Truman to reverse his harsh diplomatic approach of late April 1945, to dispatch Harry Hopkins to Moscow, and to delay the Potsdam conference despite Churchill's misgivings.[16]

More disturbing than this charge is Alperovitz's subsequent argument that Americans did not merely wish to possess the bomb but actually used it to enhance the country's position vis-à-vis the Soviets. Alperovitz repeats the charge that by the spring of 1945 most Washington officials believed neither the bomb nor an invasion was necessary to end the war. Either continued blockade or a Russian declaration of war could achieve victory. The bomb, however, would obviate the need for Soviet participation in the Pacific war, and, allegedly, the United States wanted desperately to keep Russia out. Along with hastening the technical preparations for Hiroshima, the United States supposedly had the Chinese Nationalists prolong their negotiations with Moscow so that the Sino-Soviet treaty would remain a stumbling block to Stalin's entry.[17]

Interestingly enough, the historiographical factions in this debate have crossed the usual lines. Kolko offers the most cogent response to Alperovitz and the most plausible reconstruction of Potsdam. On the other hand, Herbert Feis—the major traditionalist historian of wartime diplomacy—has so tempered his conclusions that despite himself he grudgingly gives the Alperovitz view considerable credence.[18] Alperovitz has indeed documented a reversal in May 1945 of some initial efforts at confrontation and then a renewed American toughness after Potsdam. But whether calculations about the bomb were decisive remains unproven. The evidence adduced must remain circumstantial: the increased hostility to Russia that was thrust upon the new President; Stimson's and Byrnes' awareness that possession of nuclear weapons might bestow significant diplomatic leverage; and the pushing back of a Big Three parley. In light of this conjunction of events a calculated strategy of delay, such as Alperovitz develops, does remain a possible component of Truman's motivation. But the initial months of the new administration formed a period of contradictory needs and approaches. For a while Truman may have been thinking in terms of disengaging from the disquieting Soviet repression in Bulgaria and Rumania by withdrawing from the Allied Control Commission rather than attempting to reverse the course of events by exerting pressure within it.[19] The Hopkins mission was well suited to many purposes: perhaps an effort to appease Stalin until nuclear weapons were at hand, but more immediately an attempt to secure agreements in their own right and to halt further deterioration of relations as a worthy goal in itself. For Truman, as even Alperovitz realizes, the Hopkins trip was probably viewed not as a reversal of his earlier harsh language to Molotov on April 23, but as a complementary démarche, another approach to a dramatic unjamming of issues.[20]

What also makes the Alperovitz view so difficult to evaluate is the fact, as the author himself admits, that the debate has been largely a retrospective one. Actors at the time hardly saw the significance of the alternatives as later historians have. The place that the idea of using the bomb might have been thrashed out was in the so-called Interim Committee dominated by Stimson and Byrnes, both of whom were committed to dropping the weapon. In this forum it was easy to dismiss any alternative to the incineration of a real city as beset with one fatal obstacle or another. And beyond the Interim Committee, except for a group of scientific dissenters at Chicago who felt they had been turned into sorcerers' apprentices, there was no fundamental challenge to using the weapon. Moreover, if the bomb represented a threshold in terms of weapons technology, it no longer represented one in terms of casualties: the Tokyo incendiary raids in March of 1945 produced about 84,000 deaths; Dresden, between 60,000 and 130,000; Hiroshima, about 70,000. The significant ethical question was that of area versus precision bombing, and the allies had long since steeled their conscience on that issue. If the Navy and Air Force, moreover, were confident that they could starve the Japanese into submission, the Joint Chiefs never gave their collective imprimatur to such a view because the Army would not endorse it. Many thought the collapse of Japan was likely; official plans were drawn up to deal with a sudden surrender; but no one in authority felt he could assume official responsibility for advocating restraint so long as some prolonged Japanese resistance was remotely possible. If Byrnes, Harriman, and Admiral Leahy would have preferred to complete the Pacific war without obligations to Moscow, Truman still felt it his duty to cling to the contingency plans of the Joint Chiefs of Staff and seek Soviet help at Potsdam. Even at Potsdam when Japanese capitulation seemed near, a host of factors militated against reappraisal: the ambivalence of the Tokyo response to the Potsdam ultimatum (itself only the vaguest of warnings); concern that die-hard Japanese militarists would seek to "protect" their monarch against those who counseled surrender; the debate in Washington over retention of the Emperor, which delayed a surrender formula both sides might accept; the belief that the nation responsible for the Pearl Harbor attack could be requited from the air hundreds of times over without any injustice; and no doubt the vested interests in making the bomb contribute to the war effort.[21] If in addition to these pressures Byrnes also entertained an ulterior anti-Soviet motive, it probably represented a marginal, additional payoff of a policy long established on other grounds.

Alperovitz seems to feel it wrong that the atomic bomb became a major factor in American policy calculations. Certainly, however, it was natural to give deep consideration to the new weapon's diplomatic implications. And despite Alperovitz's linkage, there is insufficient evidence that possession of nuclear weapons was decisive in motivating a hard line on Bulgaria and Rumania in the latter half of 1945. This approach followed naturally from the administration's view of Eastern European developments since Yalta and would have been pursued without an atomic monopoly. It is questionable, too, whether the United States could have utilized a veiled atomic threat except in regard to the distant future, for Washington was not prepared to threaten the use of nuclear weapons over Russian targets in 1945.[22] Despite the revisionist view that the United States enjoyed a preponderance of power and therefore must be charged with the greater responsibility in the generation of the Cold War, the Soviet Union still exerted effective control over the area that was central to the dispute. This is not to deny that outside its borders the United States seemed to be flaunting its nuclear capacity. Harriman reported from Moscow in November that the Soviets felt America was trying to intimidate them with the atomic bomb, while to observers in Washington Truman and Byrnes often seemed bolstered by an inner assurance of American invincibility.[23]

Indeed it may have appeared by late 1945 and early 1946 as if the United States were wrapping iron fist in iron glove; but even had there been a far more sophisticated and reserved approach, the simple fact of one-sided possession of the bomb was bound to evoke mistrust. There was no way for its influence to be exorcized from international relations.

Alperovitz's charges are, of course, profoundly disquieting. But at least he suggests that things might have been different. Had Roosevelt lived he might have smoothed out differences with Moscow. Had Stimson been heeded, the United States might have bargained by offering to share atomic secrets and not by seeking, as it is alleged to have done, to intimidate with the weapon itself. Gabriel Kolko, in contrast, can dismiss Alperovitz's arguments about atomic diplomacy because they are unnecessary for what he considers the more important indictment, namely, that the United States, in order to serve its economic needs and ambitions, opposed any threat to its world-wide military and political power.

This view produces a more radical interpretation of both American foreign relations and the country's internal history. William Appleman Williams, for instance, argues that the long-term American quest for universal market and investment arenas, even into Eastern Europe, naturally collided with quite moderate Soviet wartime aspirations and thereby helped the Kremlin's own hardliners and ideologues to prevail.[24] For both Williams and Kolko, moreover, a critique of United States foreign policy forms only part of a wider reassessment of American liberal institutions. The anti-communist effort is depicted as the natural product of an industrial society in which even major reform efforts have been intended only to rationalize corporate capitalism.[25]

The more the revisionists stress the continuity of American capitalist goals and de-emphasize the importance of the Roosevelt-Truman transition, the more they tend to condemn all of America's earlier policies as contributing to the Cold War. The revisionists in general have stressed the direct pre-1945 clashes with the Soviets. They emphasize the significance of the Allies' delay in opening a Second Front in

Europe; [26] and while anti-Soviet historians duly cite Russia's non-aggression pact with Germany, the revisionists usually argue that the Soviets were forced into this arrangement by the Western powers' appeasement policies and their exclusion of Moscow from any common defense plans.[27] Finally, revisionists like Fleming recall the United States' original hostility to bolshevism and the interventions of 1918–1920.[28] In short, all revisionists are mindful of the Western treatment of the Soviets as a pariah regime.

The more radical revisionists, however, go on to depict all of twentieth-century foreign policy as woven into a large counter-revolutionary fabric of which the Cold War itself is only one portion. Their logic links a hesitant and ineffective anti-Nazi foreign policy with a zealous anti-communism and thus finds that the issues of the 1930's adumbrate Cold War attitudes. Similarly, revisionists who discuss pre-war diplomacy have attacked the usual image of American isolationism by stressing the country's persistent economic stakes abroad. All this vaguely serves to hint that the lateness of United States enlistment against Nazism is no longer explainable in terms of deep internal divisions about involvement in European quarrels: the United States responded only as it perceived threats to foreign economic interests.[29] Receding even further, the revisionists view Woodrow Wilson as a major architect of liberal but counter-revolutionary interventionism.[30] And even before Wilson the roots of the Cold War can be discerned, they feel, in the economic lobbying that backed the Open Door policy and the capitalist expansion of the late nineteenth century.[31] Finally, under the stresses of a market economy, even the otherwise virtuous farmers felt it necessary to seek world markets and back imperialist expansionism. The private economy, for Williams and others, taints with acquisitiveness the Jeffersonian Eden that America might have been.[32]

There is a further aspect of this radical revisionism. Since it concentrates on American expansionism in general, its focus shifts from the Soviet-American conflict to the alleged American imperialist drive against all forces of radicalism, or what Kolko loosely calls the New Order. Not an insouciant blundering, and not the arrogance of power, but only capitalist megalomania suffices to explain American efforts to prop up an international Old Order of discredited and outworn parties and elites. Within this perspective, Kolko's explanation of the events of 1943–1945 becomes most clear. He offers three major areas of evidence: United States policy in respect to its future enemy, that is, the effort to reduce Russia to dependency; United States policy against its own ally, that is, the insistence on an economic multilateralism designed to reduce Great Britain to dependency; and United States policy in respect to the "Third World" and the Resistance, the effort to smash all truly independent challenges to American hegemony.

Under Kolko's scrutiny the policies once adjudged to be among the most enlightened emerge as the most imperialistic. Where, for example, previous critics attacked the abandonment of Morgenthau's intended ten-billion-dollar loan to Russia, Kolko sees the proposal itself as devious. Coupled with the destruction of German industry, the contemplated loan was allegedly designed to prevent Russia from refurbishing her industrial base from German factories and thus to force her into a dependency on United States capital for which she could return raw materials. Ironically enough, the plans of Harry Dexter White—abused as a communist in the 1950's—represented a massive effort to place the USSR in a state of semi-colonial subservience.[33]

American aid to England emanates from analogous motives, according to Kolko and Lloyd Gardner who have concentrated most closely on this issue. Kolko asserts that American policy aimed at keeping Britain in a viable second-rank position: rescuing her from utter collapse for reasons of world economic stability yet profiting from her distress. State Department officials, congressmen, and businessmen supporting assistance to Britain intended to penetrate the sterling bloc and the Commonwealth markets protected by tariffs since the 1930's. The celebrated Article Seven of the Mutual Aid Agreement of February 1942, the revisionists emphasize, demanded that Britain consider reduction of Commonwealth trade barriers in return for Lend-Lease, a stipulation repeated with each renewal of Lend-Lease. Finally, all the projects for post-war financial credits and arrangements, as they took form at Bretton Woods and in the 3.75-billion dollar loan negotiated in December 1945, envisaged a sterling-dollar convertibility that would also open the Commonwealth to American goods and severely test the pound.[34]

As the revisionists see it, the interest in convertibility and multilateralism represented the answer of post-Depression America to the chronic domestic under-consumption of a capitalist economy. In the final analysis American efforts amounted to a subtle neo-colonialism. While classical economic theorists helped to justify the international division of labor by comparative-advantage doctrine no matter how unequal the partners, the revisionists evidently feel that the costs to the less powerful or industrial nation outweigh the benefits. They emphasize that specialization can act to perpetuate relations of dependency and they view American policy as dedicated throughout the twentieth century to fostering the bonds of economic subordination.[35]

In this interpretative framework the Cold War, in its European aspects, arose because Soviet Russia refused to allow herself or Eastern Europe to be integrated into the American neo-colonial network.

This analysis is often illuminating but sometimes exaggerated and tendentious. One can certainly differentiate between the values of the arguments about the Soviet Union and Britain. To see de-bolshevizing Russia as Morgenthau's underlying concern in 1944–1945 is simply to ignore the central quest of his public life, which was to deny Germany any future as a world industrial power. In the policy alternatives shaping up in Washington, a bitterly anti-German policy could, moreover, only mean a desire to collaborate with the Soviet Union and not to dominate it. And by late 1944 Morgenthau viewed those opposing his projects as themselves motivated primarily by anti-communism. The major purpose of the loan to Russia was, in fact, to make it easier for the Soviets to accede to the dismantling of German industry. The economic destruction of the Reich was not designed to make the Russians dependent upon America: if the Soviets would receive no reparation from future German exports they would get many factories that would have produced the exports.[36]

Revisionist analysis of American economic relations with Great Britain is more convincing. Kolko's discussion of Anglo-American financial relations in the framework of overall United States goals probably forms the most innovative and substantive contribution of his study. Americans did push against British trade barriers and mentally relegated the country to a secondary role in a Western economic system. The pressure upon the beleaguered Ally could be harsh: "What do you want me to do," Churchill asked about Lend-Lease renewal at Quebec in the fall of 1944, "stand up and beg like Fala?"[37] Nevertheless, revisionist judgments tend to neglect the powerful ties of sentiment that motivated Roosevelt's policy, and they minimize the critical fact that British financial commitments were over-extended in terms of her own resources. Moreover, the focus by the revisionists on the free-trade rapacity of an Eastern banking establishment is inappropriate. Insofar as banking representatives formed a coherent interest it was often the friendliest to London's needs. Pressures came as much from a conservative Congress as from Wall Street.[38]

Still, as the revisionists stress, economic self-interest was woven into American policy even when it was most generous. The hard fact is that until they both felt mortally threatened by Soviet power London and Washington had conflicting economic interests. There was a desire for currency convertibility on the part of the United States Treasury which Britain naturally felt was potentially disastrous. For Britain to meet the American wishes for sterling convertibility at a moment when she had liquidated four billion pounds of overseas assets in order to fight the war meant subjecting her economy to great deflationary pressure. During the war Keynes had already asked priority for full employment and strong domestic demands over considerations of exports and stable exchanges. After the war the Labour government even more fervently stressed easy money to banish the specter of unemployment. They did not want planning, investment, and new social-service transfers to be impeded by worries about sterling outflow. The American enthusiasm for currency convertibility threatened havoc to all the delicate equilibriums in London; and it was only dire necessity that led the English to pledge an effort at convertibility as a condition for the massive credits the United States extended in late 1945. When finally the dissenting historians reach the story of 1947–1950, they will no doubt be able to depict in their terms a further effort at world economic supremacy. For similar Treasury pressures for convertibility were to continue into the America-sponsored negotiations for intra-European payments agreements in 1949 and the European Payments Union of 1950. Once again, Britain feared a flanking attack on the sterling area, and once again many of her Labour leaders worried about a deflationary thrust against schemes of economic planning.[39]

One can agree that American objectives clashed with British economic policy without accepting the larger revisionist accusation of a pervasive neo-colonialism. As of 1945, American thinking on foreign trade and investment (as well as more general questions of colonialism) was often marked by reformist ideas. American spokesmen such as Eric Johnston of the Chamber of Commerce or Donald Nelson of the War Production Board certainly emphasized the need for sustained American exports as a safeguard against renewed depression,[40] but a sense of the need for exports assumed that countries rich and industrialized enough to offer extensive markets were more helpful to the United States than economies kept in perpetual underdevelopment or one-sided dependency.[41]

Underlying much revisionist criticism of United States foreign economic relations is a desire for socialist self-sufficiency: a virtuous autarchy inflicts the least damage on the rest of the world. Indeed, in theory, there might have been one alternative for the American economy that did not require either unemployment or international trade: a great program of domestic investment to remedy urban blight, improve transportation, build new TVA's—in short an expansion of the New Deal into a semi-socialized economy. But after the domestic emphasis upon small business and competition in the "Second New Deal," and after the massive infusion of business leaders into the government to run the war economy, such a public-sector commitment was not likely.[42] In the absence of such a program the stress on international trade was probably the most reasonable United States response. Finally, one must note that a United States public-sector solution for full employment would not necessarily have benefited foreign countries. Their problems were not entirely owing to outsiders' exploitation; they needed investments, and socialist governments, whether British or Soviet, were no less likely to draw profits from abroad where they could.

The revisionists' reasoning on this point fits in analytically with one of their major current preoccupations: the role of the United States in the third world of peasant movements. The same revisionist argument that sees foreign trade as a means to subordination and control also suggests that the United States had to be hostile to movements seeking genuine self-determination and local independence. Thus American hostility to popular resistance movements, including those of World War II, forms one more logical extension of the country's counter-revolutionary and imperialist drive in the wake of World War II. Kolko makes much of the British suppression of the Greek resistance movement in December 1944, of the American preference for continued dealings with Vichy, of the dislike of Tito's partisans, and of the joint Anglo-American efforts to restrain the left-wing forces in the Italian resistance. When it is remembered that the United States is still fighting the heirs of the Vietnamese resistance to the Japanese and later the French, or that the Haiphong incidents between French and Vietminh occurred within two years after the British put down the Greek resistance cadres in Athens, the emotional thrust of the revisionist argument becomes more understandable.[43]

This concern with the continuities of counter-revolution arises in part from the natural fact that revisionists want to explain the origins of cold war against the background of Vietnam. Ironically enough, the result is to downgrade the importance of the Soviet-American antagonism that originally preoccupied revisionist authors. What in fact increasingly distinguishes the more radical historians is their emphasis upon a Soviet "conservatism" that sought to discourage revolutionary action for the sake of acquiring territorial buffers. Stalin's treaty with Chiang at the expense of Mao, his distrust of Tito, and his abandonment of the Greek Communists, complement American objectives. In view of this supposed convergence of Moscow and Washington, the Cold War becomes little more than a mistaken enmity deriving from the United States' panicky idenification of Soviet policies with indigenous Marxist or merely democratic movements. This finding confirms a "third world" viewpoint which can indict both major world powers and supply a "usable past" for those morally overwhelmed by an updated Holy Alliance between Moscow and Washington.[44] Through the mid 1960's, in short, the revisionists could still be fixed upon explaining the origins of conflict with Moscow; by the end of the decade they were concerned with the antagonism with Havana, Hanoi, and Peking.

Attractive though it may be in light of current events, this third-world perspective has serious analytical deficiencies. First of all, its Marxian basis imposes an overly schematic view of motivation; it precludes any possibility that American policy makers might have acted from genuine emancipatory impulses or even in uncertainty. The war had united the country around democratic ideas that were genuinely held, even if too abstract for implementation in the areas they were aimed at. It can be argued that the economic aspirations that State Department draftsmen grafted onto the policy statements the revisionists cite were just as ritualistic as the political formulas,[45] and that there was still cause for a genuine dismay at the developments in Eastern Europe. The revisionist presentation conveys no sense of America's anti-totalitarian commitment and thus little understanding of the seeds of the post-1945 disillusionment.

Furthermore, the new revisionist writings composed under the impact of Vietnam attribute too consistently ideological an opposition to the resistance movements in Western Europe. For anyone with sympathy for the "vision" of the Resistance, vague as it was, American policy often does appear as misguided or willful. At times tactical considerations were influential; at times the wartime authority that devolved upon conservative proconsuls such as Robert Murphy was critical; at times United States policy acquiesced in a joint allied position more rightist than Washington alone would have preferred, as when the exigencies of coalition warfare led Roosevelt to accede to Churchill's reactionary policies in Italy and Greece.[46] Yet most basically what militated against the Resistance was a big-power paternalism and the wartime habit of viewing military success as an end in itself. United States spokesmen accused Resistance leaders of seeking their own political advantage above the destruction of the Germans, though what Americans saw as narrow partisanship was to Resistance leaders a battle against collaborators and a fascist or semi-fascist right—a struggle for regeneration within to match the fight against the occupying power. The British and Americans preferred to think of the Resistance as a vanguard of saboteurs who might soften up the Germans and pin down their troops but not as an army or regime in embryo. Centralization and control, the distrust of independent authority and pretensions, characterized all three great powers. But unless decentralization itself is made synonymous with radicalism while centralization is defined as reactionary *per se,* it is misleading to condemn American behavior toward the Resistance movements as consistently conservative.[47]

Finally, what is perhaps most misleading about the neo-Marxian point of view is its suggestion that Europe in 1945 was as socially malleable as underdeveloped societies today. By projecting a third-world image upon the West the revisionists overestimate the power of the radical forces and the structural possibilities for change. The United States did help to brake fundamental change especially after V-E Day, but the major limits on reconstruction were set by the internal divisions within the Resistance and the conservative attitude of the Communist parties and the other two allies.[48]

No more in institutional than in political terms did America alone abort a New Order. Kolko's New Order represents a normative image of revolution borrowed from predominantly peasant countries or Yugoslavia and applied to industrial Europe. But not even 1945 Europe was so shaky: the Germans, not the Russians, had occupied the area and left most elites intact. Even where nominally socialist remedies such as nationalization were to be tried, they rarely incorporated any revolutionary tendencies.[49] Pre-war economies had already evolved toward pluralist balances among labor, heavy industry, and small producers and merchandisers. The communists were concerned primarily with retaining their share of the trade-union component in this equilibrium of forces. They sought a social and economic buffer as Stalin sought territorial buffers. A renovation of society on new principles would have required smashing the corporate pluralism in which left-wing as well as conservative leaders found comfort. America did not really have to rescue Europe from radical change because no significant mass-based elements advocated a radical transformation. The so-called New Order—an amalgam in the revisionist mind of Yugoslavian factory councils and Algerian, Vietnamese, or Greek national resistance movements—had no solid peacetime constituency in the West.

What in fact was new in the West was precisely the conglomeration of business, labor, and government that the revisionists lament. In America the New Deal and the wartime economic effort worked to dissolve many of the old lines between public and private spheres.[50] In Fascist Italy, Vichy France, and Nazi Germany a similar interweaving occurred, as it did in a democratic Britain that submitted to extensive planning and welfare measures.[51] Revisionists such as Kolko would accept this description of trends—in fact, Kolko examined the precursor of this private-public interpenetration in his critique of Progressivism—but the revisionists regard these developments as clearly elitist and conservative. Ultimately their general interpretation conceives of the issues behind the Cold War in terms of inequality and class: the Cold War represents to them a continuation of an international civil war in which Russian and later peasant revolutionary forces have successively championed the cause of the oppressed in all countries, while the United States has become the leader of the world's elites.

But no matter what importance this conceptualization may have for today's world, it obscures the historical development. If there has been a growth in international class conflict over the past generation, so too in Western societies there has been an increase of bureaucratic and administrative solutions for social conflict—solutions to which labor contributed, solutions that were conservative in leaving intact private control and ownership, yet still social compromises that commanded wide assent. The forces for compromise sprang from the bureaucratic trends of modern industrial society as they existed in Europe as well as in the United States. The revisionist view splits the world into an industrial half that America supposedly stabilized on behalf of a bureaucratic capitalism and a peasant world where the United States has since met its match. But if peasant society has proved hard to manipulate, Western industrial society has also proved refractory; the neo-Marxians overestimate the fragility of its capitalist order, and overvalue the American contribution to counter-revolution as well as the will to impose it. There is still no well-modulated portrayal of what the United States sought in the world, even less of the real possibilities of institutional change.

No full evaluation of revisionist history, however, can be content with weighing particular interpretations against available evidence. For beneath the details of specific revisionist arguments are more fundamental historiographical problems—implicit conceptual models and underlying assumptions about the decisive factors in American foreign relations.

The revisionists' approach to international conflict and foreign policy formation is a narrow one. They are interested in certain specific modes of explanation and no others. Rejecting any model of international society that sees crucial impulses to conflict as inherent in the international system itself, they seek explanations in American domestic conditions. But for them all domestic conditions are not equally valid. They are unwilling to accept any description that tends to stress the decentralized nature of decision-making or that envisages the possibility of expansionist policy taking shape by imperceptible commitments and bureaucratic momentum. Above all, they approach history with a value system and a vocabulary that appear to make meaningful historical dialogue with those who do not share their framework impossible.

The revisionists presuppose international harmony as a normal state and have a deep sense of grievance against whatever factors disturb it. This common assumption shapes their work from the outset in terms of both analysis and tone. But is international harmony a normal state? The division of sovereignty among nation-states makes it difficult to eliminate friction and tension, as theorists from the time of Machiavelli and Hobbes have pointed out.[52] The disputes of 1944–1945 especially were not easy to avoid. With a power vacuum in Central Europe created by the defeat of Germany and with the expansion of American and Soviet influence into new, overlapping regions, some underlying level of dispute was likely. Angered by the scope that the Cold War finally assumed, the revisionists do not really ask whether conflict might have been totally avoided or what level of residual disagreement was likely to emerge even with the best intentions on both sides.

Once mutual mistrust was unchained—and much already existed—all disputes were burdened by it. The initiatives that would have been required to assuage incipient conflict appeared too risky to venture in terms either of domestic public opinion or international security. By late 1945 the United States and Russia each felt itself to be at a competitive disadvantage in key disputes. Each felt that the other, being ahead, could best afford to make initial concessions, while gestures on its part would entail disproportionate or unilateral sacrifice. Perhaps more far-sighted leaders could have sought different outcomes, but there were pressures on all policy makers to take decisions that would harden conflict rather than alleviate it. Some details on this point are particularly worth considering.

In retrospect there appear to have been several areas of negotiation where compromise might at least have been possible, where accommodation demanded relatively little cost, and where the continued absence of greater concession probably deepened suspicion. Some additional flexibility on the issues of both atomic control and financial assistance might have helped to alleviate the growing estrangement. Innovative and generous as our plans for atomic energy control appeared to Americans at the time, the provisions for holding all United States weapons until controls were complete, as well as the demand that the Russians renounce their United Nations veto on all atomic-energy matters, probably doomed the proposal. With such an imbalance of obligations the Soviet advocates of their own country's atomic arsenal were likely to prevail over those willing to acquiesce in nuclear inferiority for a decade or so. As so often after 1946, the reluctance to give up an advantage that at best could only be transitory led to a further spiral in the arms race.[53]

With far less objective risk than was presented by the nuclear issue, liberality with aid might also have offered United States policy makers a chance to dissipate quarrels. Unfortunately, Lend-Lease was brusquely cut off in a way that could not help but offend the Russians, although it was slated to end with the close of the war in any case.[54] Had transitional aid or a significant post-war loan been available, the termination of Lend-Lease might not have proved so abrasive. But the loan proposal was always keyed to the extraction of political concessions, and the Russians had no need to become a suppliant.[55] As it turned out a post-war credit was less crucial to the Soviets than to the British, who faced a mammoth balance of payments crisis that Russia did not have to cope with. Washington could not really use the loan to wrest concessions; instead her failure to provide funds precluded any chance for postwar credits to help improve the general international atmosphere and re-establish some minimal trust.

Disagreement at the start over Eastern Europe had undermined the chances of those peripheral initiatives that might in turn have helped to alleviate overall tension. By becoming trapped in a position where apparently unilateral démarches were needed to break a growing deadlock, policy was far more likely to be vetoed by State Department, Congress, or the President's immediate advisers. It was far harder to justify financial assistance or atomic renunciation when Russia was already felt to be uncooperative. Domestic constraints and the suspicions fed by international rivalry interacted to intensify a serious deadlock.

Although the revisionists do not readily soften their judgments about American policy makers in light of these pressures, they do use them to make Soviet responses appear more acceptable. They explain that the Russians had to reckon with the death of an exceptionally friendly President and the replacement of his key policy makers by tougher spokesmen; with a tooth-and-nail resistance to the German reparations that Russia felt she clearly deserved; and with the curt United States dismissal of a Soviet voice in the occupation of Japan, an influence over the Dardanelles, and a base in the Mediterranean. Neither side was likely to see in the opposing moves anything but a calculated effort to expand power, or, with a little more subtlety, the upshot of a contest between the other power's doves and hawks with the doves increasingly impotent. Such interpretations tended to produce a re-

sponse in kind. In the absence of any overriding commitment to con-
ciliation, the Cold War thus contained its own momentum toward
polarization and deadlock.

It would, however, also be inappropriate to fix too much blame for
the origins of the Cold War upon the Hobbesian nature of the international system, though it is a major element the revisionists ignore.
As revisionists insist, domestic factors are clearly required to explain the
timing and trajectory of the Soviet-American antagonism. But significantly absent from revisionist writing is any sense of the bureaucratic
determinants of policy—an element of increasing interest to historians
and social scientists seeking to respond to the revisionist indictment. In
the view of these writers, decisions are seen as the outcome of organizational disputes within an overall government structure. Policy emerges
not so much as a way of maximizing a well-defined national "interest"
as the outcome of struggles among bureaucratic forces each seeking to
perpetuate its own *raison d'être* and to expand its corporate influence.
Recent studies have shown for instance that much of the impulse toward
a cold-war defense posture after 1945 came from the fact that both the
Air Force and the Navy sought out new strategic conceptions and justi-
fications to preserve their wartime size and status.[56]

Study of the German and reparations issues also reveals how American foreign policy emerged from inter-departmental contention, in this
case between Henry Morgenthau and the Treasury on the one hand,
and on the other a more conservative State Department desirous of
recreating economic stability in Central Europe. After V-E day the
Army military government agencies also demanded that their American occupation zone be as economically self-sufficient as possible. The
result of these pressures, and of Morgenthau's loss of influence under
Truman, was that the United States quarreled bitterly with the
Soviets to limit reparations. The American insistence at Potsdam that
each power largely confine its reparations to its own zone helped lead
to the very division of Germany that the United States officially de-
plored. The intent was not to build Germany up at the expense of
Russia: Byrnes after all offered the Soviets a 25- or 40-year treaty
against German aggression in late 1945 and the spring of 1946. But
each agency's struggle for the priorities it set in terms of its own
organizational interest helped shape a narrow policy that was not
subordinated to a clear sense of our more general relations with the
Soviet Union.[57]

This approach to policy analysis, which opens up a new range of
motivation and offers an alternative to an undue emphasis on personal
factors, contrasts with the explanatory model suggested by the neo-

Marxist revisionists.[58] For the latter group what ultimately explains policy is a "system" arising out of the property and power relations within a society, a system causative in its own right and within which institutions and organizations do not lead independent lives but relate to each other dialectically. For these revisionists the explanation of events in terms of intra-governmental structure and struggles is simply formalistic, oriented to the procedural aspects of policy formation and begging the substantive questions. For them, the processes of government might as well be a black box: if one understands the distribution of wealth and influence then policy follows by an almost deductive logic. To attribute decisive influence to bureaucratic pressures seems additionally frivolous to the revisionists since allegedly only certain elites ever rise to the top of those bureaucracies.[59] For those, on the other hand, who stress the political infighting among bureaucracies what is important about history tends to be the successive modifications of action—in short, political process not social structure.

Both of these approaches are deceptive and limiting if taken to extremes. For those who stress history as bureaucratic process, all questions of historical responsibility can appear ambiguous and even irrelevant. Foreign policy emerges as the result of a competition for fiefs within governmental empires. Bureaucratic emphases can produce a neo-Rankean acquiescence in the use of power that is no less deterministic than the revisionist tendency to make all policies exploitative in a liberal capitalist order. But what is perhaps most significant about these alternative causal models is that they are addressed to different questions. The non-revisionists are asking how policies are formed and assume that this also covers the question why. The revisionists see the two questions as different and are interested in the why. And by "why?" revisionists are asking what the meaning of policies is in terms of values imposed from outside the historical narrative. The revisionists charge that the historian must pose this question of meaning consciously or he will pose it unconsciously and accept the values that help to uphold a given social system. History, they suggest, must serve the oppressors or the oppressed, if not by intent then by default. The historian who wishes to avoid this iron polarity can reply that social systems rarely divide their members into clear-cut oppressors and oppressed. He can also insist that even when one despairs of absolute objectivity there are criteria for minimizing subjectivity. On the other hand, he must also take care that the history of policy making not become so focused on organizational processes that the idea of social choice and responsibility is precluded.

In the end it is this attempt by the revisionists to analyze specific historical issues on the basis of *a priori* values about the political system that most strongly affects the controversies their writings have touched off. For their values cannot be derived from the mere amassment of historical data nor do they follow from strictly historical judgments, but rather underlie such judgments. This is true in some sense, no doubt, of history in general, but the whole of Cold War historiography seems particularly dependent upon defined value systems.

For the revisionists, on the one hand, the key issues hinge not upon facts or evidence but upon assessments as to how repressive or non-repressive contemporary liberal institutions are. These judgments in turn must be made within ground rules that allow only polar alternatives for evaluating political action. What is non-revolutionary must be condemned as counter-revolutionary, and reformist political aspirations are dismissed in advance. Similarly, the foreign policies of Western powers cannot escape the stigma of imperialism, for imperialism and exploitation are defined by the revisionists as virtually inherent in any economic intercourse between industrialized and less developed states, or just between unequals. But how can one decide whether the economic reconstruction that America financed was beneficial or "exploitative" for countries brought into a cooperative if not subordinate relationship to the United States? How does one judge the value of multilateral or bilateral trading relations that benefit each side differentially? Judgments must rest upon definitions of exploitation or fairness that logically precede the historical narrative and cannot be derived from it.

The non-revisionist, on the other hand, can refuse to accept the ground rules that presuppose exploitation, dependency, or automatic neo-colonialism; he can refuse to accept the definitions that allow no choice between revolution and reaction. But traditional Cold War historians no less than the revisionists have been involved in tautologies. Historical explanations are normally tested by efforts to find and weigh contradictory evidence, but Cold War analyses on both sides have relied upon propositions that cannot be disproven. Sometimes disproof is precluded by prior assumptions, and while revisionists may believe America's capitalist economy necessitates a voracious expansionism, Cold War theorists have similarly argued that any commitment to communism is *ipso facto* destructive of a "moderate" or "legitimate" international order.[60] Often disproof is impossible because the explanations are totalistic enough to accommodate all contradictory phenomena into one all-embracing explanatory structure. So writers who condemned the Soviets cited Marxist ideology as evidence of real intention when it preached revolution and as evidence of deviousness when it envisaged United-Front coalitions. Conversely, according to the revisionists, when the United States withdrew foreign assistance it was seeking to bring nations to heel; when it was generous, it sought to suborn. When the United States bowed to British desires to delay the Second Front it justified Soviet suspicions; when it opposed Churchill's imperial designs it did so in order to erect a new economic hegemony over what England (and likewise France or the Netherlands) controlled by direct dominion. Spokesmen for each side present the reader with a total explanatory system that accounts for all phenomena, eliminates the possibility of disproof, and thus transcends the usual processes of historical reasoning. More than in most historical controversies, the questions about what happened are transformed into concealed debate about the nature of freedom and duress, exploitation and hegemony. As a result much Cold War historiography has become a confrontation *manqué*—debatable philosophy taught by dismaying example.

Notes

1. Herbert Feis, *Roosevelt-Churchill-Stalin. The War They Waged and the Peace They Sought* (Princeton, 1957), p. 655.

2. Adam Ulam, *Expansion and Coexistence: The History of Soviet Foreign Policy, 1917–1967* (New York, 1968), p. 377.

3. William H. McNeill, *America, Britain, and Russia, Their Cooperation and Conflict, 1941–1946* (London, 1953). For recent explorations in the same spirit: Walter LaFeber, *America, Russia, and the Cold War, 1945–1966* (New York, 1967), which stresses growing ideological militancy; Louis J. Halle, *The Cold War as History* (London, 1967), a treatment that verges on fatalism; Martin F. Herz, *Beginnings of the Cold War* (Bloomington, Ind., 1966); William L. Neumann, *After Victory: Churchill, Roosevelt, Stalin, and the Making of the Peace* (New York, 1967); André Fontaine, *History of the Cold War*, trans. D. D. Paige (2 vols.: New York, 1968); cf. also Arthur Schlesinger, Jr., "Origins of the Cold War," *Foreign Affairs*, 46 (1967), 22–52.

4. Denna F. Fleming, *The Cold War and its Origins, 1917–1960* (2 vols.: Garden City, N.Y., 1961). Unfortunately the book relies almost exclusively on newspaper accounts and commentary. Relying heavily on Fleming for its historical analysis is David Horowitz, *The Free World Colossus* (New York, 1965).

5. Harriman's assessments in Department of State, *Foreign Relations of the United States* (henceforth: *FRUS*), especially November 5, 1943 foreseeing disagreements on reparations and Poland but generally pleased with Russian cooperation (*FRUS*, 1943, III, 589–593), August 15, and August

21, 1944 (*FRUS*, 1944, III, 1376, 1382 n. 1.), March 17, 1945 (*FRUS*, 1945, III, 732), and April 4, 1945—"the Soviet program is the establishment of totalitarianism"—(*FRUS*, 1945, V, 819).

6. For the Teheran discussions of the Polish frontier, Feis, *Churchill-Roosevelt-Stalin* pp. 284–285. Harriman advice in *FRUS*, 1944, III, 1322ff.

7. For the revisionist view of the Polish dispute, Gabriel Kolko, *The Politics of War, The World and United States Foreign Policy, 1943–1945* (New York, 1968), pp. 99–122, 147–152; Gar Alperovitz, *Atomic Diplomacy: Hiroshima and Potsdam* (New York, 1965), esp. pp. 243–256; Fleming, *The Cold War and its Origins*, I, 222–248. Cf. Feis, *Churchill-Roosevelt-Stalin*, pp. 283–301, 453–460, 518–529; official summary in *FRUS, The Conferences at Malta and Yalta (1945)*, p. 202ff.; and for strong anti-communist presentations, Arthur Bliss Lane, *I Saw Poland Betrayed* (Indianapolis, 1948), and Edward J. Rozek, *Allied Wartime Diplomacy: A Pattern in Poland* (London, 1958).

8. Alperovitz, *Atomic Diplomacy*, pp. 250–253, 261–267, on Roosevelt after Yalta, and 188–225 on post-Hiroshima aggressiveness. In judging Roosevelt's correspondence it is important to remember that by March 1945 the Polish issue was just part of a larger concern about keeping the alliance together in view of the upcoming United Nations conference and preventing broad public disillusion about the Crimean agreements. Roosevelt was acting more as a mediator than as a defender of a particular Polish position. For the President's misgivings about the agreement even at Yalta see William D. Leahy, *I Was There* (New York, 1950), pp. 315–316; the mingled exultation and disillusion in the post-Yalta atmosphere is conveyed in Robert Sherwood, *Roosevelt and Hopkins* (New York, 1948), pp. 869–876. For the quarrel about the composition of the Polish government, Winston S. Churchill, *The Second World War*, vol. VI, *Triumph and Tragedy* (Boston, 1953), pp. 418–439; cf. also the reports from the Commission on Poland sitting in Moscow: *FRUS, 1945*, V, 134ff.

9. But see the American point of view in James F. Byrnes, *Speaking Frankly* (New York, 1947), pp. 72ff., 89–101, 115ff.; also the critical reports of Byrnes's observer in Rumania, Mark Ethridge, who urged firm resistance to growing aggression: *FRUS*, 1945, V, 627–630, 633–641.

10. See Kolko, *The Politics of War*, pp. 168–171 (an analysis marred by the remarkable judgment that absence of civil war in Eastern Europe showed the "flexibility and subtlety of the various Communist parties and the Russians"); also Alperovitz, *Atomic Diplomacy*, pp. 217ff.; Fleming, *The Cold War and its Origins*, I, 203, 208–210, 242–243, 250–258.

11. For a spectrum of opinions on Stalinist objectives see Ulam, *Expansion and Coexistence*, pp. 377, 381, 388–408, an anti-revisionist but rich and subtle account; J. M. Mackintosh, *Strategy and Tactics of Soviet Foreign Policy* (London, 1962), pp. 1–17, for a traditional view; also Philip E. Mosely, "Soviet Policy in a two-world System," *The Kremlin and World Politics* (New York, 1960), who sees the Russians reverting to revolutionary goals from November 1944; Kolko, *The Politics of War*, pp. 164–165, stressing Soviet conservatism; McNeill, *America, Britain, and Russia*, pp.

564–565, 609–610; LaFeber, *America, Russia, and the Cold War*, pp. 14–18, 23, 28–32, which couples Stalin's electoral address and Churchill's speech at Fulton, Missouri; Isaac Deutscher, *Stalin, A Political Biography* (New York, 1960), pp. 518–521, 529ff.

12. Cf. Kolko, *The Politics of War*, pp. 37–39, 128–131 for the Italian-Rumanian parallel; Churchill, *Triumph and Tragedy*, pp. 227–235, for the percentages agreement; cf. Alperovitz, *Atomic Diplomacy*, pp. 133–134.

13. For a pro-Western account of Balkan party politics: Hugh Seton-Watson, *The East European Revolution* (New York, 3rd ed., 1956), pp. 31–36, 174–175, 184, 197–198, 202–219.

14. For official American disavowal of spheres of influence, Cordell Hull, *The Memoirs of Cordell Hull* (London, 1948), II, 1168, 1298; *FRUS, The Conference of Berlin (The Potsdam Conference) 1945*, I, 262–264. For Stimson's dissent, Alperovitz, *Atomic Diplomacy*, p. 54; for Kennan's, George F. Kennan, *Memoirs, 1925–1950* (Boston, 1967), pp. 211–213, 222, 250; for Henry Wallace's coupling of political spheres of influence with economic universalism, LaFeber, *America, Russia and the Cold War*, pp. 37–39.

15. H. Stuart Hughes, "The Second Year of the Cold War: A Memoir & an Anticipation," *Commentary*, 48 (1969), 27–32, esp. 31.

16. Alperovitz, *Atomic Diplomacy*, pp. 19–33, 55–90, 270–275.

17. *Ibid.*, pp. 117–120 on military estimates, 176–187 and 226–242 on nuclear calculations, 120–126 and 183–186 on the Sino-Soviet treaty. The delays in the final arrangements of the treaty, however, did not all stem from the American or Chinese side; the Russians themselves were raising the price of a treaty with Chiang's government. Cf. Kolko, *The Politics of War*, pp. 556–560.

18. Kolko, *The Politics of War*, pp. 560–565: "Mechanism prevailed"; Herbert Feis, *The Atomic Bomb and the End of World War II* (Princeton, N.J., 1966), p. 194, who now feels that "to monitor" Russian behavior may have been a motive for using the weapon. Cf. Alperovitz's critique of Feis's vacillation now included as "The Use of the Atomic Bomb," in his collection of *New York Review of Books* pieces: Gar Alperovitz, *Cold War Essays* (Garden City, N.Y., 1970), pp. 51–74. A variant of the Alperovitz thesis was first advanced by P. M. S. Blackett, *Fear, War, and the Bomb* (New York, 1949). Important in the earlier debate was Henry L. Stimson's justification, "The Decision to Use the Atomic Bomb," *Harper's Magazine*, February 1947, reprinted in H. L. Stimson and McGeorge Bundy, *On Active Service in Peace and War* (New York, 1948); also Louis Morton, "The Decision to Use the Atomic Bomb," *Foreign Affairs*, 35 (1957), 334–353.

19. See Memorandum of Conversation, May 2, 1945 with President Truman, Generals Schuyler and Crane, in Joseph Grew MSS., Conversations, vol. 7, Houghton Library, Harvard University.

20. Alperovitz, *Atomic Diplomacy*, p. 80. As grounds for pushing back a summit conference, Truman himself claimed newness to office and the need to complete the preparation of a budget before the end of the fiscal

year (Grew-Eden-Truman conversation, March 14, 1945, Joseph Grew MSS, Conversations, vol. 7). Alperovitz dismisses the budget considerations as implausible (p. 67). Much of Alperovitz's case hinges upon the timing and intent of the Hopkins mission. Truman's decision to dispatch Hopkins was made earlier than Sherwood said, although the suggestion was still Harriman's; hence Alperovitz argues it should be read as a response to Stimson's atomic briefings and not the disputes usually cited. Cf. Harry Truman, *Year of Decisions* (Garden City, N.Y., 1955), pp. 108–110 for April 30 date; Sherwood, *Roosevelt and Hopkins*, p. 885, for mid-May, and cf. Alperovitz, *Atomic Diplomacy*, p. 71n, and pp. 270–275. In fact by the end of April there were many indications of urgent troubles warranting an envoy's talk with Stalin: see Churchill's major letter of April 29 to Stalin, which foresaw a divided Europe and a quarrel "that would tear the world to pieces." *Triumph and Tragedy*, pp. 494–497.

21. For the recommendations of the Joint Chiefs of Staff see *FRUS, The Conference of Berlin (Potsdam)*, I, 903–910, which records the White House meeting of June 18, 1945, where Marshall outlined a November 1 landing on Kyushu, and the President said he would seek Russian help at Potsdam and wanted to prevent an "Okinawa from one end of Japan to another." See also the text of the JCS report, pp. 910–911, and the Combined Chiefs of Staff report as approved by Truman and the Prime Minister on July 24, in Vol. II, 1462–1463. Cf. Alperovitz, *Atomic Diplomacy*, pp. 117–120, for discussion of this point. For divisions on the surrender debates within the respective combatants: Waldo H. Heinrichs, Jr., *American Ambassador: Joseph C. Grew and the Development of the United States Diplomatic Tradition* (Boston, 1966), pp. 372–380; Robert J. C. Butow, *Japan's Decision to Surrender* (Stanford, 1954), pp. 158ff. for the post-Hiroshima situation.

22. Cf. Kolko, *The Politics of War*, p. 560; Halle, *The Cold War as History*, p. 173.

23. Harriman's assessment is in *FRUS, 1945*, V, 922–924. On Truman and the bomb, see Alperovitz, *Atomic Diplomacy*, p. 227; cf. Nuel Pharr Davis, *Lawrence and Oppenheimer* (Greenwich, Conn., Fawcett ed., 1969), pp. 257–260.

24. William Appleman Williams, *The Tragedy of American Diplomacy* (New York, rev. ed., 1962); for similar analysis as applied to the whole Roosevelt period cf. the work of Williams' student, Lloyd C. Gardner, *Economic Aspects of New Deal Diplomacy* (Madison, 1964).

25. For this theme, Gabriel Kolko, *The Triumph of Conservatism* (Chicago, 1963); William A. Williams, *The Contours of American History* (Chicago, 1966), pp. 390ff.; James Weinstein, *The Corporate Ideal in the Liberal State, 1900–1918* (Boston, 1968); Barton J. Bernstein, "The New Deal: The Conservative Achievements of Liberal Reform," in Barton J. Bernstein, ed., *Towards a New Past: Dissenting Essays in American History* (New York, 1969), pp. 262–288.

26. See John Bagulley, "The World War and the Cold War," David Horowitz, ed., *Containment and Revolution* (Boston, 1968), pp. 77–97;

Kolko, *The Politics of War,* pp. 12–30. For non-revisionist discussions of this thorny issue cf. Feis, *Churchill-Roosevelt-Stalin,* pp. 47–80, 93–102, 114–119, 134–136; Maurice Matloff and Edwin M. Snell, *Strategic Planning for Coalition Warfare, 1941–1942* (Washington, 1953), pp. 229–244, 328–349; also Maurice Matloff, *Strategic Planning for Coalition Warfare, 1943–1944* (Washington, 1959). Valuable insight into the "technical" restraints on Allied policy is provided by Robert W. Coakley and Richard M. Leighton, *Global Logistics and Strategy, 1943–1945* (Washington, 1968), pp. 3–6, 173–245.

27. See Fleming, *The Cold War and its Origins,* I, 106–134; also A. J. P. Taylor, *The Origins of the Second World War* (New York, 1962), pp. 240–241, for defenses of Stalinist diplomacy, and George F. Kennan, *Russia and the West under Lenin and Stalin* (Boston, 1960), pp. 312–336, 347–348, for a harsh critique. The recent accounts on both sides—Kolko, *The Politics of War,* pp. 13–14, and Ulam, *Expansion and Coexistence,* pp. 250–279—stress the prevailing Machiavellism and cynicism of the late 1930's and sensibly tend to divorce the period from an integral role in cold war origins.

28. Fleming, *The Cold War and its Origins,* I, 20–35.

29. One can usefully separate those accounts that stress the ineffectiveness and hesitations of Roosevelt's foreign policy—Arnold Offner, *American Appeasement: United States Foreign Policy and Germany, 1933–1938* (Cambridge, Mass., 1969); Robert A. Divine, *The Illusion of Neutrality* (Chicago, 1962)—from those questioning the old view of isolationism from economic or ideological criteria: Gardner, *Economic Aspects of New Deal Diplomacy,* pp. 86–98; Williams, "The Legend of Isolationism," in *The Tragedy of American Diplomacy,* pp. 104–159; Robert Freeman Smith, "American Foreign Relations, 1920–1942," in Bernstein, *Towards a New Past,* pp. 232–256.

30. For a presentation of Wilsonian aspirations parallel in some respects to Kolko, Arno J. Mayer, *Politics and Diplomacy of Peacemaking: Containment and Counterrevolution at Versailles, 1918–1919* (New York, 1967). Cf. also N. Gordon Levin, Jr., *Woodrow Wilson and World Politics* (New York, 1968). Common to both Mayer and Kolko, is the subordination of the German problem to the Russian one; on the other hand, Wilson exerted a more genuinely reformist impulse in Europe according to Mayer than Roosevelt did according to Kolko.

31. See Marilyn B. Young, "American Expansion, 1870–1900: The Far East," in Bernstein, *Towards a New Past,* esp. pp. 186–198, for a tempered interpretation; also Williams, *The Tragedy of American Diplomacy,* pp. 37–50; Walter LaFeber, *The New Empire: An Interpretation of American Expansion, 1860–1898* (Ithaca, N.Y., 1963).

32. See William A. Williams, *The Roots of the Modern American Empire* (New York, 1969), based upon an extensive reading of agrarian opinion, and a learned and moving, if problematic, book.

33. Kolko, *The Politics of War,* pp. 323–340.

34. For detailed treatment of these issues, see Richard N. Gardner,

Sterling-Dollar Diplomacy (Oxford, 1956), which covers the entire wartime period; cf. also E. F. Penrose, *Economic Planning for Peace* (Princeton, 1953). Revisionist critiques are in Lloyd Gardner, *Economic Aspects of New Deal Diplomacy,* pp. 275–291, and Kolko, *The Politics of War,* pp. 280–294, 488–492, 623–624.

35. For critiques of "exploitative" international economic relations from a Marxist viewpoint, see Harry Magdoff, *The Age of Imperialism: The Economics of United States Foreign Policy* (New York, 1969); and Paul A. Baran, *The Political Economy of Growth* (New York and London, 1957), pp. 177ff.

36. John Morton Blum, *From the Morgenthau Diaries: Years of War, 1941–1945* (Cambridge, Mass., 1967), pp. 323–347; Paul Y. Hammond, "Directives for the Occupation of Germany: The Washington Controversy," in Harold Stein, ed., *American Civil-Military Decisions* (Birmingham, Ala., 1963), pp. 348–388.

37. Cited in Blum, *From the Morgenthau Diaries,* III, 273.

38. For impulses to cooperation, Richard Gardner, *Sterling-Dollar Diplomacy,* pp. 54–58; for the spectrum of domestic opinion on aid to Britain, *ibid.,* pp. 192–199, 226–253, 208–210; cf. also Thomas Lamont's call for restoration of British prosperity, cited in Lloyd Gardner, *Economic Aspects of New Deal Diplomacy,* pp. 275–276; also Blum, *From the Morgenthau Diaries,* III, 324–326 for opposed views (Morgenthau's and Baruch's) on what to demand of Britain.

39. Richard Gardner, *Sterling-Dollar Diplomacy,* pp. 306–347; J. Keith Horsefield, *History of the International Monetary Fund* (Washington, D.C., 1970), I, 3–118. For the difficulties that convertibility presented to English policies: Sidney Pollard, *The Development of the British Economy, 1914–1950* (London, 1962), pp. 365–407; Hugh Dalton, *High Tide and After: Memoirs, 1945–1960* (London, 1962), pp. 68–89, 178–184, 254ff. For American policies of 1949–1950, William Diebold, Jr., *Trade and Payments in Western Europe: A Study in Economic Cooperation, 1947–1951* (New York, 1952), pp. 34–110.

40. See Thomas G. Paterson, "The Abortive American Loan to Russia and the Origins of the Cold War, 1943–1946," *The Journal of American History,* 56 (1969), pp. 71–72, 75–77.

41. Cf. Sumner Wells, *The Time for Decision* (New York, 1944), p. 409.

42. See Under-Secretary of State Dean Acheson's condemnation of any such tendency as bordering on Soviet autarchy cited in Williams, *The Tragedy of American Diplomacy,* p. 236; for a spectrum of economists' thinking about post-war possibilities, see Seymour Harris, ed., *Postwar Economic Problems* (New York, 1943).

43. Cf. Kolko, *The Politics of War,* pp. 55–71, 154–155, 172–193. For a pointed Greek EAM-NLF comparison, see Todd Gitlin, "Counter-Insurgency: Myth and Reality in Greece," in Horowitz, *Containment and Revolution,* pp. 140–181. The major pro-EAM Greek account is now André Kédros, *La résistance grècque (1940–1944)* (Paris, 1966).

44. Cf. Isaac Deutscher, "Myths of the Cold War," in Horowitz, *Con-*

tainment and Revolution, pp. 17–19; Gabriel Kolko, *The Roots of American Foreign Policy* (Boston, 1969), esp. pp. xi–xii and 85–87 on the United States relation to the third world; also Kolko, *The Politics of War,* pp. 449–451, 594–595ff. For an extensive critical discussion of the American attitudes toward the third world and Greece since the '1940's see Richard J. Barnet, *Intervention and Revolution: The United States in the Third World* (New York and Cleveland, 1968).

45. For a view of economically determined aims for Eastern Europe, see Kolko, *The Politics of War,* pp. 167–171. But is it really so true, as Kolko claims, that trade and investment were "so central to objectives in that area"? The aims stated by Stetinnius (*FRUS, 1944, IV,* 1025–1026) that Kolko cites were more inconsistent than imperialist: their cardinal point was self-determination of political and social systems. Briefing papers prepared for Yalta also said that the United States should insist on access for trade and investment, but still recognized that the Soviets would exert predominant political influence in the area. They expressed a willingness to accept the fact so long as American influence was not completely nullified, and ventured, furthermore, to say that precisely the safe assurance of a pro-Russian political orientation would let the Soviets admit United States loans. (See *FRUS, The Conferences at Malta and Yalta,* pp. 234–235.) For definition of aspirations in a concrete situation see Harriman's report on the Polish agreement, June 28, 1945, in *FRUS, The Conference of Berlin (Potsdam),* I, 728, where the matter of concern cited is administration of the Ministry of Internal Security: "the crux of whether Poland will have her independence, whether reasonable personal freedoms will be permitted and whether reasonably free elections can be held."

46. On Vichy policy: William L. Langer, *Our Vichy Gamble* (New York, 1947); Robert Murphy, *Diplomat Among Warriors* (Garden City, N.Y., 1964), pp. 49–64, 124–185; Cordell Hull, *The Memoirs of Cordell Hull,* II, 1127–1138, 1222–1226, 1241–1246. For allied differences in Italy: Norman Kogan, *Italy and the Allies* (Cambridge, Mass., 1956); for British policy in Greece, Kédros, *La résistance grècque (1940–1944),* pp. 479–513; William H. McNeill, *The Greek Dilemma* (London, 1947); and Churchill's defense in *Triumph and Tragedy,* pp. 283–325.

47. Cf. Norman Kogan, "American Policies toward European Resistance Movements," *European Resistance Movements, 1939–1945. Proceedings of the Second International Conference on the History of the Resistance Movements Held at Milan, 26–29 March 1961* (London, 1964), pp. 74–93; cf. F. W. Deakin, "Great Britain and European Resistance," and the veiled criticisms of Allied policy by Ferruccio Parri and Franco Venturi, "The Italian Resistance and the Allies," in the same collection xxvii–xxxvii.

For a critique from the Left of Allied pressure against the Northern Resistance movement in Italy (the CLNAI) see Franco Catalano, *Storia del C.L.N.A.I.* (Bari, 1956), pp. 283–315, 326–350; Kogan, *Italy and the Allies,* pp. 90–110; Kolko, *The Politics of War,* pp. 53–63.

48. It is often overlooked that the political decisions of late 1944, which led to the British suppression of the Greek resistance and the Allied pres-

sure for a compromise between the reformist Northern Italian resistance groups (the CLNAI) and the more conservative Rome government, grew out of Anglo-American differences as much as out of any quarrel with the Soviets. At the second Quebec Conference in September 1944 Roosevelt had pressed the Morgenthau plan upon the reluctant British and had threatened Lend-Lease curtailment. At the same time the President, in view of the upcoming elections, was advocating an Italian policy more favorable to the Rome government or the Resistance parties than Churchill desired and was more obdurate on the Polish issue. It was immediately after Quebec that Churchill flew to Moscow to make his "percentages" agreement with Stalin on the demarcation of Balkan spheres of influence. In the months to come Stalin increased his own domination over the Eastern European countries, but in contrast reaffirmed his policy of having Western communist leaders support the established forces in Rome and Paris. Churchill and Eden could act with a freer hand in the Mediterranean and also explore a West European bloc. In short, both Allies adopted policies that envisaged a possible falling-out with America, although the Soviet push into Central Europe was to bring Churchill quickly back into an anti-Russian posture. In the interim it was the independent forces of the local Resistance movements that bore the cost. But for the divisions within the Resistance forces themselves, which was also an important factor, see Kolko, *The Politics of War*, pp. 428–456, esp. 450–456; Franco Catalano, "Presentazione," and "Italia," in *Aspetti sociali ed economici della Resistenza in Europa: Atti del convegno . . . (Milano 26–27 marzo 1966)*, pp. xviii, 114ff., 121ff.; Georgio Bocca, *Storia dell'Italia partigiana* (Bari, 1966), pp. 466–484; cf. also Leo Valiani, "Sulla storia sociale della resistanza," *Il movimento di Liberazione in Italia*, 88 (1967), 87–92 on the limits of the Resistance Left. For France, Henri Michel sees American and inherent limits on the resistance: "France," *Aspetti sociali ed economici*, pp. 17, 32–33; cf. also his *Les courants de pensée de la résistance* (Paris, 1962), pp. 387–410, 518–529, 685–706, 711–721.

49. A brief exception may have been the Communist efforts at syndical control in France, but even these appear to have been only a means to entrench the Party in a new labor fief. See Maurice Bye, Ernest Rossi, Mario Einaudi, *Nationalization in France and Italy* (Ithaca, N.Y., 1955), pp. 96–109.

50. Ellis Hawley, *The New Deal and the Problem of Monopoly* (Princeton, 1966), pp. 449ff., 489; Sherwood, *Roosevelt and Hopkins*, pp. 157–164; Barton J. Bernstein, "America in War and Peace: The Test of Liberalism," in Bernstein, *Towards a New Past*, pp. 292–295; also his "Industrial Reconversion: The Protection of Oligopoly and Military Control of the War Machine," *American Journal of Economics and Sociology*, 26 (1967), 159–172. For a good case study of military-industrial collaboration, Robert H. Connery, *The Navy and the Industrial Mobilization in World War II* (Princeton, N.J., 1951).

51. Derek H. Aldcroft, "The Development of the Managed Economy before 1939," *Journal of Contemporary History*, 4 (October 1969), 117–

137; W. K. Hancock and M. M. Gowing, *British War Economy* (London, 1949). For French initiatives, Stanley Hoffmann, "Paradoxes of the French Political Community," in Stanley H. Hoffmann, et al., *In Search of France* (New York, Harper Torchbooks, 1965), pp. 38–39. For descriptions of the German situation, Arthur Schweitzer, *Big Business in the Third Reich* (Bloomington, Ind., 1954); Franz Neumann, *Behemoth, The Structure and Practice of National Socialism* (New York, Harper Torchbook ed., 1966), pp. 221–361; David S. Landes, *The Unbound Prometheus* (Cambridge, Eng., 1969), pp. 402–417. For the origins of the IRI, Rossi, Bye, Einaudi, *Nationalization in France and Italy*, pp. 191–200.

52. For an introduction to the large body of theory that stresses the inherent logic of the international system in shaping bipolar or balance-of-power competition, see Morton Kaplan, *System and Process in International Politics* (New York, 1957), also his "Variants on Six Models of the International System," in James N. Rosenau, ed., *International Politics and Foreign Policy* (New York, 1969 ed.), pp. 291–303; cf. Karl W. Deutsch, *The Analysis of International Relations* (Englewood Cliffs, N.J., 1969), pp. 112–140. In its most abstract form in terms of an international system, the Cold War to 1948 can be reconstructed as a transition in which each side raised its criteria of tolerable political conditions in third countries from acceptance of regimes so long as they allowed some influence for its own respective supporters to an insistence on regimes that excluded its opponents' clients from any voice in policy. For elaboration of a similar logic in mathematical terms as applied to arms races, see Anatol Rapoport, "Lewis M. Richardson's Mathematical Theory of War," now included as "The Mathematics of Arms Races," in James N. Rosenau, ed., *International Politics and Foreign Policy* (New York, 1961 ed.). For a useful discrimination between causal models of war according to their focus on international, domestic, or psychological factors see Kenneth Waltz, *Man, the State, and War* (New York, 1959).

53. Richard G. Hewlett and Oscar E. Anderson, *The New World, 1939–1946* (University Park, Pa., 1962), pp. 455–481, 531–619; David Lilienthal, *The Journals of David E. Lilienthal: The Atomic Energy Years, 1945–1950* (New York, 1964), pp. 27ff.; Dean Acheson, *Present at the Creation: My Years in the State Department* (New York, 1969), pp. 151–156; critical views in Fleming, *The Cold War and its Origins*, I, 363–379; cf. also Robert Gilpin, *American Scientists and Nuclear Weapons Policy* (Princeton, 1962), pp. 52–63.

54. The best recent summary is in George Herring, Jr., "Lend-Lease to Russia and the Origins of the Cold War, 1944–1945," *The Journal of American History*, 56 (1969), 93–114. Herring emphasizes that Lend-Lease to Russia always depended upon Roosevelt's constant intervention to smooth requirements that might have disqualified the Soviets. The 3 (c) clause of the Lend-Lease agreement provided for transitional aid after the war, but the negotiations were dropped in March 1945 on the recommendation of Joseph Grew and Leo Crowley—who also engineered the cut-off in May. Grew and Crowley pleaded Congressional difficulty, but this seems

exaggerated. Cf. Morgenthau's objections to 3 (c) delays in *FRUS, The Conferences at Malta and Yalta*, p. 320.

55. See Paterson, "The Abortive American Loan to Russia and the Origins of the Cold War, 1943–1946," pp. 70–92.

56. Vincent Davis, *Postwar Defense Policy and the U.S. Navy, 1943–1946* (Chapel Hill, 1966), pp. 164ff., 186ff., 219ff.; Perry M. Smith; *The Air Force Plans for Peace, 1943–1945* (Baltimore, Md., 1970). The Army, on the other hand, was interested in maintaining Soviet participation in the war because they were unwilling to concede that air and naval power would defeat Japan; moreover Eisenhower needed Russian cooperation in administering Germany, and was personally impressed by Marshall Zhukov. See Dwight D. Eisenhower, *Crusade in Europe* (New York, 1948), pp. 458–475; Feis, *Between War and Peace*, pp. 74–76, 141–144.

57. For inter-agency contention on Germany see Hammond, "Directives for the Occupation of Germany," pp. 408–443. State Department conservatism and backwardness are well evoked in Acheson, *Present at the Creation*, pp. 17, 22–36, 38–47, 64ff; Kolko, *The Politics of War*, pp. 511–521, 569–575, and for criticism of reparations policy, 578; John M. Gimbel, *The American Occupation of Germany: Politics and the Military, 1945–1949* (Stanford, 1968), pp. xii, 9–30, 52–61, 85–87, stresses the economic needs of the American zonal administrators and the resistance of the French. For the hard-fought reparations negotiations, see also Feis, *Between War and Peace*, pp. 234, 246–258, and *FRUS, Conference of Berlin (Potsdam)*, I, 510–511, 519–554; II, 274–275, 277–287, 295–298 and passim to 512–518, 830–949. Cf. Alperovitz, "How did the Cold War Begin?" *Cold War Essays*, p. 48, for recognition of the complexities of the German questions.

58. For some examples of this approach see Hammond's and other studies in Stein, *American Civil-Military Decisions;* also the studies in Werner Schilling, P. Y. Hammond, and G. H. Snyder, eds., *Strategy, Politics and Defense Budgets* (New York, 1962); Werner Schilling, "The H Bomb Decision: How to Decide Without Actually Choosing," *Political Science Quarterly*, 76 (1961), 24–46. For a methodological statement, see Graham T. Allison, "Conceptual Models and the Cuban Missile Crisis," *The American Political Science Review*, 63 (1969), 689–718.

59. See most recently Gabriel Kolko's emphasis on the permeation of business influence in the United States foreign-policy elite and his attack on bureaucratic formalism in *The Roots of American Foreign Policy*, esp. pp. xii–xiii, 3–26.

60. See Henry Kissinger's influential distinction between legitimate and revolutionary orders in *Nuclear Weapons and Foreign Policy* (Garden City, N.Y., 1958), pp. 43–49; also Henry Kissinger, "Conditions of World Order," *Daedalus*, 45 (1966), pp. 503–529.

2

Franz Schurmann

Selections from The Logic of World Power

Franz Schurmann is a scholar of Communist China who teaches at the University of California at Berkeley. He has contributed a major study in his area of specialty: Ideology and Organization in Communist China *(Berkeley and Los Angeles: University of California Press, 1968). The book, from which the following selections are taken (pp. 8–17, 46–53, 56–62, 64–68, 91–100, 105–109) with the permission of the publisher, Pantheon, and the author, represents an effort to place the Vietnam war in the longer perspective of three-power conflict among the United States, the Soviet Union, and China. Frankly theoretical, Schurmann's work seeks to link the foreign policies of the major states with economic structures, political and bureaucratic institutions, and ideology. The close attention paid to American "capitalism" indicates the author's debt to various strands of Marxism. But the differential analysis of United States economic interests, the critique of revisionism, and the emphasis given to the autonomous imperialist drives generated by ideas represented in the Democratic Party and the logic of nuclear weapons, all make for an unorthodox and independent critical stance. It is, of course, always problematic to link up the broad outlines of theory with day-to-day outcomes; any grand scheme will be vulnerable to charges of glossing over particular historical events that fit less well. Moreover, Schurmann's summary that American imperialism provoked the cold war regardless of Soviet aspirations will seem too clever for many readers. Still, Schurmann's theory, I think, satisfies a major criterion that should be set for any explanation in the social sciences, namely, the uncovering of testable relationships between areas of activity not otherwise plausibly linked together.*

Vision and Executive Power:
Toward a Theory of Ideology and Interests

If Roosevelt's vision of "one world" was an emerging doctrine of American imperialism, then one obvious and central fact about it has to be noted: it was conceived, formulated, and implemented at the highest levels of governmental power, by the President himself. Moreover, if one takes seriously the conflict between isolationists and interventionists, that vision was put forth against the opposition of a major part of the American business class, who constitute the great bulk of America's particular interests and were traditionally the most expansionist segment of American society. This points to something that people raised in or influenced by the Marxist tradition are prone to reject: the autonomous, innovative, and powerful role of the state. But one must go even further and see what was obvious at the time: that it was not from the state as a whole, the aggregate of executive, bureaucratic, and legislative agencies, but from the very pinnacle of the state that the vision originated.

Although I have begun with some historical observations, my real intent is theoretical, to sketch out a theory of relations between states in the last quarter-century. A theory is an explanatory device, neither true nor false in itself, which demonstrates its worth by generating a continuous chain of derivative explanations of phenomena that are not in conflict with conventional wisdom or certain testable hypotheses. In other words, a good theory is a satisfyingly productive one. People feel the need to construct theories when they are persistently faced with anomalies in important problems which existing theories cannot explain away. When such anomalies exist in the realm of human affairs, it is usually the historians who take command. They gather the salient facts, sort out the patterns, and construct generalizations. The process of generalization works from the bottom up, that is, from generally accepted facts. Theory construction, on the other hand, works from the top down, from the logical mind. Both, however, demonstrate their productivity by generating hypotheses that can be tested against generally accepted canons of evidence. The most exciting situation for learning occurs when theory, hypotheses, and generalization constitute a thriving, interacting trinity in which all grow.

The important problem that has produced anomalies during the quarter-century of the nuclear age is the nature of state-to-state relations. If one accepts the notion that America has been the prime mover in this new network of relations, then the important problem becomes the nature of American foreign policy since 1945, when the nuclear age began. Mounds of popular and scholarly material have been written on this subject. All the points of view, which implicitly are kinds of theories, agree that the world since 1945 has become a political whole: even minor events in a distant part of the world affect the global skein of relations. But, since the points of view are usually ideologically inspired, they naturally differ in their basic assumptions. The most popular point of view in America has been the notion that communism has been the prime aggressive force in the world, seeking to undermine and destroy the free world. The opposite point of view, initially held in the socialist countries and by the international left wing but increasingly prevalent among "revisionist" scholars, is that America has been the prime aggressive force in the world, seeking to undermine the socialist camp and destroy revolutionary movements. A third point of view, much more esoteric, is held largely by trained experts in the field of international systems. It sees global politics as a game in which the key actors are the great powers (primarily America and Russia), the key pieces are elements of power (notably nuclear), and the other pieces are a changing variety of political actors. While the first two points of view have produced the bulk of the literature, they have not been particularly theoretical. There has been little theoretical thinking in American popular anticommunist approaches. There appears to be a great deal in the Russian and Chinese approaches, particularly as expressed in their polemics during the early 1960s, but theory, dogma, and politics were too intertwined there to allow the theory to appear in simple and elegant form. "Revisionist" writers on the left in the West have only begun the process of theory construction, much of which tends to follow Marxist lines. . . .

When people do a lot of writing about a particular subject, it always means that they are bothered by it. One hardly has to press the argument that state-to-state relations since 1945, particularly with the ever-present threat of nuclear destruction, deeply bother people throughout the world. The phenomenon of nuclear power has produced the major anomaly demanding satisfying explanation in the contemporary world—not only is this power, which can virtually burn up the planet, the product of stupefyingly sophisticated technology, but the power to use it is so centralized that, at least in the United States, one person alone can make the final decision. This is symbolized by the little black box always in the presence of the President of the United States, which contains the signals to activate, deploy, and fire the nuclear weapons. This concentration of political power of enormous scope in the hands of the chief executive, only barely modified by fail-safe devices, seems to contradict all notions of politics. Politics is the realm of power, and power can be simply defined as the command over men and resources for the achievement of goals. The notion of goals is basic to politics. Men achieve power in political structures to advance or protect their own interests or those of constituencies with whom they identify. The President of the United States is presumed to wield power in the interests of all Americans, his constituency, although it is generally believed that he does so primarily for some and less so for others. In any case, politics presumes that he acts to achieve someone's interests, even if his overriding interest is entirely personal, such as assuring his re-election. Radical and liberal views of politics in America may differ on whose interests are being advocated by the President, but they agree that his power serves interests. Whether the President is the instrument of certain constituencies or their leader does not affect that argument.

The notion of politics as serving interests runs into a dilemma when one enters the nuclear field. That the President of the United States (and presumably also the chief executives of Russia and China) exercises nuclear power is obvious—he wields command over men and resources (nuclear strike forces) to achieve goals (the destruction of an enemy). But what and whose interests are served by nuclear war? Conventional (non-nuclear) wars serve real interests: that one side capture from or deny to the other side territory, populations, resources, prestige, or time. Even a war so murky as the Vietnam war can be explained in terms of interests. Nuclear war, however, does not envisage the capture or denial of anything to an adversary. It is theoretically designed to assure maximum destruction of an adversary with maximum survival for one's own side. Since it is in the "interest" of all living beings to survive, the concept of interest loses any theoretical force, for it has meaning only where interests can be differentiated into various kinds. At first, nuclear weapons were seen as just another kind of weapon with which to punish or threaten an aggressor. Then it was realized that no nation would pursue a deliberately suicidal course in order to get something it wanted, such as a chunk of another nation's territory. Notions of deterrence then became popular, implying that massive nuclear power could in effect deter a nation from trying for illegitimate gains. As the two superpowers, America and Russia, achieved overwhelming arsenals of nuclear weapons, deterrence lost its credibility, because each side simultaneously paralyzed the other with its power, thus presumably allowing the more normal politics of gain to go on. If power cannot be used, it can serve no interests. Under such circumstances, common sense and utilitarian assumptions indicate that the power should wither away to be replaced by more useful forms. Obviously nuclear power is not only not withering away, but achieving greater dimensions than ever before. If nuclear power only deters an adversary from using his own nuclear power, then we are forced to the conclusion that it exists in and for itself. Even this notion, however, can be explained in some sort of interest terms: there are productive facilities that make the weapons and thereby gain profit, research is stimulated which benefits other sectors of the economy, bureaucratic and corporate bodies get a share of the power deriving from involvement in nuclear programs. But this is true of all weapons procured by a government. The argument about a "military-industrial complex" implies that the real purpose for the vast accumulation of arms of all kinds is to service private corporate and public bureaucratic interests. It explains the baffling problem of why the government acquires weaponry far beyond the dictates of utility in terms of conventional political wisdom, which assumes that politics always serves interests. While there is some truth to this argument, closer examination quickly shows that too much is left unexplained and too much just is not so. It does not explain the quality, nature, and purpose of the strategic weapons the government decides it needs, and overlooks the fact that much military production is not particularly profitable for the corporations concerned. To say that the government acquires immense stockpiles of nuclear weapons just to fatten the profits of corporations and expand the power of certain bureaucracies strains the public imagination, which rightly senses something anomalous about the realm of nuclear weaponry. . . .

Nuclear power is obviously a realm of politics, for if politics is the game of power, and power involves command over men and resources to achieve goals, then the immense organizational and technical systems that nuclear power has generated are political. But it is a realm of politics in which interests do not play the decisive role. Governments create nuclear systems not to benefit this or that particular interest but to give security to all the people or to the free world or even to the world as a whole. Security is intangible and unquantifiable, a mood which skilled politicians sense and can take advantage of. But public moods are clearly a reality, and for centuries organizations have existed to create and service them. The Catholic Church, for example, is a gigantic organization whose basic purpose is to cultivate the faith of its adherents. It also does many more practical things, such as teaching Christian ethics, ministering to the poor and the sick, solving problems in its communities. But faith remains the living core of its entire corporate existence. It is no coincidence that the largest organized religious body in the world is headed by one man, the Pope. A sense of security is somewhat like religious faith in its belief that there is a higher being with the power, knowledge, and presence to protect people in a threatening world constantly in turmoil. Similarly, the essence of the faith from which a sense of security derives is that there is a supreme being at the apex of the political system who is the fountainhead of that faith. Nuclear power therefore has created the need for a god. This notion should not be surprising. Most civilized societies have gone through periods when kings and emperors assumed some kind of divine form. Europe had its "divine right of kings" and China had its "celestial emperors." Much of the modern political process has resulted in the erosion of supreme and autonomous executive power—absolute monarchies have turned into constitutional monarchies and democracies have turned rulers into chief executives, periodically chosen leaders who are supposed to be little more than chairmen of the board. It is obvious that supreme executive power has made its reappearance in socialist societies (Stalin and Mao Tse-tung, for example), and now the nuclear phenomenon has also generated it in America. Never in American history has executive power been so centralized, far-reaching, and autonomous as at the present time. America is making a transition comparable to that of ancient Rome from republic to empire.

The anomaly people feel when trying to explain nuclear politics in terms of an interest theory begins to dissipate if we accept the notion that there is not just one but two realms of politics: the realm of interests and the realm of ideology. Nuclear systems belong in the realm of ideology; conventional weapons in the realm of interests. There is a qualitative gap of great importance between these two kinds of weapons systems and the power and politics they represent. This, however, reflects a much more basic gap between presidential power (the White House) and all other bureaucracies of government, including the Cabinet. The theme of qualitatively different presidential and bureaucratic politics is one of the main arguments in this book.

Understanding the realm of ideology requires an analysis of the Presidency. The analysis need not just flow outward from the personality and position of the President, but can flow inward from the context of power, issues, and conflicts in which he operates. The office makes the man as much as the man makes the office. Thus, one can learn as much about presidential power from understanding nuclear politics as from analyzing a specific decision or his decision-making powers. The President is the leader of a big political world which influences him as he influences it. He also is the only one who deals with the chief executives of other countries in an international game which has generated certain rules. Understanding that game, particularly the relations among the great powers, tells us much about presidential power. But to analyze it in terms of interest quickly leads to a dead end. It has to do with intents and intentions, actual and projected capabilities, all of which must be conceived of in a systematic sense, which I call ideological. More theoretical exposition is necessary, however, before the notion of a presidential realm of ideology can become productively useful.

Roosevelt's Vision

Roosevelt's vision involved a new world order based on the principles laid out in the Bretton Woods and Dumbarton Oaks conferences. In retrospect, one can also say that nuclear power, which today has the most powerful global force of all, had its roots in another of Roosevelt's visions. Roosevelt probably never anticipated that this new weapon, which had not even been successfully tested at the time of his death, would be one of the great determining factors of world politics for the latter half of the twentieth century. Nevertheless, the immensely costly program to develop an atomic bomb never would have been undertaken in the United States were it not for his inspiration. It can be argued that had Truman, a man steeped in interest politics, become President a few years earlier (had he been Vice President then), the atomic bomb would not have been developd. Similarly, as most historians concede, it is doubtful that the United Nations would have been formed without Roosevelt's driving force. It is also questionable whether a new monetary system and something like the World Bank would have come into being even before the war had ended without the combination of Franklin Roosevelt and Henry Morgenthau.

Roosevelt is remembered outside the United States as a visionary, a man who would have brought world peace had he lived. Within the United States, those old enough remember him either as a man devoted to peace and justice or a dictator willing to destroy the free enterprise system to feed his dreams of world grandeur. Roosevelt started out as a master politician whom even conservatives supported as a smart and forceful leader. But as he moved to resolve the crisis of depression, he evolved dreams of a new America, and as he entered the crisis of war, he began to evolve his visions of a new world. Roosevelt's long-standing interest in the Navy, in faraway places, his early global travels, gave him a world consciousness, but whatever visions he had in his earlier years went little beyond those of most stamp collectors. The conclusion that Roosevelt's global visions grew as America became involved in World War II is inescapable. War and vision were closely interrelated in Roosevelt's mind. . . .

Roosevelt's vision of atomic power, a United Nations, and a postwar monetary system was not just passive prediction that all this would come about anyway. As with scientific prediction, the President of the United States could, by virtue of his vast political power, create the conditions that would bring these new military, political, and economic systems into being. Also like scientific prediction, Roosevelt's vision was based on elements of hard realities: on a considerable array of scientific, technical, and human resource facts which convinced him—and many others—that it could be done. Many of the bricks used to build the United Nations had been available since the pre–World War I period, before the League of Nations had been formed. The most active period for the formation of international agencies dated from the turn of the century. The bricks for the new monetary system were contained in the world-wide sterling system, which survived the abandonment of the gold standard in the early 1930s and only weakened because Britain was so badly hurt during World War II. Like so many Arab mosques in Spain, which were built with older Christian masonry, Roosevelt's vision was made up of elements already in existence. What was new was the whole structure, the product of a series of flashes of insight.

Roosevelt's vision of the postwar world was, thus, a prediction of what would be, made by the only man in the world at that time who had the power to bring it about or to set up the conditions that would show that the predictions were wrong. If atomic power had fizzled, if the United Nations had quickly collapsed, and if the dollar had not been able to sustain the international monetary system, Roosevelt's visionary experiment would have been reckoned a total failure. Only America and, in America, only Roosevelt had the power to generate a global vision. Indeed, the great international structures and systems of the postwar world were American creations: nuclear power, the United Nations, and the international monetary system. Russia, which symbolically abdicated from its own internationalism during the war by dissolving the Comintern and ordering the dissolution of the American Communist party, eventually reverted to it, but only *after* the cold war had begun.

Some Propositions and Observations

Nations (or even cities and tribes) have turned into empires in the past, and, in spite of the vast historical differences, all these transformations have something in common. I shall make some general propositions on the subject, though they relate particularly to America of the postwar period.

A nation turns into an empire not simply by direct or indirect conquest, but by creating, developing, and maintaining a larger political system to govern its new dominions, clients, and dependents.

When a nation becomes an empire, a new political realm comes into being which I call the realm of ideology. This realm centers on the chief executive, and the military and political agencies he creates or assumes power over to carry out his global policies. In empires, the dominant ideology is imperial.

A nation is primarily concerned with national interests. Empires, in addition to pursuing their own interests as nations, also pursue goals deriving from the imperial ideology, which are frequently incomprehensible in terms of national interest.

The sources of imperial ideology are popular, but it is the great leader or executive projecting a vision who succeeds in transforming ideological beliefs into structures of organizational power.

Powerful realms of ideology turn outward to impose their will abroad, that being a mark of empire, except in the case of revolutionary countries, which project their power inward to revolutionize society.

I shall also make some practical observations on the basis of the theory developed so far. America became an empire in the closing days of World War II. For reasons that have yet to be explored, America made a qualitative leap from its traditional expansionism to a new global role whereby it tried to create and implement a world order. In this it succeeded, not in the form of Roosevelt's "one world," which would have included Russia, but in the form of the later "free world," which excluded Russia. America's assumption of an imperial role was obviously in part a response to the political vacuum brought about by World War II. But the theory also points to the enormous expansion of governmental power, particularly of the executive branch, as an element in this process. This expansion began in the crisis environment of the Depression but was greatly accelerated by the war. America's transition from nation to empire cannot be understood except in terms of the political visions of Franklin D. Roosevelt, which he had already gone far to implement before his death.

What I propose, in effect, is that when any nation has a political realm of ideology concretely visible in the form of a powerful chief executive, military and political structures with global concerns, and deep ideological currents purporting to bring about peace, progress, and justice in the world, it is on the way to becoming an empire. . . .

Interests Against Ideology

By giving Roosevelt his fourth term in 1944, the American electorate did more than signify acceptance of the United Nations. It reaffirmed a progressive New Deal philosophy widely regarded as crypto-revolutionary by many conservatives. In 1944 it was already clear that the war would soon end and that New Dealism would be the dominant ideology of the postwar period. The New Deal probably saved American capitalism by preventing the labor-business struggles of the Depression from turning into class war. But it did so with an ideology which, in the eyes of people of the time, was more leftist than centrist. In retrospect, one can say that in 1944 the American electorate voted for imperialism. In subsequent years they would do this again and again, not because they were hoodwinked by labor fakers or reactionaries in liberal clothing, but because they perceived American imperialism as a progressive force, which would bring benefit to themselves and to the world as a whole. Both during the Depression and during the war, the American people had an overriding desire for security—security of employment and income and security from external attack. They wanted security to overcome the miasma of fear that had come over the country after the euphoria of the 1920s. They looked to government guided by the progressive values of social welfare to provide this security, and they looked equally to government to provide such military power that never again would a Hitler or a Tojo threaten world peace. Because of the Depression and the war, the American electorate swung to the left. Thus, when Roosevelt went to them to secure a mandate for his postwar plans, his vision had a populist and progressive aura to it. Like Wilson, the progressive quality of his vision assured him world-wide support and acclaim, regardless of what the interests thought of it.

Whatever the end result of American imperialism, its origins were democratic. But what was to become the real imperialism in the postwar years was not a simple expansion of Roosevelt's vision, but the product of a struggle with two other major ideological currents springing from the realm of interests. These two currents, which I call internationalism and nationalism, have roots deep in American history and persist to the present time. They are also rooted in basic American interests, particularly economic. Prior to 1945, as universalism and isolationism, they sought to restrain Roosevelt's flights of vision and channel presidential policy into more conventional directions. But once the war was over, they fought to replace Roosevelt's vision with policies of their own.

[Early in this study], I noted three great events at the end of World War II which shaped the postwar world: the founding of the United Nations, the re-establishment of an international monetary system and world bank, and the development of atomic weapons. While not so intended, each of these events addressed itself to the key concern of one of the three currents. For the current that was to flow out of Roosevelt's vision, the establishment of the United Nations promised a new world of peace, security, and progress, a New Deal on a world-wide scale. The structures emerging from Bretton Woods addressed themselves to the key concern of the universalist current: free trade fueled by sound money. And the atomic bomb eventually became a symbol of the nationalist and isolationist obsession with military power. Actually, Roosevelt himself expressed all three currents. He was not a starry-eyed internationalist willing to disarm America, but a hard-headed military thinker devoted to the notion of American military power serving American interests—he was always interested in military bases. Although not adept at handling intricate economic problems, his Eastern patrician heritage made him sympathetic to the world trade concerns of Wall Street. And his growing stature as the leader of the free and the friend of the poor did as much as anything to make the United Nations into something above and beyond the League of Nations. Roosevelt was full of contradictions, which made him a superb politician. They sprang not so much from his pliant personality as from the facts of American political life.

Universalism or Internationalism

The universalist current ran strong in the State Department, the agency of American government traditionally close to international business. It was the obvious agency to concern itself with postwar planning, and, as a bureaucracy with a long history, it did so from the perspective of its own interests. The main business of the State Department was, in fact, business. The main duties of its vast diplomatic network, particularly its consular corps, were to aid American businessmen in their dealings with foreign governments. Since the time of John Hay, the predominant ideological current governing the State Department was an "open door" policy, a commitment to free trade and protection of American property and businessmen in foreign countries. The State Department feared that postwar economic chaos could lead to a repetition of what happened after World War I: revolution followed by fascism and war. Cordell Hull, as Secretary of State, regarded the United Nations as a political instrument which, by universality of membership, could compel members to adopt the principles of free trade and respect for property. Free trade, fueled by loans from the prosperous United States, could revive the devastated economies and thereby provide the firmest guarantee against new troubles. Peace would be the product of universally accepted free trade. The hope was entertained that even Bolshevik Russia might depart from its rigid hostility to free trade practices and thereby gradually rejoin the world community.

Free trade versus protectionism was an old issue in American politics, and the State Department traditionally stood on the side of free trade. The State Department has always been the most elitist governmental agency (its foreign service officers were recruited largely from graduates of Ivy League schools), and it is not surprising that it took its cues from the most elitist segment of American business, the Eastern Establishment. It was also the most internationally minded bureaucracy in the government. Only the State Department felt that it really understood how much America was intertwined with larger world systems, and within America only the Eastern Establishment with its far-flung business interests abroad was directly involved in the world scene.

The primary concern of the Eastern business establishment was making and keeping money on a grand scale through investments and trade that covered the world. Built into this basic commitment to money were a series of attitudes arising out of two centuries of practical experience. The Eastern Establishment loathed war and revolution. War destroyed property and increased the power of governments. Revolution was a mortal threat to property. The State Department traditionally reflected both of these attitudes. In its postwar planning, the assurance of peace was, next to free trade, its major concern. On the other hand, the State Department also held some of the most ferocious anticommunist views in government, reflected by many of its ambassadors. The coincidence of these two attitudes was manifested in State Department policies toward the Vichy government and in the person of the United States Ambassador to Vichy, William Leahy. The State Department maintained friendly ties with Vichy partly to prevent the war from spreading over the rest of France and the French Empire and partly out of instinctive support for a conservative, anticommunist regime determined to prevent Bolshevism from arising in France. It opposed de Gaulle because he wanted to drag the French Empire back into the war and create the kind of chaos that would permit the Communists to resurrect themselves.

The State Department was intellectually the heir of the Hamiltonian tradition that regarded government, particularly foreign policy, as too intricate a matter to be entrusted to the ignorant masses. How could the people be relied on to make judicious judgments about something so complex as international monetary policy? The State Department's elitism did not arise from a reactionary fear of the masses but from the comfortable conviction of men who, like bankers and financiers, held a monopoly of knowledge about the ethereal world of international relations. Its universalism was the reflection of a basic reality, that of the world market system. For two centuries, capitalism, spearheaded by Great Britain, had woven a nexus of economic and political interests spanning the entire world, on which all nations were dependent to one degree or another. The energizing force of this world market system was world trade, which, of course, was monopolized by the advanced and civilized nations. Trade brought profits to national enterprises and the raw materials which an expanding capitalism needed. While America did not approve wholeheartedly of the British Empire as the political expression of the world market system, it was regarded as irreplaceable for the preservation of that system. The pound sterling was the symbol both of the world market system as the leading reserve currency and of the British Empire by virtue of its Englishness. The British Empire was the closest thing to a world order since the Roman Empire. If World War II weakened Great Britain's ability to maintain that empire, this did not mean and should not mean that the world order too should disappear. Universalism was a further elaboration of the world order which the British Empire did most to bring about in the modern world and for the maintenance and further development of which America was to assume the guiding role in the post-1945 world.

Cordell Hull's universalism was an expression of the realm of interests. The interests were the international economy which for two centuries had been under the control of Englishmen and Americans. The internationalists saw both world wars as attempts by ferocious nationalisms to destroy the international economy. Conversely, they regarded the destruction of the international economy as the main cause for the rise of fascism, Bolshevism, and other barbaric political forms. The Bolsheviks took people's property away and the Nazis threatened to undo the world market system. While the Anglo-American elites exhibited natural tendencies to seek accommodations with both in order to avoid war, the Bolshevik and the Fascist/Nazi dangers had to be resisted when they came too close to the core of the international economic system. Hullian universalism was quite different from the American imperialism of the postwar period. It was politically and economically conservative. It wanted to restore what was and do as little new as possible. What had to be restored above all else was the world market system. If this was done, the Anglo-American business elite would have its power reaffirmed and, as the best custodian of a peaceful world order, could then do what was necessary to improve mankind's lot and prevent new barbarisms from arising. The State Department believed that if the world could be brought back to where it was before the turn of the century, before an ambitious Kaiser Wilhelm threatened its peace and security, the greatest good for the greatest number would be vouchsafed.

The insulated atmosphere of the State Department, like that of the great international banking offices, made it easy for them to think in terms of the logic of international relations and difficult for them to understand the popular furor which produced wars and revolutions. But visionary ideologies and innovative policies do not arise out of the realm of interests. Conservatism in the modern world means nothing more than a commitment to certain existing interests. Attempts to portray it as a moral or visionary force have failed for the simple reason that it can never conjure up hope and anticipation in people's minds. Hullian universalism would have liked to see a postwar world where governments came back into the hands of responsible conservatives (as eventually happened in the former enemy nations with Adenauer, Yoshida, and De Gasperi), where outlaw nations like Russia assumed international responsibilities by recognizing the obligations of participation in the world market system, and where the small and poor nations took the sensible path of slow, deliberate efforts toward improving their lot.

Universalism was, in essence, a benign, conservative internationalism. It flourished during World War II through close Anglo-American cooperation for the preservation of the existing world order. It was not nationalistic, and was willing to make major sacrifices in the area of national sovereignty. That this was possible without sacrificing national identity was due to the overriding fact that in the eyes of the universalists the English-speaking world was the world itself. No language was more widely spoken than English. Through the British Empire and America's far-flung private activities (businessmen, missionaries, educators), Anglo-American culture had become the predominant world culture, just as Roman culture had covered the known Western world two thousand years before. Above all, nowhere in the world could one find cultivated men with as deep a sense of moral responsibility as in London and the eastern seaboard of the United States. Moreover, these men had access to the greatest power in the world, the command over wealth. It seemed natural that the American and British worlds should eventually coalesce in an English-speaking union in which both would surrender archaic notions of sovereignty to the interests of a peaceful new world order.

The universalists, like all conservatives, were hostile to huge governmental power and above all to militarism. Like the Marxists, they believed that capitalism knew no boundaries. They thought that power was best invested in a class of wealthy, educated, and propertied men who had been taught responsibility in the finest schools. Government was to be their instrument, in which they served often at cost to themselves. Huge bureaucracies and huge armies would only produce the barbaric monstrosities of Nazi Germany and Bolshevik Russia. The universalist conservatives mistrusted the state as an irrational force. From it sprang lust for power and, above all, the drive toward war, which of all policies in government the conservatives most opposed. They tried to stem the drive toward war until it was inevitable, and during the war they tried to plan for postwar structures that would make a new war impossible. The universalist conservatives instinctively sympathized with Chamberlain's efforts to avoid war by appeasing Hitler. Roosevelt, as a sometime universalist, actively supported his efforts to settle the Czech crisis in 1938. The basic concern of the universalist conservatives was stability, and nothing was more conducive to stability than peace. The conservatives abhorred revolution, but they also abhorred war. Therefore, *both* Nazi Germany and Bolshevik Russia were abominations in their eyes. Yet if Germany ceased making war against other nations and Russia refrained from exporting revolution, there was no reason one could not coexist with them. It was regrettable that the German and Russian peoples allowed themselves to be governed by barbarians, but if they would just leave other people alone, there was no reason to make war against them.

This theoretical proposition suggests that conservative universalism, inclined toward a world order dominated by Anglo-American capital, was also committed to peace and to peaceful coexistence. Free, unfettered trade fueled by a stable international monetary system was the indispensable basis for any kind of rational world order. War as much as revolution was the deadly enemy of trade. Peace assured stability and stability was the necessary prerequisite for the accumulation and preservation of wealth. Peace was to be preserved at all costs except where the threat became mortal.

The universalist current, as the world view of international business, retained its power during the postwar years. It fueled postwar economic reconstruction of Europe, foreign aid to poor nations, and participation in United Nations activities, and argued for peaceful coexistence with Russia. It was not accidental that the breakthrough to peaceful coexistence with Russia came under the conservative Eisenhower and that the breakthrough to China came under Nixon. Once Russia and China opened their iron and bamboo curtains respectively, the conservatives were more ready than others to espouse peaceful coexistence. While the right-wing military opposed it and the ideological liberals (like organized labor) shrank, back, the conservatives made the move. In both Eisenhower's approach to Russia and Nixon's approach to China and Russia, trade played a major role. Peaceful coexistence could be meaningful only if Russia and China agreed to join the world market system. If they did, the conservatives foresaw that conservatizing forces would set in in both countries. The more these militantly revolutionary countries were involved in world trade, the more their barbaric regimes would be civilized under the weight of international responsibility. It would be too much to hope that they would once again accept the principle of private property, but accepting foreign investment was a step in the right direction.

Universalism was a World War II expression of capitalist conservatism. As the cold war made "one world" meaningless, universalism took on more modest postures. It advocated greater unity within the "free world," fought against trade barriers, supported internationalist programs. The conservatives eagerly joined the anticommunist crusade and needed little convincing that the Russians were intent on expanding Russian national power, as well as revolutionary communism, throughout the world. But they never lost their conviction that peace was best for profits, and it mattered little from which side of the Iron Curtain profits came. When the Russian threat was proclaimed contained, they were the first to initiate steps toward peaceful and profitable coexistence. . . .

Isolationism or Nationalism

The isolationist current was opposed to universalism. On the surface, it seemed to imply doctrines that the United States should not get involved in the wars of other nations unless directly attacked. Historically, it appeared to derive from one of George Washington's basic principles of foreign policy, that the new United States must avoid "entangling alliances." In fact, isolationism was a form of American nationalism clearly expressed in its favorite slogan: America first.

Much has been written on the diverse interests and attitudes isolationism represented. Yet, as James MacGregor Burns wrote, what was common to all isolationists was the view "defense, yes; aid to the Allies, perhaps; but foreign wars—never." [1] The isolationists, except for their transient left-wing fringe, believed in American military power. Their congressional representatives voted eagerly for defense build-ups and displayed a typically nationalist admiration for the flag propped up by guns. They believed fervently that America should defend its interests by military force where threatened. Since those interests were obvious in Asia and Latin America, they were more prepared to challenge Japanese expansionism than that of Germany in Europe, and Mexico's nationalization of United States-owned oil companies aroused an angry furor. What they could support in Roosevelt was his espousal of a strong navy, but they distrusted the uses to which he was going to put American military power. The key issue of debate was the European war.

The isolationists were anti-imperialist, which, in the 1930s and 1940s, meant being against the *only* world imperialism of the time, the British Empire. They regarded it as a global conspiracy on the part of vast financial interests centered in London abetted by similar interests in New York to dominate the world economy. The ultimate aim of Britain, they believed, was to create a world economic and political monopoly which would stifle the natural expansionist desires of late-comer powers, such as America. The isolationists were indeed expansionists, the true heirs of "manifest destiny." They saw a glorious future for America beyond its borders, but not particularly in Europe or Africa or Western Asia. They looked westward to East Asia and southward to Latin America. They believed in laissez-faire capitalism and were hostile to big government, whose only result could be to suppress freedom, the natural right of every individual to deploy his enterprise in the pursuit of his own interests. They believed in the individual, particularly the individual who decided to rise above the masses by acquiring wealth. They had a classical commitment to freedom, to a society subject only to minimal governance. Above all, they saw themselves as Americans, a definite, distinct, and proud nationality with a mission in the world. American, in the understanding of the day, meant white, Protestant, and male.

One can get a sense of the social nature of the isolationists by looking at the Americans who expanded into the Pacific during the late nineteenth century and on into the twentieth. There were three types: merchants, soldiers, and missionaries. Nowhere else in the world, save in Central America, could one find comparable numbers of such Americans. American traders found lucrative new enterprise in Hawaii, the Philippines, China, and in the interstices left open by other empires. Since the Spanish-American War, America had acquired major military bases throughout the Pacific. Missionaries were everywhere in the region preaching more by example than by word the superior nature of American man. Free enterprise in Hawaii showed what honest enterprise could achieve. By the end of the nineteenth century, a few American families, largely of missionary origin, had developed vast sugar and pineapple plantations, recruited Asians to work them, and made immense fortunes. All this occurred under conditions of "freedom" granted to them by the Hawaiian monarchy and then further assured by a beneficent American takeover. Through the Navy, the American military began to develop imperial qualities in the Pacific, most evident in the Philippines, which was run pretty much as a military domain. The effort of the missionaries was ideological, the preaching of Protestant Christianity. Nowhere else in the world did America assume such an ideological role. Europe was regarded as hopelessly corrupt, Latin America as lost to the Catholic Church, and Africa of little interest. Only Asia with its billion heathen seemed within the reach of conversion to Christianity. China, in particular, was the most ardently pursued target for full conversion.

The dreams and visions that the Pacific engendered were not greatly appreciated in the pro-European parts of the American east coast. The westward expansion of the United States was taken for granted, and, of course, America should pursue its interests in the Pacific. But the highly educated men of the Eastern Establishment could not understand the passion which motivated these dreams and visions, and hatreds which arose when they were thwarted. The Pacific symbolized a general American expansionism which in the 1920s appeared to have scored fantastic successes. In 1919, America rejected internationalism, returned to pursue its own narrow interests, and enjoyed an unprecedented boom. By 1930, the boom had collapsed. The expansionists saw the crash of the stock market and the subsequent breakdown of the international monetary system as conspiracies aimed at destroying them. When unions began to organize with the active support of the patrician Roosevelt, the expansionists saw an even greater conspiracy between the mighty of the Eastern Establishment and the communist-inspired labor unions to crush them in the middle. They saw themselves as the real driving force in America, the people who created enterprise and made the wealth which others, bankers and organized labor, then usurped. Expansionism and nationalism were identical in the minds of those who took the isolationist stance prior to 1941; the history of America in the Pacific had forged that identity.

If the nationalists saw expansionism and nationalism as identical, they pretended to see a similar identity between internationalism, communism, and imperialism. The big bankers of Wall Street were internationalist—so were the communists with their Marxist doctrines, and so were the British with their empire. Moreover, the growing alliance between the Roosevelt-led administration and the unions seemed to indicate a real alliance between the forces of international capital and their ostensible enemies, the revolutionary proletarians. All this could only be aimed at capitalism, as the nationalists saw it. The expansionist image of capitalism was that of the National Association of Manufacturers, which saw the corporation, producing and marketing things, and not the banks as the core of free enterprise capitalism. Socialism to them meant monopoly domination of the economy whether by immense finance capital, big government, or communist revolutionaries. When Hitler began to preach that an international conspiracy of capitalists, Jews, and Bolsheviks was trying to crush the expansionist drive of the German nation, many in the United States understood and sympathized. By the late 1930s, the Roosevelt-labor union alliance had expanded to include an emerging British-American alliance to oppose Germany. And after June 22, 1941, the archenemy of mankind, Bolshevik Russia, had joined. The conspiracy became horrifyingly real both domestically and internationally. At home, an Eastern Establishment-dominated administration was colluding with labor unions and Red-sympathizing intellectuals to establish an American socialism. Abroad, an alliance between America, imperial Britain, and Bolshevik Russia was developing against Germany, a country that was nationalist, expansionist, and capitalist in the best sense of the word. A climax was reached in the great lend-lease debates when Roosevelt was ready to turn over a significant number of American warships to Britain, which the isolationists construed as a weakening of American military power, an infringement on American sovereignty, and involvement in a war whose only favorable outcome could be a victory for British international bankers and Russian Bolsheviks.

American nationalism remained isolationist until December 7, 1941. When Japan attacked America, militant nationalism immediately joined the fray. Japan was a welcome enemy for the nationalists. It was a nonwhite power threatening American interests in the Pacific. It was already at war with America's special responsibility in the Far East, China. It was not at war with Bolshevik Russia, thus precluding Russian-American collaboration in the Far East, and, above all, the Japanese had the effrontery to attack their most admired symbol of American military power, the Navy. Hitler's declaration of war against America completed the picture of an attack on two fronts, and war against both Germany and Japan was accepted by all American nationalists.

Prior to December 7, 1941, the interventionists wanted war in Europe and the isolationists opposed it. War against Japan, however, was acceptable to both. It can be argued that the multifaceted Roosevelt was a nationalist and expansionist in the Far East but an internationalist and imperialist in Europe. Roosevelt was a Navy man, and believed in America's pre-eminent role in East Asia. The war in the Pacific was run along nationalist lines on the American side. Unlike the European theater where America and Britain had to conduct a joint war, the war in the Far East, except for Burma, was a strictly American affair. The Americans carried out their special relationship with China without benefit of British advice, and where, as in Burma, British and American actions came into contact, the relationships were bad, such as those between Stilwell and Mountbatten. Roosevelt easily assumed that British power had been shattered in the Far East and only America was able to oppose Japan. The nationalism of the war against Japan was evident, for example, in the racism that accompanied it. While there was deep ideological revulsion against the Germans, there was little anti-German feeling in a racial sense, as in World War I. But the Japanese were hated as an upstart race. Japanese, but not Germans and Italians, were interned in concentration camps in the United States. Japanese captives in the Pacific were much more cruelly treated than German captives.

Whereas the core belief of the internationalist current was the need for international systems, particularly economic, that of the nationalist current was the need for pre-eminent American military power. In a dangerous world, this was the only guarantee for American safety, for the defense of America's interests, and, in particular, for the assurance of the ever-continuing outward expansion of American enterprise. America must have a powerful navy and develop new technologies, such as air power, to the hilt. It must have a powerful army, although the nationalists were always suspicious of universal military service. . . . The nationalists regarded military power as the main force supporting expansionism. It was, therefore, legitimate and necessary to destroy the military power of countries threatening America, such as Japan and Germany, and to do everything possible to prevent new military powers from arising which could threaten America, such as Russia.

Contradictions Between Internationalism and Nationalism

The debate over America's role in the postwar world found both internationalists and nationalists making expected arguments. The internationalists wanted international systems which would guarantee a world market based on free trade, monetary stability, and political responsibility. The nationalists cared for little else beyond the assurance of American power, particularly military, in the postwar world. In 1919, these two currents had clashed and nationalism won out, although internationalism resurfaced with the Dawes and Young plans. During World War II, they clashed again. This time the outcome was not a synthesis or a compromise but something new—an American imperialism, which neither internationalists nor nationalists had envisaged.

The practical internationalists still thought in pre-1914 terms of a world led by the key powers, America and Britain, working closely together, with Russia's role to be worked out in a manner satisfactory to the world market system. The nationalists believed neither in "one world" nor in the Anglo-American partnership, and felt that America would only get into trouble if it departed from the sound utilitarian principle of self-interest first. Roosevelt's vision of a Pax Americana was in many ways a reincarnation of Wilson's earlier vision, but, unlike Wilson, Roosevelt had the good fortune to appear as a nationalist (in the Pacific), an internationalist (in Europe), and, above all, a popular leader spreading revolutionary ideas to the downtrodden masses of the world.

Both internationalism and nationalism, when stimulated or attacked, generated ideologies of their own, as we shall see. In the postwar period, they became prominent on the left and right of the American political scene. But they were not creative ideologies, and in themselves launched no new vision or policies. Internationalism was too elitist to elicit much popular response except where it coincided with left-wing internationalism. And left-wing internationalism had too little support within the American people to constitute a powerful popular ideology. The popular weakness of both forms of internationalism made them easy targets for nationalism, particularly when it assumed virulent anticommunist forms. Nationalism achieved its own greatest popular success during the McCarthy period, but as an ideology it collapsed when McCarthy began hitting too close to the Establishment. While internationalist and nationalist sentiments are deeply grounded in the American people, the ideologies they generated have remained confined to the left and right extremes of the political spectrum. Since Roosevelt's time, the dominant ideology in America has been one or another form of liberalism, and Roosevelt's role during the 1930s and during World War II was crucial in its fashioning.

A question widely discussed among historians is, Why did the cold war begin? A more appropriate question, in the light of my discussion, is, Why did American imperialism arise? Even Establishment journals such as *Fortune*, musing over the great changes coming over the world in the 1970s, speak of a Pax Americana that governed the world in the post–World War II period. It is my contention that the cold war erupted as a result of America's decision to create an empire, not the reverse. Inspired by Roosevelt's vision, America began to plan a postwar order in which it would be the dominant, guiding force and the source of morality. Russia did not or could not or appeared not to go along with this new order, and, *therefore,* the cold war began. Assuming the burdens of empire is a task not to be taken lightly, and virtually nothing in America's tradition, not even its expansionism, prepared it to assume responsibility for the entire world. Roosevelt did not propose that America join a new League of Nations, but that instead a United Nations be conceived and located on American soil and other nations be invited to join. The United Nations was an American creation which other nations joined largely out of the simple power-political realization that World War II had made America the mightiest nation on the globe. What, then, impelled Roosevelt and his closest advisers to undertake such a novel task? The simplest answer is fear—fear that the world would again degenerate into bloody conflicts, fear that civil wars would erupt, fear that economic and political systems would disintegrate not only from revolutionary pressures but perhaps even more from bitter conflicts within ruling classes themselves. Roosevelt's most profound experience from the American Depression was the vision of America's ruling classes turning against each other with a violence reflected in the bitter struggles waged in and around Congress during the 1930s.

There has been a current in revisionist scholarship that sees the determination of the United States to suppress revolution as the key moving force behind the development of the cold war. While there is much truth to this notion, it overlooks some of the basic fears weighing upon the men who ruled America during the 1940s. If the phenomenon of Bolshevik Russia was loathsome to them, equally if not more loathsome and frightening was the phenomenon of Germany. How could a country in the forefront of civilization and eminently successful in capitalist enterprise have turned into a barbaric monstrosity which showed little hesitation at plunging the world once again into a war? The internationalists were convinced that virulent nationalism was as deadly an enemy of capitalism as Bolshevik Russia. Twice within the century that had not yet reached its halfway point, German nationalism had attacked the world market system, turning what could have been a viable international order for keeping the peace, assuring economic stability, growth, and profits, and allowing the international elites to resolve their countries' problems, into a cauldron for unbelievably destructive war. How to prevent a new Germany, either Germany itself or some other nation, from arising was the central problem for the internationalists during the post–World War II period. . . .

That internationalism and nationalism were contradictory currents in America is evident from the great conflicts that rent the country between 1945 and 1950. The most general form this conflict took was "Europe-first" versus "Asia-first." The word "first" implied a conflict not just of priorities but of different world views. By and large, the pre-1941 interventionists emerged as Europe-firsters and the isolationists as Asia-firsters. The Europe-firsters believed that a healthy Western Europe was the major prerequisite for American security, and demanded that considerable monies be spent to bring this about. The Asia-firsters, who were mainly in the Republican opposition, saw the vast spending that such a program entailed as another New Deal measure to soak business for obscure international purposes whose end result would be only to create an even more powerful and dictatorial federal government. Meanwhile, legitimate American interests were being threatened by communism in Asia, chiefly China. To the Asia-firsters, the Democratic administration's tolerance of communism in Asia was an ominous replay of the worst features of the Roosevelt Administration. Here again, the American people were called on to bail out "Britain" in the West while in the East "Russia's" tentacles, in the form of Chinese communism, were painted as "agrarian reformers," movements of the poor for justice, to be accepted as legitimate forces. In the period 1945–1950, "Asia," especially "China," became the symbol of American nationalism. Senator William Knowland's advocacy of Chiang Kai-shek, so intense that he was nicknamed the Senator from Formosa, would seem ludicrous in retrospect except for the fact that Chiang Kai-shek had become much more than the symbol of determined anticommunism. Methodist by religion and married to an American-educated woman, a leader viewed by them as determinedly loyal to America, he was more American than most Americans. Like General Douglas MacArthur, America's most shining examplar of militant nationalism, Chiang was a beleaguered fighter struggling against an international communist conspiracy directed against him not only by Moscow and its Chinese tools but by Washington, New York, and Harvard as well. In that great conflict, the nationalists felt on the defensive, finding themselves threatened by a range of powerful forces intent on doing away with American nationality and sovereignty. The backlash of McCarthyism indicates how violent the conflict had become.

The bitter conflict for which McCarthyism was more symbol than substance eventually ebbed away in the 1950s for one major reason— "bipartisanship in foreign policy." Spearheaded by Senator Arthur Vandenberg's wartime rallying to Roosevelt's conception of a United Nations, the "liberal" wing of the Republican party accepted the premise that consensus must prevail over the basic issues of foreign policy.

That they were able to force bipartisanship on the party against the opposition of conservatives like Robert Taft was manifest in their candidates in 1948 and 1952: the New York liberal Thomas Dewey and the wartime commander of Allied forces in Europe, Dwight Eisenhower. If bipartisanship had not been achieved in the postwar years, it is likely that the Republican party as the chief political vehicle of American nationalism would have mounted an even greater attack on the Democratic internationalist liberals, which could only have resulted in a foreign policy much different from the Pax Americana, which the United States succeeded in constructing.

A new ideology, different from both internationalism and nationalism, forged the basis on which bipartisanship could be created. The key word and concept in that new ideology was *security*.

Security as an Operational Idea

No word better characterizes the New Deal of the 1930s than security, just as no word better characterizes the climate of that Depression period than fear. The institution of Social Security for the aged by Roosevelt's Administration typified the New Deal's ideology: unless people had assurance that they would not remain destitute victims of unpredictable business cycles, society would disintegrate into chaos. Only one institution in society, the government, could provide that assurance. If wealth had to be redistributed so that security could be achieved, the more affluent had to pay the price, lest by not doing so they lose everything. An important corollary to these Social Security policies was that injecting money into the economy to "prime the pump" would stimulate a business upturn. What appeared to be waste in order to calm people's fears was essentially similar to private investment, spending in order eventually to produce more income. It would be wrong, however, to see Social Security, loans and payments to farmers, relief measures, small business loans, and so on as simply devices to get corporate capital functioning again. There were twenty-five million unemployed in the 1930s, and class war in the form of militant industrial union organizing threatened to tear the country asunder. The crash providing of even a small degree of economic security was viewed as essential to prevent matters from getting worse. This ideology of security, deeply implanted in the administration, gave rise to an entire range of social legislation, most notably the Wagner Labor Relations Act, which gave unions unprecedented protection under the law. Unions were perceived as a form through which security could be achieved for the most dangerous element of the population, the blue-collar workers. The union meant protection.

The fear that gripped America in the 1930s was domestic. By the 1940s, it had become external as well. In 1941, American soil was attacked by a foreign power for the first time since the War of 1812. Moreover, German and Japanese armies were threatening to take over the entire Eastern Hemisphere, leaving America alone and isolated in the Western Hemisphere. Later as postwar planning proceeded in Washington, the concern for security became the dominant theme, uniting the universalists in the State Department, the ex-isolationist nationalists in the Republican party, and, of course, the key Rooseveltian liberals in the Treasury Department. Whatever form the postwar order took, above all, it had to provide security for the United States against another threat arising such as had provoked World War II. While the talk of security still roused the hackles of conservatives, who saw in it just another cloak for New Deal big government, the great majority of the people responded to it. They finally realized that the world was fundamentally chaotic, something few people had accepted in the nineteenth century. War and depression were endemic to people's existence unless active measures were taken to curb them. If "struggle" is the word most characteristic of Maoism and symbolic of its world view, then security and fear were symbolic of the major world view that governed the United States at the end of World War II—chaos produced fear which could only be combatted with security.

It has been said many times that Roosevelt's vision of the postwar world was an extension of his New Deal to the world as a whole. The United Nations was to become the nucleus of a world government which the United States would dominate much as the Democrats dominated the American Congress. The essence of the New Deal was the notion that big government must spend liberally in order to achieve security and progress. Thus, postwar security would require liberal outlays by the United States in order to overcome the chaos created by the war. It is not accidental that the most ambitious New Dealish schemes for the postwar period came out of the Treasury Department, which was more Rooseveltian in ideology than any other governmental bureaucracy. But even when its plans assumed absurd forms, as in turning the Germans into a nation of farmer/herders, the Treasury most closely expressed Roosevelt's own ideas. It proposed the destruction for all time of the world's most virulent nationalism, that of Germany. If German and to a lesser extent Japanese nationalism were destroyed, the world would never again have to fear that an advanced capitalist nation would threaten the international system. Aid to Russia and other poor nations would have the same effect as social welfare programs within the United States—it would give them the security to overcome chaos and prevent them from turning into violent revolutionaries. Meanwhile, they would be drawn inextricably into the revived world market system. By being brought into the general system, they would become responsible, just as American unions had during the war. Helping Britain and the remainder of Western Europe would rekindle economic growth, which would stimulate transatlantic trade and, thus, help the American economy in the long run. America had spent enormous sums running up huge deficits in order to sustain the war effort. The result had been astounding and unexpected economic growth. Postwar spending would produce the same effect on a world-wide scale. By destroying Germany and paying off Russia, America and the world would achieve security from their two greatest fears—nationalist aggression and violent revolution.

By portraying America as an aggressively imperialist nation since the end of World War II (if not before), revisionist scholarship has washed away one of the most important factors that made American imperialism possible—the tremendous ideological appeal of New Deal doctrines of security. Wilson's Fourteen Points aroused widespread response from peoples throughout the world seeking national self-determination, much to the chagrin of the Versailles peacemakers. But Roosevelt's appeal was of a different order. America was the liberator with the power and money this time to prevent war from recurring. While American anticolonialism was to have a great impact on the Third World countries, the biggest impact on Europe was the American ideology personified by Roosevelt and his New Deal. Virtually the entire communist movement from America to Russia to the European and Asian parties believed that America was coterminous with Roosevelt and the New Deal. Ho Chi Minh was so taken with America that he made the American Declaration of Independence the model for Vietnam's own declaration of independence from France. At the end of World War II, the dominant sentiment in the advanced countries was a yearning for peace and security, not for revolution. Nor was it different in a poor country like China. The Chinese Communists looked to America for some support in their efforts to secure a coalition government with Chiang Kai-shek so that they could cease at last the wars that they had been fighting since 1927. They wanted security from Kuomintang attack, which, when it came in 1946, impelled them back onto the path of revolution. America in 1945 held a virtual ideological monopoly in the world. "Communism" as a global ideology had withered as the result of defeats in Spain, the Nazi-Soviet pact, the disbanding of the Comintern and the American Communist party, the growing awareness of Stalin's purges of Russian and foreign Communists, and the obvious national character of the Russian resistance to the Germans during the war. At the end of World

War II, people did not yearn for class struggle but for an end to struggle. War was so horrible an evil that nothing could be worse. No other nation seemed so dedicated to and capable of providing the security that the world wanted than America. The ideological power that this gave America was one of the most important weapons it wielded in the postwar period, and was decisive in enabling it to construct the Pax Americana, its own imperialism. . . .

Containment

By the summer of 1947 a new current in American foreign policy became evident, symbolized by the word "containment." This doctrine ostensibly derives from George Kennan, who, from his post as ambassador to Russia, wired home dire cables about the inexorable character of Russian expansionism. Russia might be communist in ideology, he noted, but the real force for its expansionism was nationalist and went far back into Russian history. Unless the free nations put up powerful walls to contain this expansionism, Russian power would ooze out over Western Europe and Asia, and before long America and its allies would be faced with a threat as great as that from Nazi Germany. Kennan's "cable from Moscow" came a little less than a year after former Prime Minister Churchill had given his famous Iron Curtain speech at Fulton, Missouri, in March 1946. Throughout 1946 there was no lack of voices within America speaking of the growing danger emanating from Russia. That a case could be made for Russian expansionism is obvious. Stalin had concluded that great power cooperation was no longer feasible and he might as well fasten his hold on Eastern Europe, as well as on the Soviet zone of Germany. The great atomic test at Bikini on July 1, 1946, was a bad sign, indicating that America was pushing the development of new atomic bombs to the hilt with the ever-present threat that they might be used against Russia. Negotiations for a coalition government in China had broken down, making civil war a certainty. Everywhere Russian-American relations were getting worse. In the euphoric days after Yalta, Stalin had been in the mood for concessions to the British and Americans, but as the months of the Truman Administration passed, he realized that concessions were always followed by more demands. Undoubtedly remembering his experiences with Hitler, Stalin decided that the only language the capitalists understood was power, and moved to consolidate Russia's control over its front entrance in Eastern Europe.

Whether Russia was or was not expansionist is not vital to understanding why the new foreign policy current of containment arose. The facts marshaled by such eminent experts as George Kennan served an already existing ideological need in Washington. The allegedly electrifying impact of his cable of February 1947, and later his "Mr. X" article in *Foreign Affairs,* was hardly due to their analytical brilliance. The rising national security bureaucracy clustered around the White House needed a view of the world that would fit the policies they were beginning to develop.

Kennan's cables and articles, while meant for the bureaucracy rather than the public, had the same ideological impact as *Mein Kampf* had earlier in showing a nation bent on eating up the entire world. Kennan's portrayal of Russia in terms reminiscent of Germany was more welcome to Washington than the rising theme of an international communist conspiracy. Then in the forefront of an effort to uplift, liberate, and reform the world, Washington had no stomach for an anticommunist crusade which would line it up with the international right wing. But an expansionist Russia could allow for the same kind of global united front that was mounted to resist German and Japanese expansion.

The Democrats who ruled Washington in the postwar years were committed to the notion that the American government had the key role in bringing security, peace, and progress to the world. But they did not yet have an operational ideology for America's new role in the world comparable to New Deal ideology on the home front. The nationalists and the internationalists already had world views that envisaged a definite external role for America. For the nationalists, what mattered was dealing with other nations on an *ad hoc* basis for one purpose: serving American interests. To make sure that those interests were respected, America had to remain strong, and what better way to remain supreme than to keep and enforce its own atomic monopoly. The internationalists wanted an economic world based on trade and free enterprise with threats and opportunities handled in utilitarian terms. What Kennan's contributions made possible was the elaboration of a world view that gave the government—not the military or the corporations—the leading role in the new adventures abroad.

The origin of these imperialist policies cannot be dissociated from the Anglo-American alliance which developed at this time and proved to be closer and more harmonious than it was during the war. Laborite Britain, which had aroused feelings of horror among American free enterprisers, turned out to be America's staunchest ally in the development of its imperialist policies. During the war, America and Britain collaborated mainly in the campaign against Germany. Elsewhere in the world, the two nations went their separate ways. In fact, to Churchill's fury, Roosevelt even showed inclinations to break up the British colonial empire. But after the war, America and Britain became close collaborators not just in Western Europe but throughout the world. Britain was in a precarious position when the war ended. It was heavily in debt not only to the United States but to many of its colonies as well, notably India. Moreover, with the Laborite victory in August 1945, Britain launched the welfare state, which imposed a new drain on its limited resources. Most significant of all, the tide toward independence from colonial rule seemed irresistible. The Laborites were more prepared ideologically than the Tories to grant political independence to the colonies, but they were still faced with the heavy burden of maintaining military forces in faraway places. Where "responsible governments" (mainly British-trained elites) would assume political leadership, London was usually glad to grant independence, since this did not involve jeopardy to British economic interests and political influence (after all, the newly independent countries elected to remain within the Commonwealth). But in too many parts of the world either there were no such responsible governments or real threats demanded the continued presence of British military force, at great cost.

In the five years following 1945, Britain had to keep a powerful military presence in Greece, Malaya, the Suez Canal, Jordan, and Iraq, and had to maintain far-flung naval and air units to preserve its credibility as a world military power. In addition, it had to maintain occupation forces in Germany and other parts of Western Europe. In Greece and Malaya, Britain fought Communist revolutionary movements which threatened to bring into power governments that could not be counted on to cooperate with Britain. In the Middle East (which included Greece), nationalist unrest and Arab-Jewish conflict threatened to spill over into regions from which most of the world's oil came. Iran was turbulent because of a left-wing government in Azerbaijan. Rebellious Kurds threatened the Mosul oil fields. King Farouk's rule in Egypt was unstable. Southeast Asia had the same kind of turbulence. Indonesian nationalists were threatening Dutch rule and Vietnamese insurgents would not let the French back into Indochina.

The British feared that the chaos that had beset Europe after the First World War would this time erupt in Asia and the Middle East. Almost everywhere in Asia, civil wars were threatening: between Hindus and Muslims in India, between Jews and Arabs in Palestine, between procommunist Turks and proroyalist Persians in Iran, and between procolonialist and anticolonialist elements in Indochina, Malaya, Indonesia, and Burma; in Greece, the struggle was between Communists and anti-Communists. The Laborites did not share the Tories' confident assumptions that a few staunch British soldiers could easily restore law and order. In fact, they suspected old empire loyalists in India and Palestine of causing more trouble than was necessary. The Laborites shared one attitude with the Tories: they were deeply anti-communist. Like Walt W. Rostow two decades later, they believed that the communists were trouble exploiters who misused natural class and racial conflicts to obtain power. They regarded them as a naked organizational force blindly loyal to Moscow, from whom they expected moral and material support. Like their American labor counterparts, the British Laborites had had considerable experience fighting communists in the labor movement. Bevin criticized Churchill's easygoing friendliness with Stalin and himself preferred to spit in Molotov's face. In Greece, the Communists were receiving weapons from Tito, Moscow's loyal ally in the Balkans. In Iran, the communist Tudeh movement was headed by an out-and-out Soviet agent, Pishavari. In Malaya, Chin Peng was a Moscow-oriented Communist. Thank God that the Communists were still weak in India, where responsible socialists like Jawaharlal Nehru or Islamic nationalists like Muhammad Ali Jinnah could assume power from the British. And while the Glubb Pashas favored the Arabs in Palestine, London knew that Ben-Gurion was a socialist Zionist who could be expected to keep the communist virus out if a Jewish state came into being.

The postwar Anglo-American alliance had several facets. One was the cooperation that flowed naturally out of Bretton Woods where, despite strong disagreements about the postwar monetary system, America and Britain assumed joint responsibility for maintaining the dollar and sterling as key world currencies. Anglo-American cooperation was vital for the resolution of the German question and the eventual creation of a separate Western zone ("Bizonia") out of which the German Federal Republic emerged. Anglo-American cooperation was further necessitated by the fact that the British, even without American know-how, were developing an atomic bomb. These and the many other strands of the alliance naturally facilitated cooperation on the most difficult problem facing Britain: how to extricate itself from its outmoded empire without going bankrupt, while assuring an orderly transition of power to "responsible" governments. The Laborites were opposed to empire but committed to the Commonwealth. With the enormous economic burdens weighing on Britain, London could not afford to lose its share from participation in a world market system that it enjoyed by virtue of far-flung foreign investments, from its central role as a capital market and banking center, and from access to markets in the sterling area.

While Britain felt it could still mount the military power to protect the emerging Commonwealth, it lacked the economic means to do so. If the Commonwealth, comparable formations like the "French Union," and sundry new nations were to be kept afloat, vast sums of money would have to be spent. The only source of such monies was the United States. With a combination of British (and French) military power and American money, the West would be able to maintain control over the emerging countries even while granting them political independence. For over a year after the war, Britain tried to struggle along with monetary infusions from the United States and Canada, but by early 1947 it was facing economic collapse. The British informed Washington then that Greece was on the verge of being taken over by the Communists, which, if it happened, would inevitably produce a domino effect in the fall of Turkey. Truman rose to the challenge and proclaimed his Truman Doctrine for Greece and Turkey. This was the first and most important policy action expressing the new doctrine of containment. It drew a line along the Greek and Turkish borders with Russia and its allies in Eastern Europe. In subsequent years, containment would pursue its line-drawing policies over the entire globe, each time proclaiming the line of demarcation an inviolable frontier. With the proclamation of the Truman Doctrine on March 12, 1947, the United States formally became an imperial power by assuming the mantle of empire from faltering Britain.

Assuming that mantle required, above all, an American commitment to provide the military means necessary to prevent threatened parts of the empire from falling into hostile hands. Defending the empire demanded military means of a particular nature: *conventional* forces (troops, ships, and planes) which could establish bases in threatened regions, engage in ground combat where necessary, or be introduced in sufficient numbers to prop up threatened regimes. As America found out during the Second World War and as it was to rediscover during the Korean and Vietnam wars, conventional forces are exceedingly costly. In contrast to strategic weapons whose initial heavy costs for research and development subsequently decline, conventional weapons, particularly troops, require constant or increasing outlays. By demobilizing its vast armies just after World War II, Washington was able to effect drastic cuts in its budgets. Aside from occupation forces in Germany and Japan, it no longer needed to maintain large standing forces. Britain, on the other hand, was unable to make a similar cutback in its budgets. Along with the increased burden of welfare spending, it was faced with the crushing costs of maintaining occupation armies in Europe and fighting forces in Malaya, the Middle East, and Greece, as well as vast naval installations throughout the world. To make things even worse, Britain also was committed to developing its own atomic capability. In March 1947, Britain formally requested America to take over this burden and Truman responded with alacrity. The Truman Doctrine on Greece and Turkey aroused vigorous opposition within the United States, from both nationalists and internationalists. But when Truman invoked the specter of Russian expansionism, the voices were silenced and "bipartisan" support was given to America's new global imperial role.

Without the Russian threat, neither the nationalists nor the internationalists would have so meekly accepted the new American imperialism. The nationalists were horrified by the vast new spending which these commitments brought with them. They wanted to concentrate on strategic weapons, to maintain the American atomic monopoly, and to enforce that monopoly by a preventive strike against Russia if necessary. When the issue of universal military training was raised, the nationalists opposed it bitterly. They saw it as a device for creating a federal dictatorship which would bankrupt corporate enterprise and usher in a *de facto* socialism, while involving America in a whole range of conflicts where basic American interests were not threatened. America had no real interests in Greece worth defending, and money spent there was designed only to pull Britain's chestnuts out of the fire—*except* that the Greek Communists were Moscow's instrument. The extension of Russian power anywhere in the world was viewed by the nationalists as a threat, and so grudgingly they accepted the Truman Doctrine. But the Truman Doctrine involved more than providing American military protection to Greece and Turkey. Truman announced a vast program of economic and military assistance (foreign aid) to both countries, which set a precedent for the entire range of foreign aid programs which soon followed. Foreign aid to India and Pakistan could then easily be justified as preventive actions designed to avoid the creation of Greek-type insurgencies which would require even more costly military intervention (an analogy originally applied to Turkey).

The internationalists were primarily interested in Western Europe's economic recovery and wanted large-scale infusions of money into the European countries. Though inflation-conscious and not Keynesians, they did not regard these monetary infusions as waste. Economic recovery in Europe would lead to American loans being repaid, a stimulation of world trade which could only benefit America, and a climate of general economic stability which would incur new enterprise. They were as conscious of the Russian threat as the nationalists, but in a different way. The three countries of the emerging "Catholic Union" (France, Germany, and Italy) contained large, powerful Communist and Socialist movements. Italy voted to become a republic by ousting the monarchy which the American conservative internationalists regarded as a stabilizing force (like the Japanese Emperor). Communists and left-wing Socialists were growing so fast in Italy that a left-wing electoral triumph was a distinct possibility. In Germany, Adenauer's Christian Democrats were not threatened so much by Communists as by Social Democrats. True, Kurt Schumacher and Erich Ollenhauer were anticommunist and anti-Russian, but a Socialist assumption of power in West Germany was very disturbing. Socialist programs in Germany could wreck the emerging revival of free enterprise capitalism with damaging effects on the international market system. So also in France, where the Communist and Socialist threats were great and could oust de Gaulle from power. Socialism of any variety in the three great Western European countries would forever smash the dreams of a European economic union, since socialist governments would be forced to follow nationalist economic policies in order to pay for the vast social welfare schemes they wanted to introduce. The best European spokesman for this conservative internationalist current was Konrad Adenauer, who loathed Marxism, socialism, and Russia as essentially the same phenomena. Adenauer was not a "revanchist," the Russian term applied to post-Hitlerian Germans who wanted to retake lost eastern territories. He wanted to keep Russia or Russian influence out of Western Europe. If the Truman Doctrine on Greece and Turkey resulted in the United States committing itself more solidly to conservative Europe through money and troops, it was to be loudly welcomed.

Russian expansionism was the key to the acceptance within the United States of the Anglo-American program for the transfer of empire onto America's shoulders, the launching of the Marshall Plan to revive Western Europe, the institution of world-wide foreign aid, American rearmament, and especially the American government's new policy of peacetime fiscal expansionism. If Russia was expanding, that constituted a threat. A preventive nuclear strike, which the nationalists advocated, was too risky, because in the long run it would create even more chaos in the world and provide favorable conditions for anticapitalist movements. The threat could also be ignored or attempts be made to negotiate arrangements with the Russians to minimize it by mutual accord. But negotiation with the Russians was believed to be futile, inasmuch as they would not budge on opening the doors of their country to on-site inspection and control. So long as Russia was unwilling to join the international community on American terms, there was no way to convince the nationalists or the internationalists that it was becoming "responsible." The only solution was *containment,* the spirit of which is best captured in the French rendering of the word, *"endiguement." Endiguement* means building a network of dikes to hold in onrushing flood waters. Dike systems are costly, widespread, and must be hermetically sealed at even the most remote point. They not only protect populations from floods, but allow the working of fields so that wealth can be produced. Containment would not only protect the free world but allow the new world order based on the Pax Americana to flourish. It was the best possible doctrine to allow the formation of a peculiarly American type of empire. . . .

The authors of United States containment policy saw three great sources of danger. First, they were convinced that Russian development of atomic weapons and build-up of conventional forces posed a supreme danger. If the balance of power tilted away from the United States, pressures would rise from American nationalist circles and from countries contiguous to the Russian-controlled parts of the world to redress the balance, by anything ranging from a first strike against Russia to vast new military deployments or political and economic commitments. Secondly, they were convinced that any trouble in areas where Russian and American interests collided could have a Serbian effect leading from minor incidents, in domino fashion, to full-scale war. And thirdly, "chaos" in the free world could lead to changes in the geographical balance of power between Russia and America which, again, would bring pressures from within the United States and the threatened countries to redress the balance by forceful military action.

Their response to these three dangers constituted the core and essence of containment policy. First, failing any chance of achieving enforceable accords with the Russians on nuclear weapons, the United States had to undertake a crash program to develop weapons of such scope and quantity and so speedily that no matter what the Russians did, they would never be able to catch up. Furthermore, control over nuclear weapons and energy had to be removed from the military and placed in the White House. Secondly, to eliminate any doubts from the minds of the Russians as to what areas America considered part of its empire and what areas it conceded to Russia, it undertook to draw demarcation lines which eventually encircled the Soviet Union from northern Norway to the 38th parallel in Korea. And thirdly, to prevent chaos, America undertook a vast program of foreign aid to promote economic development, first in Europe, and then in a whole array of poor countries, particularly those "threatened by communism."

Russia, of course, was the common denominator of each of these fears and the responses to them. It was the only power capable of matching the United States militarily. The world's major trouble spots —Berlin, Greece, Iran, and Korea—were in areas where Russia collided with the newly emerging American empire. And the most threatening form of "chaos" came from communist revolutionary movements in such countries as Greece, Azerbaijan, the Philippines, Malaya, Korea, Indochina, and, of course, China. Cultivated gentlemen like Acheson and Kennan, machine politicians like Truman, tough lawyers like Forrestal and Dulles, all shared an overwhelming fear born of two world wars and a great depression. The only way to banish that fear was to have total security or, as James Forrestal said in December 1947: "We are dealing with a deadly force and nothing less than 100 percent security will do." [2] Russian paranoia was easily matched by American paranoia, and both countries opted for the same solution: control, control, and more control.

The World View of Containment

. . . The world view of containment made it possible to build up the realm of ideology. Concretely, that realm took the form of the enormously expanded executive branch of the United States government. Its material basis was the federal budget, in which the foreign affairs and national security component played an ever-increasing role until by the early 1960s, it constituted not only the bulk of the budget but one-tenth of the gross national product of the United States. The executive branch acquired a monopoly over "national security policy." Constitutionally, this seemed to derive from the President's role as commander-in-chief. In times of peace, foreign affairs were to be conducted with the advice and consent of the Senate, which had to approve by two-thirds vote any treaties the President entered into. But the world view of containment enshrined a new doctrine, that of the cold war. The cold war was war, and even if not formally declared by Congress, "bipartisanship" in foreign policy signified acceptance of that war. This meant that, as in times of war, foreign affairs were virtually equivalent to national security affairs. More particularly, those foreign affairs that were construed as relating to the conflict between America and Russia were considered to be within the realm of national security. The executive branch thereby acquired a monopoly over all policies relating to national security, which ensured the President a minimum of interference in his national security policies from both the nationalists and the internationalists. Nationalists were strongly represented in Congress and in the military; internationalists were also strongly represented in Congress, with the State Department as their chief bureaucratic vehicle in government.

Presidential monopoly over national security affairs, over time, produced a range of bureaucratic institutions which were direct emanations of presidential power, such as the Central Intelligence Agency (CIA), the National Security Agency, the Atomic Energy Commission, and the various agencies concerned with foreign aid and information. In addition, it led to the creation within existing bureaucracies of top-level policy-making bodies concerned with foreign policy and national security affairs. This was to become most apparent in the Defense Department under Kennedy, where the International Security Agency (ISA), ostensibly a body that advised the Secretary of Defense on foreign affairs aspects of national defense, became a virtual "State Department." The ISA, as the Pentagon Papers reveal, was closer to the White House than to the military services over which the Secretary of Defense presided. It was concerned with "policy," whereas the services, by statute, were supposed to be concerned solely with "operations," that is, implementing policy.

The presidential monopoly over national security policy was the most important achievement of the government during the postwar period—an achievement constantly in danger of assault from nationalist and internationalist currents, which were excluded from the monopoly. Policy, as I have pointed out, means goals, direction, and methods. It specifies what is to be achieved; and by what routes; and it lays down the kinds of "capabilities" (in ordinary language, political, economic, military, and other weapons) to be used. Or, in the words of Samuel P. Huntington, policy means strategy and structure. The world view of containment reserved to the supreme leadership of America a very special kind of policy-making function. Since the American-Russian relationship was the most critical matter in America's foreign relations, since nuclear weaponry had created a *de facto* global unity, and since even minor actions in faraway places (Laos, for example) could have a direct bearing on the American-Russian relationship, only that body of the American political structure which had total and comprehensive knowledge of the entire global picture could make national security policy. Congress or old established bureaucracies like the military services or the State Department, which represented particular interests, could not make national security policy because they were moved primarily by those interests and not by a disinterested awareness of the entire picture. Obviously, only the President and his national security bureaucracy could make national security policy for, by virtue of the great new intelligence agencies which surrounded them, only they had all the knowledge, all the facts, all the necessary wisdom.

Containment ideology envisioned an active role for America. The President was to be not just an arbiter who would decide from among various "options" presented to him by interest groups within the bureaucracy, a phenomenon of presidential decision-making power that was to become apparent (or seemingly so) under the Johnson and Nixon administrations. The duty of the President was to assure America's security and that of the free world primarily by creating conditions that would make it impossible for World War III to break out while preserving the interests of America and its free world clients and allies. Whether or not others shared that commitment either abroad or within the United States did not matter. The supreme criterion for judging the success of a national security policy was the fact that World War III had not occurred. If anyone argued that the fear of nuclear war was excessive and paranoiac (as Mao Tse-tung was alleged to have done), then the facts of nuclear destructive power could be presented to show that the madness was really on the side of the doubter. If a person feels threatened by an impending catastrophe of uncertain source, he will feel justified in fortifying his house and his grounds, stockpiling supplies, and keeping his family in a constant state of readiness. If the catastrophe should not occur, he can point to all the power, wealth, and internal discipline that this effort brought about. It was in this way, through the fears that nuclear weaponry generated, that the American empire came about. Abroad, the empire resulted in a degree of global organization that never before existed. At home, it created a vast American governmental power whose role is crucial to the maintenance of the economy and all other major social and political institutions in the country.

Notes

1. James MacGregor Burns, *Roosevelt: The Soldier of Freedom*, p. 42.
2. Fleming, *The Cold War and its Origins*, vol. 1, p. 487.

3

Radomír Luža

Czechoslovakia Between Democracy and Communism, 1945-1948

The nations of Eastern Europe were both the source and the principal victims of the Soviet-American antagonism. In modern times these small lands remained subject to heavy foreign influence even after they had won their right to exist as states at the close of World War I. With the collapse of German power in 1944–45 and the advance of the Red Army, it was unlikely that they could escape deep infringement of their newly recovered independence.

Nonetheless, it was not foreordained that they must be communized. In Czechoslovakia a precarious independence was maintained for almost three years. And even today Finland provides the example of a country that has preserved a democratic political life while clearly accepting an international role that respects Russian interests. Was "Finlandization" excluded for the East European nations? Stalin's own thinking remains hard to reconstruct. On the one hand, he reportedly told the Yugoslav communist, Milovan Djilas, that the country that sent its troops into a liberated area would also inevitably impose its own social system. On the other hand, he allegedly reassured the Czech leader Edvard Beneš (among others) in regard to his intentions toward Warsaw that "communism fit Poland like a saddle fits a cow." Perhaps the Russian leader never intended to allow a free choice of regimes in Eastern Europe, or perhaps he interpreted the formulae of democratic governments and free elections, which he accepted at Yalta, as being tantamount to a choice for communism. At the least he expected a strong communist role in Hungary and Czechoslovakia and worked to assure a preponderant communist influence in Poland and Rumania from late 1944 on, if not earlier. And even if the final totalitarian result were not planned at the outset of the process, the logic of conflict with Washington meant that every dispute between the two great powers led to further repression in Eastern Europe and thus to more irreconcilable Soviet-American polarization.

But what were the United States' stakes in this relatively distant area? Our economic intercourse with Eastern Europe was minimal, although neo-Marxist critics assert that if Washington was to assert the "open door" as its general stance, it had to fight for this right in Eastern Europe as well. More plausible a factor in my judgment was the ideological commitment generated within America as part of the national mobilization for World War II. After waging a messianic struggle on behalf of oppressed peoples, how could American leaders simply surrender the region where World War II had begun to a new repression? (This was all the less likely in view of the millions of votes in major industrial states that the ethnic groups from Eastern Europe represented.) "Realist" critics of American foreign policy could well answer that we ended up surrendering the region in any case and that it was illusory to believe there was an alternative. By refusing to recognize Soviet preeminence, and likewise failing to develop credible threats to deter it, we both "lost" the area to communism and envenomed relations with Moscow. Nonetheless, the wisdom of renunciation is not usually learned without difficulty. At the end of Roosevelt's war, acquiescence in the division of Europe would have demanded an implausibly rapid psychological re-education of Americans—even apart from the moral elements involved.

Most accounts of Eastern Europe in English focus upon the region as part of the larger Soviet-American struggle. For an able summary of East European developments in terms of their ramifications upon American policy, the student might well employ Bennett Kovrig's, The Myth of Liberation: East-Central Europe in United States Diplomacy and Politics since 1914 *(Baltimore, Md.: The Johns Hopkins University Press, 1973). The essay included here offers a different perspective— namely a focus upon the difficulties of the Czechoslovak republic from the viewpoint of Prague. Czechoslovakia was the country of Eastern Europe most akin to the West in terms of social and economic structure; it had enjoyed the greatest success between the wars in maintaining democratic government; it was least ravaged by the war itself; and it was the most successful in combating postwar inflation. It gave the greatest promise of being able to preserve friendly relations with Moscow and a pluralist regime at home. Thus its communization in early 1948 especially dismayed Westerners, convincing them of the gravity of the cold war much as the fall of France had pressed home the earnestness of the Second World War. But the account instructively highlights the burdens placed upon Czech democracy from its own internal problems. And it also suggests that failures of will and resolve also played a crucial role—in short, Czechoslovaks made history as well as suffered from it.*

Radomír Luža teaches history at Tulane and with Victor S. Mamatey is the editor of the volume, A History of the Czechoslovak Republic, 1914–1948, *from which this essay is taken with the permission of Princeton University Press and the author. Professor Luža has also written* The Transfer of the Sudeten Germans: A Study of Czech–German Relations, 1933–1962 *(New York: New York University Press, 1964) and* Austro-German Relations in the Anschluss Era *(Princeton: Princeton University Press, 1975).*

The Government of the National Front

The fate of postwar Czechoslovakia, like that of other small nations of East Central Europe, did not depend on the will and actions of her people alone. It was also affected by the actions of the great powers and their postwar relations.

In the winter of 1944–45, while the Red Army was fighting its way to Prague, Vienna, and Berlin, the Soviet Union, the United States, and Britain were making final preparations for the meeting of their leaders at Yalta. They were aware that the presence of the Soviet military might in Poland, Rumania, Bulgaria, Hungary and Czechoslovakia meant a basic shift of power in Europe. Nonetheless, both East and West still clung to the concept of postwar coalition and were exploring the basis for a series of agreements on European and Far Eastern problems.

The policy of President Edvard Beneš, developed while he was in exile in London, had been to restore Czechoslovakia to her pre-Munich territorial integrity and reinstitute her democratic institutions. The success of this policy depended on the continued cooperation of the Allied Powers, not only until the end of the war but afterward. Only in these circumstances could Czechoslovakia hope to recover her independence and territorial integrity and restore her traditional parliamentary-democratic system. Throughout the war, therefore, Beneš had tried to promote a cooperative effort of the anti-Nazi alliance to find a permanent settlement in Europe. Alone among the exiled leaders of East Central European countries he sought both the support of the Western powers and an accommodation with the Soviet Union. The signing of the Soviet-Czechoslovak alliance treaty in Moscow in

December, 1943, was conclusive proof of his determination to come to terms with Moscow, and appeared to be a guarantee of the success of his policy.

Beneš was, therefore, deeply disappointed and even shocked when reports reached him late in 1944 that Soviet authorities were promoting a movement in Ruthenia (Carpathian Ukraine)—which had been the first Czechoslovak province liberated by the Red Army—for its secession from Czechoslovakia and its attachment to the Soviet Ukraine. As early as 1939, in conversations with Ivan Maisky, the Soviet ambassador in London, Beneš had voiced his willingness to solve the question of Ruthenia in full agreement with the Soviet Union,[1] and had reiterated this view in his last talk with Stalin in Moscow in December, 1943. At the time the Soviet leaders did not regard the question as pressing, but they now apparently were determined to force a solution favorable to the Soviet Union. Czechoslovak complaints lodged with the Soviet government against Soviet activity in Ruthenia during December, 1944, proved to be of no avail.

At the same time Beneš became alarmed about the ultimate fate of Slovakia, which had been partially liberated by the Soviet army. Although the Communist Party of Slovakia (KSS) had abandoned its earlier agitation for a "Soviet Slovakia," it continued to press—with the approval of the leadership of the Communist Party of Czechoslovakia (KSČ) in Moscow—for a loose federation between Slovakia on one hand and Bohemia and Moravia on the other.

Beneš's tense concern was ended by a personal letter from Joseph Stalin on January 23, 1945, assuring the Czechoslovak government of his full support. The Soviet leader suggested, however, that the problem of Ruthenia should be solved by negotiations between the two countries that would take into account the desire of the province's Ukrainian population to join the Soviet Union. The underlying concern of Beneš, that the Soviet Union would use its control of Czechoslovak territory in disregard of its commitments, was thus relieved.[2] Soviet-Czechoslovak relations had for some time been regarded as an index of Soviet-Western relations. Undoubtedly, Stalin's decision to ease Beneš's fears on the eve of the Yalta conference was motivated, in part, by a desire to dissipate the suspicions of President Franklin D. Roosevelt and Prime Minister Winston S. Churchill, already aroused over Soviet designs in Poland and the other countries of East Central Europe occupied by the Soviet army.

Just before writing his letter to Beneš, Stalin discussed with Klement Gottwald, the exiled Czech communist leader in Moscow, the policy the KSČ should follow during and after the liberation of Czechoslovakia. Stalin advised Gottwald to accept Beneš as president, and to come to an understanding with him and his government.[3] This flexible Soviet policy essentially reflected the line set forth in the Comintern declaration of 1943, which asserted that "the great differences in the historical development of individual countries determine the differences of the various problems that the workers' class of every country has to cope with." Until the next reexamination of communist strategy in the summer of 1947, Stalin set the stamp of his approval on this thesis of national roads to socialism: "In private he even expressed the . . . view that in certain instances it was possible to achieve socialism without the dictatorship of the proletariat." [4]

During its Moscow exile the top echelon of the KSČ (Gottwald, Rudolf Slánský, Jan Šverma, and Václav Kopecký) worked out a policy line in terms of a special Czechoslovak road to socialism.[5] After broadening their reexamination to include a review of past mistakes, they determined that the party should lead and organize the national liberation struggle of the Czech and Slovak people against Nazism. In thus assuming the role of a responsible mass movement, the party acted upon the belief that after the end of the occupation it could win popular confidence under the banner of national independence.[6] In short, the communist leadership in Moscow envisioned liberation as a means of winning a predominant share of power. The irony of such an approach was that it visualized economic and social reform as being subordinate to the achievement of the primary political task: becoming the leading political force in the country. In conformity with this aim, the party tended to move cautiously. It set up broad national and democratic—instead of narrow socialist—demands. In fact, the program of the Czech home resistance—nationalization of industry, banks, and insurance companies—was much more far-reaching than the initial communist platform, which merely involved confiscation of the property of Czech and Slovak traitors and hostile Germans and Magyars.[7]

During the war the principal Czech and Slovak political forces at home and abroad held lively discussions on the future form of the country. In the winter of 1944–45, as the Soviet army overran a large part of Czechoslovakia, the balance of the pendulum between the democratic parties represented by Beneš in London and the communists led by Gottwald in Moscow swung in favor of the communists. It was a foregone conclusion that, at the end of the war, the London cabinet would be replaced by a new government with strong communist participation.[8] In 1945, with the Soviet armies advancing across Czechoslovakia, it became urgent for Beneš to implement this agreement and to return to the liberated part of the country with a newly constituted cabinet. To determine the composition of the new government and adopt a program, it was decided to hold a conference of

Czech and Slovak political parties in Moscow. The choice of Moscow rather than London for the conference was undoubtedly motivated by the fact that the Czechoslovak government needed the consent and assistance of the Soviet government to return to its homeland. It also gave the communists a considerable advantage in the ensuing negotiations.

After taking leave of Churchill and Anthony Eden on February 24,[9] Beneš, accompanied by some members of his cabinet, left London for Moscow, where he arrived on March 17. A delegation of the Slovak National Council (SNR), composed equally of Slovak Democrats and Communists, also arrived in Moscow from the liberated parts of Slovakia. However, since Bohemia and Moravia were still firmly in the grip of the Germans, the Czech home resistance was unable to send representatives. Altogether, the Czech Communist (KSČ), National Socialist, Social Democratic, and People's parties and the Slovak Democratic and Communist (KSS) parties were represented. All other prewar political movements were excluded from the conference, primarily because of their past anticommunist attitude.

Gottwald assumed the initiative at the conference, which opened on March 22 and lasted eight days, with the presentation of a draft program as the basis of the negotiations.[10] Beneš did not take part in the meetings, on the ground that as a constitutional president he stood above parties.[11] This left the London democratic exiles leaderless, since they were used to deferring to him in London, even in minor matters. It also weakened their position, because Beneš enjoyed tremendous prestige, particularly in the Czech provinces. Out of fear of arousing "suspicion on the part of the communists," [12] they discarded any joint political platform to counter the communist program. To the bewilderment of the disunited democratic camp, it soon became apparent that the negotiations were a controversy between two political groups, one based in London and the other in Moscow: "Here for the first time there was joined the battle of two political worlds." [13] What started out as negotiations for a governmental blueprint broadened into a survey of a program of action that would change almost every aspect of Czechoslovak life.

The democratic leaders received some satisfaction from the fact that the communist draft, to some extent, incorporated points agreed upon during previous exchanges of opinion between the parties. In the main, it reflected Gottwald's conception of the necessity for agreement with the democratic parties and articulated some of the aspirations of the Czech and Slovak people. Although the democratic and communist leaders clashed on many points, in the end their common interests proved strong enough to produce a final text that was not very different from the original draft.

The sharpest controversy during the negotiations occurred between the London group and the Slovak delegation, in which Gottwald assumed the role of benevolent arbiter.[14] The Slovaks brought to Moscow a resolution passed by the SNR on March 2, which demanded what amounted to attributes of sovereignty for Slovakia: a Slovak government, parliament, and distinct army units. The London group rejected this demand. It based itself on Beneš's speech of February 23, 1945, in which the president had recognized the special needs of the Slovaks but had insisted that the definition of Slovakia's place in the Czechoslovak state—like, indeed, all constitutional questions—should be left to the elected representatives of the people at home to decide after the war.[15] In the end the Slovaks yielded and accepted as a compromise a somewhat ambiguously worded statement proposed by Gottwald, which he later called grandly the *"Magna Carta* of the Slovak Nation."

In the negotiations to form a new government, the communists likewise imposed their will, but managed skillfully to camouflage their victory in a seeming compromise. They did not claim the premiership or a majority of posts in the cabinet. Instead, Gottwald proposed, and the other party leaders agreed, that the government should represent a "broad National Front of the Czechs and Slovaks." In strict conformance with the rules of parliamentary arithmetic, this decision was implemented by awarding three posts in the cabinet to each of the six parties participating in the conference. The prime minister and five vice-premiers, who were the heads of the six parties, were to form an inner cabinet to direct and coordinate the government's activities. It was further decided to give posts to four non-partisan experts and to create three state-secretaryships, thus bringing the total membership of the cabinet to twenty-five.

Upon the conclusion of the Moscow conference, President Beneš and the party leaders departed for Košice, a modest eastern Slovak town recently liberated by the Red Army. They arrived there on April 3 and stayed until after the liberation of Prague on May 9. On April 4 the new government was formally installed and the next day it announced its program, which, despite its origin in Moscow, came to be known as the "program of Košice."[16]

The Košice program proposed no radical transformation of Czechoslovak society along socialist lines. It was quite free of characteristic Marxist language. On the other hand, unlike the Czechoslovak declarations of independence issued in Washington and Prague in 1918, which had been idealistic professions of faith in democracy, it said little about freedom. Its tone was sober. It threatened more than it promised.

The program opened with a government tribute to the Soviet Union and a pledge to support the Red Army until final victory. For this purpose the government announced the formation of a new Czechoslovak army, trained, organized, and equipped on the model of the Red Army, with Czech and Slovak units under a unified command, and educational officers introduced into all units to extirpate fascist influences. Czechoslovak foreign policy, it said, would be based on the closest alliance with the Soviet Union on the basis of the 1943 treaty and on practical cooperation in the military, political, economic, and cultural fields, as well as in questions concerning the punishment of Germany, reparations, frontier settlements, and the organization of peace. It promised to maintain friendly relations with Poland, Yugoslavia, and Bulgaria on the "basis of Slavic brotherhood," to seek reconciliation with a democratic Hungary (after correction of injustices), and to promote a rapprochement between Hungary and Austria and their Slavic neighbors. Finally, almost as an afterthought, it thanked Britain for the aid extended during the war and promised to consolidate relations with her and the United States and promote close relations with France.

In the field of domestic policy the government pledged to hold elections at the earliest possible time for a national constituent assembly that would determine the precise form of the Czechoslovak government. In the meantime, the government guaranteed the people their political rights and set up new administrative machinery, in the form of popularly elected national committees, to administer public affairs at the local, district, and provincial levels.

The Slovaks were recognized as a distinct (*samobytný*) nation and the SNR as their legal representative and "carrier of state power in Slovak territory." The question of Ruthenia was to be settled as soon as possible according to the democratically expressed will of its people. The German and Magyar minorities were given the right of option for Czechoslovakia, with the understanding that disloyal German and Magyar citizens would be removed. The property of those who had "actively helped in the disruption and occupation of Czechoslovakia" was to be placed under national control pending a final disposal by the legislative authorities. Their land would be placed in a National Land Fund and distributed to deserving Czechs and Slovaks.

Czech and Slovak collaborators were to be deprived of voting rights and barred from all political organizations. The former agrarian party and all prewar parties not represented in the new National Front were accused of collaboration and proscribed. War criminals, traitors, and "other active, conscious helpers of the German oppressors" were to be punished without exception. President Emil Hácha and all members of the Protectorate government, as well as Jozef Tiso and all members of the Slovak government and parliament, were to be charged with high treason and brought before a "National Court." Finally, the Košice program provided for a broad system of social welfare.

In the new cabinet, according to a communist participant at the Moscow conference, the communists captured "positions which were a starting point for the assault on the actual fortress of capitalism. . . . The balance of power was such . . . from the beginning of the liberation, that the influence and weight of . . . KSČ was predominant and decisive." [17] At the Moscow conference, the communists had successfully promoted Zdeněk Fierlinger, a left-wing Social Democrat, as prime minister. From their point of view, the choice proved an excellent one. As wartime ambassador to Moscow, Fierlinger had won the confidence of the Soviet government by his display of an uncritically pro-Soviet and anti-Western attitude. As premier, he collaborated with the communists so closely that he won the popular epithet of "Quislinger."

Thanks to separate representation, the combined KSČ and KSS held eight seats in the cabinet and controlled the ministries of interior, information, education, agriculture, and social welfare.[18] The police, security, and intelligence services were in their hands. The Ministry of Defense was entrusted to Gen. Ludvík Svoboda, commander of the Czechoslovak army in Russia, as a nonparty expert. (Although a noncommunist at that time, Svoboda was a loyal friend of the Soviets.) As a concession to the democratic parties, the communists agreed to the reappointment of Jan Masaryk as minister of foreign affairs. A genuinely nonpartisan personality, dedicated only to the defense of his country's interests, the son of the first president of Czechoslovakia was by family tradition, education, and experience a thoroughly Western man. Therefore, as Masaryk's assistant and watchdog the communists insisted on appointing Vlado Clementis, a Slovak communist, to the newly created post of state-secretary of foreign affairs.

Thus far the "circumspect and purposeful course of the KSČ" [19] proved to be of particular advantage to the Communist party, whose chairman, Klement Gottwald, had given proof of his political maturity and craftsmanship. The less colorful democratic leaders let themselves be outmaneuvered. Since the central issue was one of power, it is surprising that neither Beneš nor his colleagues found it advisable to prevent the communists from assuming control of the police and security organs. A reasonable compromise on this question would have helped those forces in both camps who were willing to face up to problems affecting their common commitment to a democratic Czecho-slovakia. Despite some apprehensions, however, the democratic leaders had no reason to contradict Fierlinger's observations before their departure from Moscow that "It is an immense achievement that we can return home united. . . . The ideological borderline between Moscow and London has been removed. I am aware of the fact that not a few would criticize the composition of the new cabinet . . . but I consider it an immense success that unlike other emigrations . . . we are the first to be able to put order into our affairs abroad." [20] Neither side regarded the Moscow agreement as a final settlement; both were aware that the final battle was yet to come—at home after the war.

In the Czech provinces the approaching end of the war coincided with a rising tide of guerrilla activities. Early in 1945 the largest resistance group—the Council of the Three—the illegal trade unions, and the underground KSČ established the Czech National Council as the center of Czech resistance. The council was strengthened during the first days of May by a spontaneous popular uprising that spread through those parts of the country still occupied by the Germans. The movement reached Prague on May 5, where a fierce battle broke out with German army and SS units that raged even after the official dates of German surrender at Rheims and Berlin (May 7 and 8, respectively). In the early morning hours of May 9 the first Soviet tanks arrived in Prague. On May 10 the government returned to Prague. It was followed by President Beneš amid frenetic acclamation on May 16.

The Nazi occupation was terminated. The war was over.

Between Democracy and Cominform, 1945–1947

On its return to Prague, the Czechoslovak government took quick and firm hold of the levers of command. Under the Moscow agreement President Beneš had been given emergency powers to issue decrees with the validity of laws, at the request of the government, until the convocation of the National Assembly. These powers were first used to assert government authority throughout the country. The Czech National Council was dissolved.[21] The Slovak National Council, on the other hand, continued to function at Bratislava.[22] It soon became apparent, however, that it was necessary to define its jurisdiction and the basis of its relationship to the central government at Prague, a matter that the Košice program had noted only in very general terms. The SNR took the initiative in the matter. On May 26 it adopted a proposal for the fundamental organization of the republic, in the drafting of which both Slovak communist and democratic leaders shared. The proposal envisaged a dualistic, symmetrical organization of Czechoslovakia into two federated states—Slovakia and Bohemia-Moravia—each with a government and diet of its own. A federal government and parliament were to be centered in Prague.

The previous Czechoslovak experiment in federalism—the ill-fated Second Republic in 1938–39—had not been a happy one. The proposal of the SNR therefore encountered opposition from the Czech parties, both communist and democratic. On May 31, just before the government at Prague began a discussion of the SNR proposal, the leaders of the KSČ invited the KSS leaders to a meeting at which the KSS submitted to the "unified leadership" of the KSČ and agreed to abandon the SNR plan.[23] At the cabinet meeting on May 31 and June 1, only the Slovak Democrats defended the proposal for federalization, while the Czech National Socialists and Populists pressed for the restoration of the republic's pre-Munich centralist organization; the KSČ and KSS adopted a halfway course. The discussions ended in a compromise. Federalism was discarded, but Slovakia's autonomy was assured. The resulting "First Prague Agreement" both defined and circumscribed the jurisdiction of the SNR.[24]

The government delayed a full year before implementing its pledge, given in the Košice program, to hold general elections for a constituent assembly at the earliest possible time. Meanwhile it covered the naked strength of its power in a temporary constitutional garb. On August 25, 1945, a presidential decree provided for the formation of a single-chamber, 300-member provisional national assembly. It was to be chosen not by general elections but by a complicated system of three-stage elections through the local, district, and provincial national committees—thus allowing the parties of the National Front to determine its composition.[25] The Provisional National Assembly met for the first time on October 28, 1945, the national holiday, and confirmed President Beneš in his office. In the next few days the cabinet was formally reorganized, but no significant changes were effected in its composition.

The Provisional National Assembly's initiative remained limited. Usually, it approved unanimously and without discussion the decisions made by the party leaders at meetings of the National Front. Thus on February 28, 1946, it approved, also unanimously and without discussion, the ninety-eight presidential decrees issued from May to October, 1945, many of which affected the fundamental structure of the Czechoslovak state and society.

The delay in holding elections, however, did not indicate indifference on the part of the party leaders to public opinion. Quite the contrary. After the overthrow of Nazism all of Europe was swept by an intense popular demand for immediate reform and a certain disillusionment, or impatience, with constitutional procedures when they threatened to delay reform. Under these circumstances, to defer the pressing tasks of reconstruction and reform in order to engage in an electoral contest appeared almost frivolous to the Czech and Slovak party leaders. Their decision to preserve the interparty truce offered by the National Front and "get to work" had full public approval.

Air attacks, military operations, and the German occupation had made World War II more destructive for the Czechs and Slovaks than any previous conflict. According to an official government estimate 250,000 persons had died. In Bohemia, 3,014 houses were destroyed and over 10,000 were badly damaged; in Moravia the respective figures were 11,862 and over 19,000. In Silesia 34,986 buildings were ruined. Slovakia, because of the prolonged fighting in 1944–45, was the most seriously hit.[26] In the Czech provinces the total war damage per person was estimated at 17,000 Czechoslovak crowns (about $2,400), but in Slovakia it amounted to 35,000 crowns (about $4,900).[27] In eastern Slovakia alone 169 villages were razed and 300 damaged; 24,000 buildings were ruined or heavily damaged. The transportation system was seriously dislocated. Almost all the large factories had been badly bombed.[28] Livestock suffered heavily. Nevertheless, a large amount of food and raw materials stockpiled by the Germans during the occupation remained in the country.

The end of the war closed a struggle for the Czech nation's very existence. Since 1938 the Czechs had been humiliated and persecuted. They had also suffered from Nazi cruelties and the bloody fighting of the last days of the war. The radical mood of the country transformed resentment against the Nazis into demands for the permanent removal of all Germans. Popular support for the idea of expelling the Sudeten Germans caught even the Communist party by surprise. However, it swiftly went beyond the Košice program and espoused popular demands. A presidential decree on June 21, 1945, provided for the expropriation without compensation of the property of the Germans and Magyars as well as that of Czech and Slovak collaborators and traitors. The land that came within the scope of the decree involved about 270,000 farms covering 6,240,000 acres, which provided the communist minister of agriculture with a rich pork barrel from which to reward those who were willing to serve the party. By the spring of 1948 some 1,500,000 people had moved to the Czech borderlands left vacant by the Sudeten Germans, who had been removed to the American and Soviet zones of occupation in Germany in accordance with the mandate given Czechoslovakia by the Allied powers at Potsdam. After June 15, 1949, only 177,000 Germans were left in the Czech provinces.[29] This national adjustment wrought a profound change in the economic and social structure of the country. There was much disorder and violence—yet this is present in every revolutionary process. In the final analysis, the expulsion of the Sudeten Germans was a Czech national response—neither communist nor Soviet inspired —to a situation created by Nazi war policy and the Sudeten Germans themselves.

The Slovaks, led by the KSS, pressed for a similar removal of the Magyar minority from Slovakia. But it was one thing to press a claim against the Germans, who at that time were regarded as outlaws in all of Europe, and quite another to press one against the Hungarians, who were regarded as minor culprits. The Soviet Union tended to regard Hungary as a future satellite, like Czechoslovakia, and was not anxious to complicate its tasks by contributing to dissension between two of its prospective clients. At the Potsdam conference it failed to back the Czechoslovak demand for the removal of the Magyar minority. The matter was left to bilateral Czechoslovak-Hungarian negotiations. Under a mutual exchange agreement concluded between the two countries on February 27, 1946, 68,407 Magyars out of some 500,000 did leave for Hungary and a somewhat smaller number of Slovaks returned to Slovakia.[30] No large fund of land comparable to that in the Czech borderlands became available in Slovakia, a factor that had important repercussions in Czechoslovak politics.

Partly for this reason, the Czechoslovak delegation at the Paris Peace Conference in 1946 raised the demand for authorization to remove 200,000 Magyars from Slovakia. But by then, the Western powers were adamantly opposed to any further population transfer, and the matter was dropped.[31] They did, however, accede to the Czechoslovak demand for a small enlargement of the Bratislava bridgehead on the south bank of the Danube River at the expense of Hungary.[32]

Meanwhile, in June, 1945, the Poles suddenly reopened the Těšín (Teschen) question. On June 19 Polish troops under General Rola-Zymierski moved up to the city of Těšín. Possibly the Poles were encouraged to revive this old thorn in Polish-Czechoslovak relations by the Soviet government, which was anxious to prod Czechoslovakia into settling the Ruthenian question. In any event, on the same day the Soviet government invited Czechoslovakia and Poland to send delegations to Moscow to discuss outstanding questions affecting their relations. On June 29, after a week of discussions, the Czechoslovak and Soviet governments signed an agreement formally transferring Ruthenia to the Soviet Union.[33] When the Czechoslovak delegation returned to Prague, Prime Minister Fierlinger announced that the Polish-Czechoslovak discussions had been indefinitely adjourned. Apart from the loss of Ruthenia and the enlargement of the Bratislava bridge-head, the pre-Munich boundaries of Czechoslovakia remained intact.

The internal position of Czechoslovakia appeared to be fully consolidated. The withdrawal of Soviet and United States troops from Czechoslovakia as early as November and December of 1945 heralded a return to normalcy. By the fall of 1945 the country had also made considerable progress in economic reconstruction. Almost everyone agreed that it had bright prospects, provided that the wartime grand alliance and the internal balance between the communist and democratic forces could be maintained.

Since it had to compete with the democratic parties, the Communist party sought to be a mass party. The KSČ readily admitted members of former parties, drawing a line only at admitting former fascists and collaborators who, in Czech opinion, stood beyond the pale. The KSS, on the other hand, readily admitted even members of the former Hlinka People's party—indeed, it strenuously courted them. It posed as a Slovak nationalist party and did not hesitate to exploit religious prejudice by pointing out to the Slovak Catholic majority that the leadership of its competitor, the Slovak Democratic party, was largely Protestant. At the end of 1945 the KSS claimed a membership of 197,000, while in March, 1946, the KSČ claimed to have over 1,000,000 members.[34]

The growing strength of the Communist party was reflected in its high moral and internal consolidation. Between 1945 and 1948 the leadership of the KSČ (with Klement Gottwald as chairman and Rudolf Slánský as secretary-general) remained remarkably stable, and the party was unusually free of factional strife. The KSS experienced some internal stress, however, as its nationalist posture came into conflict with the strategy of the parent party, the KSČ. At a joint meeting of the central committees of the KSČ and KSS in Prague on July 17–18, 1945, the Czech communists sharply criticized their Slovak comrades for viewing the development from a "nationalist," instead of a "class," point of view and for allying themselves with the "reaction" in the SNR, that is, the Slovak Democrats. A resolution, passed at the meeting, demanded that the "policy of the KSS must not be to separate but to orient the party towards the progressive forces in the Czech provinces and in the central government" and delegated Viliam Široký, a dour internationalist communist, to take charge of the KSS.[35] The separation of the two parties, which was maintained for tactical reasons, thereafter became nominal.

While the Communist party was united, the Czechoslovak Social Democratic party (chairman: Zdeněk Fierlinger; secretary-general: Blažej Vilím), which had a long and distinguished history of defending the cause of the Czech working class, was increasingly rent by a tug-of-war between its right and left wings, representing its liberal-democratic and Marxian-socialist traditions, respectively. The Czech National Socialist party (chairman: Petr Zenkl; secretary-general: Vladimír Krajina), which claimed to be a socialist but non-Marxist party, suffered from no such dilemma. It came increasingly to the fore as the most resolute adversary of the communists among the Czech parties. The Czech Populist party, under the leadership of Msgr. Jan Šrámek, the wartime premier in London, was a progressive Catholic party that before the war had received its greatest support among Czech peasants, especially in Moravia. After the war it had difficulty in finding its bearings in the radical atmosphere, which affected even the countryside. The Slovak Democratic party (chairman: Jozef Lettrich; secretary: Fedor Hodža), which was largely a continuation of the Slovak branch of the proscribed agrarian party, suffered from the polarization of Slovak opinion after the war between the radical revolutionary movement and the conservative Catholic anticommunist movement. It could not compete with the communists in appealing to the former and found it distasteful and dangerous to appeal to the latter, for fear of exposing itself to the charge of catering to cryptofascists.

In retrospect it is clear that the prolongation of the provisional regime benefited the Communist party more than the democratic parties, by allowing an unusual measure of influence in public affairs to various extraconstitutional mass organizations, such as worker, peasant, youth, resistance, and other nationwide associations, that sprang up after the liberation of the country. The general European "swing to the left" immediately after the war undoubtedly helped the Communist party gain a preponderant influence in these organizations. No instrument was more important to it than the united Revolutionary Trade Union Movement (ROH) and workers' factory councils (závodní rady). This was true at least in the Czech provinces. In Slovakia, where the working class did not have the same importance,[36] the Communist party relied more on its influence in the resistance organizations, especially the association of former partisans.

The communist plans had emphasized the necessity of gaining leadership of the working class, a traditional domain of the Social Democratic movement. In the first postwar days the communists occupied positions of power in the ROH and the workers' councils in all large factories. In this situation, the predominant influence of the Communist party with the working class,[37] combined with its control of important levers of the state apparatus, became the central fact of politics.

After the party consolidated its grip on the political structure in the early summer of 1945, its initial moderation in economic affairs began to fade. President Beneš and the two socialist parties viewed the nationalization of the principal industries, banks, and insurance companies as inevitable. Moreover, the corresponding pressure exerted by the workers found widespread popular support. Under these circumstances the expropriation of German capital evolved into a wider trend that reflected a consensus of all responsible political forces. Thus, the first postwar measure of large nationalization in Europe [38] became a demonstration of a common resolve to establish collective ownership and direct state control over the chief means of production. The presidential decrees of October 24, which were mainly prepared by the Social Democratic controlled Ministry of Industry, resulted in the creation of a nationalized sector containing 61.2 percent of the industrial labor force.[39]

The nationalization decrees were the last great measures adopted without parliament's authorization. After the convocation of the Provisional National Assembly four days later, the democratic parties sought to limit the influence of the ROH and other extraconstitutional mass organizations and to confine policy-making to parliament. This encountered the opposition of the communists, who had found it advantageous to promote their aims through these organizations. They lent themselves more easily to manipulation than did the parliament, which had an orderly procedure and in which, moreover, they were a minority. The National Front began to experience increasing strains, and early in 1946 it was decided to hold general elections for the constituent assembly. May 26 was set as the date for the elections.

All parties committed themselves to maintain the National Front and the Košice program. This seemingly left no divisive issues. The electoral contest was nevertheless lively, though orderly. The difference between the parties lay in the accent they placed on specific aspects of the common program. The communists and Social Democrats stressed its social aspects and hinted that there were more to come. The democratic parties, on the other hand, maintained that the social goals of the program had largely been attained and placed a greater accent on freedom and democracy.

In Slovakia two new parties came into existence. Some of the old Slovak Social Democrats regarded the fusion of their party with the Communist party during the Slovak uprising in 1944 as a shotgun marriage, and now wished to go it alone. In January, 1946, with the assistance of the Czech Social Democrats, they formed the Labor party.[40] The other new party, the Freedom party, came into existence as a byproduct of electoral strategy by the Slovak Democratic party (DS). On March 30 Lettrich, the chairman of the DS, concluded an agreement (incorrectly known as the "April Agreement") with the Catholic leaders under which the Catholics were promised representation in all organs of the DS in a ratio of 7:3 in their favor.[41] The April Agreement promised to bolster the electoral strength of the DS, because the Catholic clergy had a powerful influence in Slovakia, especially in the rural areas, but it was fraught with dangers for the party. Many Catholic politicians were unreconstructed l'udáks. Their entry pulled the party sharply to the right and proved more than some of its leaders could stomach. The dissidents, among whom was notably Vavro Šrobár, formed the Freedom party on April 1.[42] Even more important was the communists' reaction to the April Agreement. In direct retaliation for its conclusion, the KSČ, with the concurrence of the Czech parties and the KSS, pressed through a further limitation of SNR prerogatives. Under the "Second Prague Agreement" on April 11, 1946, the SNR was deprived of the important power of making personal appointments without the approval of the Prague government.[43]

While the United States remained studiedly aloof during the electoral campaign, the Soviet Union gave a pointed reminder of its interest. On May 22, almost the eve of the elections, it was announced the Soviet troops would be moved across Czechoslovak territory from Austria and Hungary to the Soviet zone of occupation in Germany. At the outcry of the democratic leaders over this crude attempt at intimidation, the troop movement was postponed, but its psychological purpose had already been attained—it reminded the Czechs and Slovaks that the Soviet army was close by and could return on short notice.[44]

The communists approached the elections with confidence. They hoped to win an absolute majority, but were not worried if they did not. On February 4, at the outset of the campaign, Gottwald assured the party workers: "Even if it should happen, which is improbable, that we should not gain a favorable result . . . the working class, the party, and the working people will still have sufficient means, arms, and a method to correct simple mechanical voting, which might be affected by reactionary and saboteur elements." [45] In other words, if the results of the election were favorable to the communists, they would be accepted; if not, they would be "corrected."

The elections on May 26, which proved to be the last free Czechoslovak elections, passed without incident and, according to foreign observers, without any attempt at intimidation or manipulation. The ballot was secret. All citizens over eighteen years of age, except political offenders, were not only allowed, but were obliged to vote, thus assuring a heavy turnout. The results did not basically alter the existing party balance. In the Czech provinces the KSČ obtained 40.1, the National Socialists 23.5, the Populists 20.2, and the Social Democrats 15.6 percent of the vote. In Slovakia the DS obtained 62, the KSS

30.3, the Freedom party 3.7, and the Labor party 3.1 percent.[46] In the whole country the communists (the combined KSČ and KSS) secured 37.9 percent of the vote. This fell short of their hopes but was still impressive. The most surprising development was the failure of the Social Democratic party, which had at one time been the largest party in Czechoslovakia but was now the smallest. Its Slovak branch, the Labor party, likewise made a poor showing. During the electoral postmortem the democratic wing blamed the defeat on the campaign strategy of the party leadership, which had adopted an almost identical position on many issues as the communists, and demanded that in the future the party follow an independent course of action.

The most impressive gains were made by the Slovak Democrats. There is no doubt, however, that the large vote cast for the DS represented less a show of confidence by the Slovak electorate in the DS than a rebuke to the KSS. Several factors accounted for the communists' modest showing in Slovakia compared with their good record in the Czech provinces: the relative unimportance of the Slovak working class; the absence of a large reserve of confiscated land with which to entice the land-hungry peasantry, such as existed in the Czech borderlands; the greater war damages in Slovakia and consequently greater problems of reconstruction (in the winter of 1945–46 there were acute food shortages in the province); the influence of the conservative Catholic clergy, who did not hesitate to warn in their sermons against the perils of "godless" communism; and the bitter memory of the many excesses committed against the civilian population by the Red Army during its operations in Slovakia in 1944–45, for which the injured took revenge by voting against the "Russian party," that is, the communists.[47]

The communists did not mistake the fact that the large vote for the DS was really a vote against them, and at once took steps to correct the situation. "We have not won yet, the struggle continues," said Gottwald in reporting the results of the election to the central committee of the KSČ on May 30,[48] and he made it clear that the first target in the continuing struggle must be the DS. In order to limit its influence, Gottwald proposed to abolish what was left of Slovak autonomy—"even if we thereby violate formal national rights or promises or guarantees. . . . The Slovak comrades will no doubt understand." [49]

For the assault against the DS, Gottwald proposed four concrete steps: to limit further the prerogatives of the SNR, to launch a drive against the l'udáks camouflaged in the DS, to punish Jozef Tiso, and to take steps against the Slovak Catholic clergy, for the adoption of which the KSČ secured the concurrence of the National Front of the

Czech parties on June 12 and the National Front of the Czech and Slovak parties two days later.[50] The first step was implemented in the "Third Prague Agreement" on June 27–28, 1946, which placed the legislative powers of the SNR under government control and the Slovak commissioners under the appropriate ministers in Prague.[51] In practice, Slovakia reverted to the position that it had held before the Munich agreement in 1938: that of a simple administrative unit, like Bohemia and Moravia. This latest advance of centralism placed added strains not only on the relations between the KSS and DS but also—since it was supported by all Czech parties—between the Czechs and Slovaks as a whole.

The National Front had been somewhat shaken by the electoral contest. However, all parties still professed loyalty to it and it was continued. The Eighth Congress of the KSČ in March, 1946, had endorsed the strengthening of the National Front and had directed the party to implement further the national and democratic revolution.[52] (The KSČ never failed to stress that whatever the future model of the republic, it would correspond closely to special Czech and Slovak conditions.[53]) On July 2 the cabinet was reshuffled to conform with the results of the elections. Fierlinger yielded the premiership to Gottwald, as the representative of the largest party. Of the twenty-five cabinet posts, the KSČ received seven, the KSS one and one state secretaryship, the National Socialists four, the DS three and one state secretaryship, and the Czech Populists and Social Democrats three posts each.[54]

The parties were impelled to maintain a solid front by, among other things, the opening of the Paris Peace Conference on July 29. Three days earlier Gottwald and a delegation had returned from Moscow with the good news that the Soviet government had not only promised to support Czechoslovak claims at the conference but had also waived the provision of the Potsdam agreement that entitled it to claim German "external assets" in Czechoslovakia. Moreover, Gottwald revealed that the Soviet government had promised to support Czechoslovak economic plans by concluding a long-term trade treaty. On the other hand, the United States government had granted Czechoslovakia a credit of $50 million in June to buy American surplus war supplies in Europe. However, in September, before the credit was exhausted, the United States abruptly suspended it because the Czechoslovak delegates at the peace conference had applauded the Soviet delegate when he inveighed against American "economic imperialism." [55]

Czechoslovakia had been caught in the first cross fire of the cold war. On July 10, Soviet Foreign Minister Vyacheslav Molotov fired the first shot in the East-West struggle for Germany, by calling for the formation of a German national government and questioning the French right to the Saar. United States Secretary of State James F. Byrnes replied in his famous Stuttgart speech on September 6, by also calling for a German national government and by repudiating—in effect —the Potsdam agreement on the Oder-Neisse boundary and thus, by implication, reopening the whole question of the eastern settlement. Czechoslovak isolation from the West and dependence on the East had increased.

This development boded ill for the first important measure of the Gottwald government—the Two-Year Economic Plan for 1947–48, which the National Assembly approved on October 24.[56] The plan, which proposed to raise the standard of living ten percent above the prewar level, was oriented toward the long-range coexistence of the private and nationalized sectors of the economy and was predicated on the assumption that Czechoslovakia's traditional trade ties with the West would continue. At that time the Soviet Union faced gigantic problems of reconstruction and was in no position to provide economic aid to Czechoslovakia or to furnish, in exchange for Czechoslovak exports, the kind of goods and services she needed to realize her economic plans. The promised Soviet-Czechoslovak trade pact did not materialize until December, 1947.

The next important measure of the Gottwald government was political: it staged the trial of Monsignor Tiso as a deterrent to Slovak separatists. The trial, which opened in Bratislava on December 3, 1946, ended in March of the following year with Tiso's conviction of treason and a sentence of death. As calculated by the communists, the sentence placed the DS in a difficult position. The leaders of the party, chairman of the SNR Lettrich and Vice-Premier Ján Ursíny, were Protestants and former agrarians. They had led the Slovak resistance against Tiso's government during the war and had little sympathy for him, but they were put under pressure by the party's Catholic wing to save him. When the government considered Tiso's appeal for mercy on April 16, the DS ministers moved to commute the sentence to life imprisonment. They were seconded by the Czech Populist ministers, who demurred at hanging a fellow priest. However, the other ministers held firm for execution.[57] On the recommendation of the cabinet, President Beneš declined the appeal for mercy, and on April 18 Tiso was hanged.

Since the removal of the Sudeten German minority the "Slovak question," that is, the problem of satisfactorily adjusting relations between the Czechs and Slovaks, had become the foremost internal question in the country. The trial of Tiso, by deeply offending conservative Catholic opinion in Slovakia, aggravated this concern. It was to trouble the Third Czechoslovak Republic until its end—and, indeed, continued in a different form afterward.

In the spring of 1947 the Communist party adopted the goal of winning at least fifty-one percent of the votes in the next elections and thus gaining a majority in the National Assembly. This angered the other parties, but it did indicate that the communist leadership did not yet wish to take over all power, but was committed to the maintenance of the National Front. There were radical elements in the party that criticized the leadership for not following the Bolshevik way. Simultaneously, there were anticommunist groups in the country, biding their time. Both segments, however, represented politically insignificant forces. The predominant majority of the people wholeheartedly endorsed the objectives of the National Front to liberate men from economic and social domination within a democratic society.

These hopeful expectations, predicated on the belief that Czechoslovakia could eventually become the show window of a new, more humane system and the bridge between East and West were shattered in the summer of 1947 by Stalin's new policy line,[58] which called for consolidating the Soviet hold on Eastern Europe and drawing clear lines of combat with the West. On June 5, at Harvard University, U.S. Secretary of State George C. Marshall made his historic offer of American aid to Europe. Czechoslovakia was eager to share in the American aid, which it needed to complete the Two-Year Economic Plan successfully. On July 4 and 7 the cabinet and inner cabinet, respectively, voted unanimously to accept an invitation to sent a delegation to a preliminary conference of European states in Paris to discuss the Marshall Plan.[59] Immediately after the cabinet made its intention known, a government delegation led by Premier Gottwald left for Moscow where it was scheduled to negotiate mutual trade problems and to discuss the possibility of concluding a Franco-Czechoslovak treaty. When the delegation arrived in Moscow on July 9, it was given an ultimatum by Stalin to choose between East and West. On the following day the Prague government reversed its decision to send a delegation to Paris.[60] It had chosen the Soviet alliance.

At the end of September, the Information Bureau of the Communist parties (Cominform), including the KSČ, was founded at Szklarska Poreba in Poland as the institutional device of the communist international control system.[61] The delegates aimed "to apply the final touches to a general plan for easing the 'National Front' allies out of power and establishing a Communist dictatorship" in Eastern Europe.[62] The Cominform, then, was founded at the moment when "the Soviet Union had finally decided to take under her direct control a number of East European states," particularly Czechoslovakia.[63] The secretary general of the KSČ, Rudolf Slánský, informed the conference that the first task of the party was "to deal a death blow to reaction in Slovakia," [64] and added ominously: "It will be necessary to throw reactionary forces out of the National Front." [65] The road was opened for the Stalinist take-over in Czechoslovakia.

From the Cominform to the Prague Coup

By the fall of 1947 the struggle for power in East Central Europe was almost decided. Czechoslovakia remained the sole exception. It still had a coalition government. During the summer her hitherto favorable economic development suddenly ceased. A severe drought caused the harvest to fall to one-half of its normal level. As the leading party in the government, the communists received the major blame for the deteriorating economic situation. Feeling that the tide of public opinion was turning against them, they sought to postpone the elections that they had proposed in the spring. The democratic parties, on the other hand, aware that their chances in an electoral contest had improved, pressed for holding them at an early date. After much bickering it was decided to hold them in May, 1948.

As the parties girded for another electoral struggle, the communists displayed a wide arsenal of political and psychological weapons. In August they proposed that the owners of property in excess of one million Czechoslovak crowns pay a 'millionaires' tax" to provide aid to the ailing rural districts. Millionaires had never been numerous in Czechoslovakia and their ranks had been further reduced by the war and the subsequent expulsion of the German minority. Even the Social Democrats demurred at supporting so demagogic a measure. However, when communist propaganda succeeded in arousing popular support for it, the Social Democrats hastened on September 11 to conclude an agreement with the KSČ providing for their cooperation. The social democratic leadership thus sought to bind the KSČ to their own democratic practices. However, a large number of party members sharply criticized the agreement and Minister Václav Majer even tended his resignation.[66]

A strident note crept into communist propaganda. The communist press began systematically to impugn the loyalty of the other parties to the republic and to vilify their leaders. The public was shocked by the revelation on September 10 of an abortive attempt on the lives of non-communist ministers Jan Masaryk, Petr Zenkl, and Prokop Drtina, who had received parcels containing bombs. The communist Minister of Interior Válav Nosek and the communist-dominated police showed a curious lack of interest in the case. Instead, with much fanfare, the

Slovak Commissioner of Interior, Mikuláš Ferjenčík, announced on December 14 the discovery of a plot by the l'udák underground to assassinate President Beneš and overthrow the republic. Subsequently, the police linked the alleged plot to the l'udák exiles Karol Sidor and Ferdinand D'určanský. Widespread arrests, ultimately of more than 500 persons, followed. Among the arrested were three DS members of the National Assembly and a secretary of Vice-Premier Ján Ursíny. Although Ursíny himself was not implicated in the plot, he was forced to resign from the cabinet.

The affair served as a smoke screen behind which the communists prepared to purge the Slovak board of commissioners of its DS majority and to restructure the National Front of Slovak parties to make it more responsive to their wishes.[67] To set the stage for this coup, they arranged for the Slovak Trade Union Council (SOR—the Slovak counterpart of ROH) to meet in Bratislava on October 30 and for the Slovak Peasant Union to meet there two weeks later. At its October 30 meeting the SOR passed a resolution blaming the board of commissioners for the breakdown in food distribution and a failure to safeguard the security of the state and calling for its dismissal. Another resolution called for the reorganization of the Slovak National Front to include trade union, resistance, and peasant organizations. On the following day, in response to this "voice of the people," the communist chairman of the board of commissioners, Husák, four other communist commissioners, and the nonparty Commissioner of Interior Ferjenčík resigned from the board. Husák declared that the board was thereby dissolved and opened negotiations with the minute Freedom and Labor parties, until then unrepresented on the board, to form a new one. The DS leaders naturally protested against this novel constitutional concept whereby a minority could dismiss the majority from the caginet. They refused to resign from the board or to admit the mass organizations into the National Front.

The government in Prague then stepped into the situation, but to the dismay of the communists the National Socialists and Populists refused to associate themselves in a communist measure of coercion against the DS. On November 18, after prolonged negotiations, a new board of commissioners was formed in which the DS was deprived of its majority and the Freedom and Labor parties received representation.

The Slovak "November crisis" proved to be a dress rehearsal for the Prague "February crisis." The communists had effectively used their control of the police and mass organizations and had ruthlessly exploited every weakness in the ranks of the DS to achieve their objective. The democratic parties were alerted to what was in store for them. An early symptom of their reaction was the reassertion by the Social

Democratic party of its independence of the KSČ. At its congress at Brno on November 16 the procommunist Fierlinger was removed as chairman of the party and replaced with centrist Bohumil Laušman.[68] The democratic parties were encouraged by this development to believe that the Social Democratic party would cooperate with them. Laušman, however, personified the inability of the party to decide whether to fight on the side of the Communist party for social demands or on the side of the democratic parties for democracy. Under his leadership the party wavered in Hamlet-like indecision between the communist and democratic parties.

The communists increased their pressure on the other parties through the winter of 1947–48, with each issue exacerbating the political atmosphere and widening the divergences between the two camps.[69] The noncommunist parties made common complaint about police use of false confessions and *agents provocateurs*. Accusations levelled at the KSČ for attempting to monopolize control of the police engendered popular demands for the preservation of basic democratic freedoms. The time remaining for any possible settlement was running out. In November, 1947, the upper echelons of the KSČ began concerted action according to a plan based on their experience in the Slovak crisis. This involved a call by the ROH for a meeting of the workers' factory councils and peasant committees to formulate new popular demands. The party would then endorse their program, which would be adopted subsequently by all the mass organizations and those personalities within the existing parties who had secretly been won over by the communists. The ensuing "renovated" National Front would draw up a unified list of candidates for the elections.[70] The new alliance would then mount an electoral campaign aided by the mass media of communication, national committees, and police machinery—all controlled by the party.[71]

On February 12, 1948, the ROH issued a call to the workers' factory councils to meet in Prague on February 22, an action that convinced the democratic leaders that the communists were about to move. In a cabinet meeting the following day, the National Socialist ministers precipitated a crisis by protesting against the demotion and transfer of eight high noncommunist police officers by Minister of Interior Nosek. All ministers except the communists approved a motion introduced by the National Socialists to instruct Nosek to reinstate the police officers and desist from further personnel changes in the police forces. The communists were placed in a minority position in the cabinet and appeared isolated. Encouraged by their success, the National Socialists decided to take the offensive against them and try to upset their timetable. On February 20 the National Socialist ministers, followed by the Populist and Slovak Democratic ministers, resigned from the cabinet in protest against the failure of Nosek to carry out the cabinet decision of February 13 in the police matter. The "latent crisis" was thus transformed into "open crisis." [72]

The dramatic return of two old adversaries, U.S. Ambassador Laurence A. Steinhardt and Soviet Deputy Minister of Foreign Affairs and former ambassador to Czechoslovakia Valerian A. Zorin, to Prague on February 19 appeared to give the crisis an international dimension. Steinhardt declared to the press that the door to the Marshall Plan was still open to Czechoslovakia.[73] Zorin arrived ostensibly to expedite deliveries of grain, which the Soviet government had promised in December to alleviate the food shortage. The Western press speculated widely that he had really come to Prague to direct the communist takeover. Actually, no evidence ever turned up indicating that he had directly intervened in the crisis.[74] He did not have to. Gottwald and his associates had matters well in hand.

The ministers who had resigned constituted a minority, since neither the Social Democrats nor nonparty ministers Jan Masaryk and Ludvík Svoboda had been consulted and thus had not resigned. Consequently, Gottwald remained legally in power. The ministers who had resigned counted on President Beneš to refuse to accept their resignations. In that case, they would compel Gottwald either to call new elections or to carry out the decision of the cabinet in the police matter. They thought in strictly parliamentary terms, regarding their resignation as a mere cabinet affair, and called on their supporters "to remain calm under all circumstances." But the communists refused to abide by the rules of parliamentary democracy. While the democratic ministers and parties passively awaited Beneš's decision, the communists used their control of mass organizations and the police to take over power.

On the morning of February 21 Gottwald addressed an organized mass meeting in the Old Town Square in Prague. He accused the resigned ministers of having formed a "reactionary bloc" in the cabinet to obstruct the popular policies of the communists. They had precipitated the crisis, he alleged, to prevent the holding of elections, the outcome of which they feared. By their action they had "excluded themselves from the National Front," and the communists could have no further dealings with them. They would be replaced "with new people, who had remained faithful to the original spirit of the National Front." Gottwald put his proposal for the "renovation" of the cabinet into a resolution that was approved by acclamation, and on the spot a workers' delegation was "elected" to carry this expression of the "will of the people" to the president.

At the same time the communists deployed the instruments of their takeover—party activists, workers' militia, the police, and "action committees"—in Prague and outside it, according to a carefully prepared plan. On February 24 armed workers lent Prague a certain spurious aura of Petrograd in 1917, but their military value was slight, if any. In the event of an armed conflict with the other parties, the communists relied on the police, particularly on specially trained police regiments composed exclusively of communists. On the morning of February 21 the police assumed guard over the Prague radio station, post and telegraph offices, and railway stations. The most original instrument of the communist takeover was the action committees, which had been secretly organized earlier among men within and outside the KSČ whom the party could trust. Action committees sprang up in every government bureau, factory, and town—in fact, in every organized body in the country—and proceeded to purge them of democrats.[75]

By mass demonstrations centered on Prague and the mere threat of violence, the communists isolated and silenced the democratic parties, split the Social Democratic party, and awed the president. In such an unprecedented situation, naturally, the majority of the population expected word from Beneš—word that never came. After resisting the communist demands for five days, Beneš yielded. On February 25 he accepted the resignation of the democratic ministers and simultaneously appointed a new cabinet handpicked by Gottwald, which—in addition to communists and Social Democrats—included some members of the National Socialist, Populist, and Slovak Democratic parties, who had secretly agreed to cooperate with the communists. The façade of the National Front was thus maintained.

The only force that could have prevented the communist takeover was the army. But the army under General Svoboda, a friend of the communists, remained neutral throughout the crisis. In any event, Beneš never considered opposing force by force. The behavior of the noncommunist party leaders was, if possible, even worse. While the communists were brilliantly using the instruments of power, "the non-Communist parties . . . had no organization, no plan" [76] and finished in complete disarray, despite the support they enjoyed from the helpless and baffled majority of the Czech and Slovak people. By their precipitate and ill-considered resignation, the democratic ministers had made it possible for the communists to take over power by constitutional means. They were not forced out of the government by the communists; they had walked out of it.

Meanwhile, the zealous Husák had anticipated Gottwald's coup at

Prague with one of his own at Bratislava.[77] But the events in Bratislava lacked the drama of those in Prague, because they constituted, more or less, only a mopping-up operation, designed to complete what had been left undone in November. Unlike Gottwald, Husák did not have to contend with Beneš. Moreover, while Prague was swarming with foreign correspondents who had come to observe and report on the death of Czechoslovak democracy, none troubled to go to the provincial backwater of Bratislava. Husák, therefore, dispensed with the elaborate *mise en scène* that Gottwald felt compelled to arrange at Prague. Unlike the DS ministers in Prague, the DS commissioners in Bratislava did not resign; they had to be expelled from the board. On February 21, without awaiting the outcome of the cabinet crisis in Prague, Husák wrote them that the resignation of the DS ministers from the central government bound them to resign too, and against the eventuality that they might dispute this ruling he posted policemen at the doors of their offices to turn them away. They did not choose to resist, for the DS had been emasculated and cowed in November and had nothing left with which to fight. The communists took a majority of seats on the board (eight out of fifteen), and distributed the rest among the other parties (including two pliant DS members) and representatives of the communist-controlled mass organizations. Action committees completed the mop-up.

After appointing the new government on February 25 and receiving its members when they were sworn in on February 27, Beneš retired to his country residence at Sezimovo Ústí. On June 7 he resigned and withdrew from further participation in the conduct of state affairs. The communists were left the sole masters of the republic—free to reorganize it according to their beliefs and concepts.

Notes

1. Edvard Beneš, *Memoirs: From Munich to New War and New Victory* (Boston, 1954), p. 139.

2. See the account of Eduard Taborsky, Beneš's former secretary, "Benešovy moskevské cesty" ["Beneš's Trips to Moscow"], *Svědectví,* 1, Nos. 3–4 (1957), 203ff. Taborsky stated that in his wartime conversations with Soviet leaders Beneš held that Ruthenia should belong either to Czechoslovakia or to the Soviet Union. "As much as he wished" this area "to be Czechoslovak again, he was by no means ready to insist on it as the price of Soviet friendship" (p. 207). On March 24, 1945, Soviet Foreign Minister Vyacheslav M. Molotov asked Beneš to repeat in writing his acceptance of the loss of Ruthenia (p. 212).

3. Gustáv Husák, *Svedectvo o Slovenskom národnom povstaní* [*Testimony about the Slovak National Uprising*] (Bratislava, 1964), pp. 554–55; Zdeněk Fierlinger, *Ve službách ČSR* [*In the Service of the Czechoslovak Republic*] (2 vols.; Prague, 1947–48), II, 599ff.

4. See Miroslav Soukup, "Některé problémy vzájemných vztahů mezi kommunistickými stranami" ["Some Problems of the Mutual Relations between the Communist Parties"], *Příspěvky k dějinám KSČ*, IV (Feb. 1964), 13ff.

5. Gottwald's report to the central committee of the KSČ, September 25–26, 1946.

6. Milan Hübl, "Lidová demokracie V 1946" ["Popular Democracy in 1946"], *Slovanský přehled*, No. 2 (1966), 65–70.

7. See Karel Kaplan, *Znárodnění a socialismus* [*Nationalization and Socialism*] (Prague, 1968), *passim*. This tendency was discernible in other European communist parties, notably in France and Italy.

8. See the discussion Beneš had with Gottwald and other communist exiles in Moscow in December 1943, in Beneš, *Memoirs*, pp. 268–75, and, from the communist point of view, Bohuslav Laštovička, *V Londýně za války* [*In London during the War*] (Prague, 1960), pp. 310–30.

9. See Libuše Otáhalová and Milada Červinková, eds., *Dokumenty z historie československé politiky 1939–1943* [*Documents on the History of Czechoslovak Politics 1939–1943*] (2 vols.; Prague, 1966), II, 750–51.

10. For the minutes of the negotiations see Miloš Klimeš *et al.*, eds., *Cesta ke květnu* [*Road to May*] (2 vols.; Prague, 1965), I, 380–453. For accounts see Laštovička, *V Londýně*, pp. 496–553, and Husák, *Svedectvo*, pp. 578–89.

11. Josef Korbel, *The Communist Subversion of Czechoslovakia, 1938–1948* (Princeton, 1959), p. 114. Korbel rightly blames Beneš for his withdrawal from what the President wrongly considered to be a matter of party politics. For revealing conversations between President Beneš and U.S. ambassador in Moscow, W. Averell Harriman, on March 22 and 31, 1945, see U.S. Department of State, *Foreign Relations of the United States. Diplomatic Papers 1945*. Vol. IV: *Europe* (Washington, 1968), pp. 427–29 and 430–33.

12. Korbel, *The Communist Subversion*, p. 114.

13. Minister Jaroslav Stránský's recollections, ibid., p. 114.

14. Jaroslav Opat, *O novou demokracii, 1945–1948* [*For a New Democracy, 1945–1948*] (Prague, 1966), pp. 44–48; Jozef Jablonický, *Slovensko na prelome* [*Slovakia in Transition*] (Bratislava, 1965), pp. 227–85; Jaroslav Barto, *Riešenie vzťahu Čechov a Slovákov, 1944–1948* [*Solving the Relations Between the Czechs and the Slovaks, 1944–1948*] (Bratislava, 1968), pp. 30–34; and Samo Falťan, *Slovenská otázka v Československu* [*The Slovak Question in Czechoslovakia*] (Bratislava, 1968), pp. 186–200.

15. Edvard Beneš, *Šest let exilu a druhé světové války. Řeči, projevy a dokumenty z r. 1938–45* [*Six Years of Exile and the Second World War: Speeches, Declarations, and Documents in 1938–45*] (Prague, 1946), pp. 423–24.

16. The full text of the Košice program may be found in *Za svobodu českého a slovenského národa: Sborník dokumentů* [*For the Freedom of the Czech and Slovak People: a Collection of Documents*] (Prague, 1956), pp. 368–90, published by the Institute for the History of KSČ in Prague. For an English translation of point six of the program dealing with the Slovaks, see Jozef Lettrich, *History of Modern Slovakia* (New York, 1955), pp. 317–18.

17. Bohuslav Laštovička, "Vznik a význam košického vládního programu" ["The Origin and Importance of the Košice Government Program"], *Československý časopis historický*, VIII (August 1960), 465.

18. For the negotiations leading to the formation of the government and its composition, see Opat, *O novou demokracii*, pp. 48–50. In the SNR and its executive organ, the board of commissioners, the Communist party of Slovakia (KSS), and the Democratic party (DS) continued to share power equally.

19. Laštovička, "Vznik," p. 463.

20. Klimeš, *Cesta*, I, 447.

21. During the war both the Moscow and London exiles emphasized the primary importance of the home front. Upon returning to Prague, however, both united in refusing to offer the Czech resistance leaders any representation in the cabinet. See Josef Belda et al., *Na rozhraní dvou epoch* [*On the Frontier of Two Epochs*] (Prague, 1968), pp. 40–41.

22. Apart from the fact that the SNR was recognized in the Košice program, it had functioned continuously since February, 1945. By the time the government was established in Prague in May, the SNR was well entrenched and carried on as a quasi-government.

23. Falt'an, *Slovenská otázka*, pp. 206–207; Barto, *Riešenie*, pp. 54–58.

24. Barto, *Riešenie*, pp. 67–79; Falt'an, *Slovenská otázka*, pp. 207–12; Belda, *Na rozhraní*, p. 43.

25. The four Czech parties received forty seats and the two Slovak parties, fifty seats each. The remaining forty seats were distributed among representatives of mass organizations.

26. Radomír Luža, *The Transfer of the Sudeten Germans* (New York, 1964), p. 262.

27. V. Jarošová and O. Jaroš, *Slovenské robotníctvo v boji o moc, 1944–1948* [*The Slovak Workers in the Struggle for Power, 1944–1948*] (Bratislava, 1965), p. 69.

28. Luža, *The Transfer*, p. 262.

29. Ibid., pp. 271, 291; Karel Kaplan, "Rok československé revoluce 1945" ["Year of the Czechoslovak Revolution"], *Sborník historický*, 15 (1967), p. 115.

30. Juraj Zvara in *Historický časopis*, No. 1 (1964), 28–49, and in *Příspěvky k dějinám KSČ* (June 1965), 409–27.

31. U.S. Department of State, *Foreign Relations of the United States 1946*. Vol. IV: *Paris Peace Conference: Documents* (Washington, 1970), 727–28; A. C. Leiss and R. Dennett, eds., *European Peace Treaties after World War II* (Boston, 1954), pp. 93–96.

32. For Article I of the Hungarian peace treaty, defining the bridgehead, see ibid., p. 274.

33. F. Němec and V. Moudrý, *The Soviet Siezure of Subcarpathian Ruthenia* (Toronto, 1955), pp. 251–53. For the text of the Soviet-Czechoslovak treaty of June 29, 1945, on the cession of Ruthenia, see *British State and Foreign Papers*, Vol. 145 (1943–45) (London, 1953), pp. 1096–98.

34. Opat, *O novou demokracii*, p. 69. For a good survey of the strength, aims, and leadership of the KSČ and all parties after liberation, see Belda, *Na rozhraní*, pp. 22–39. For the KSČ, see Zdeněk Eliáš and Jaromír Netík, "Czechoslovakia," in William E. Griffith, ed., *Communism in Europe. Continuity, Change, and the Sino-Soviet Dispute* (Cambridge, Mass., and London, 1966), II, *passim*.

35. Barto, *Riešenie*, pp. 98–100; Jarošová and Jaroš, *Slovenské robotníctvo*, p. 97. The resolution was implemented at a conference of the KSS at Žilina on August 11–12, 1945, when Široký replaced Karol Šmidke as chairman and Štefan Bašťovanský replaced Edo Friš as secretary of the party. Neither Šmidke nor Friš was a Slovak nationalist but both had been swept along by the nationalists since the Slovak uprising. Široký had not participated in the uprising, being in prison at the time. Of Slovak origin but a Magyar by education, he was a bitter enemy of Slovak nationalists whether in or out of the party. The true spokesman of the nationalists in the KSS, Gustáv Husák, saved himself, for the moment, by abjuring nationalism—also for the moment—and turning on his wartime nationalist allies, the Slovak Democrats.

36. In Slovakia 25.58 percent of the population derived an income from industry, mining, and the trades, compared to 39.5 percent in Bohemia and Moravia. On the other hand, 52.59 percent of the Slovak population worked in agriculture, forestry, and fisheries, while only 20.37 percent of the population of the Czech provinces did. See Jarošová and Jaroš, *Slovenské robotníctvo*, p. 65.

37. June, 1945, the prominent communist trade unionist Antonín Zápotocký became chairman of the ROH. The membership amounted to 2,249,976 on December 31, 1947. See V. Pachman, "Boj o odborovou jednotu v letech 1945–1948" ["Struggle for the Unity of the Trade Union Movement in 1945–1948"], *Československý časopis historický*, VIII, No. 6 (1960), 810.

38. Czechoslovakia was the second state after the U.S.S.R. to nationalize its industry and banks.

39. Opat, *O novou demokracii*, p. 115; Kaplan, *Znárodnění*, pp. 7–58.

40. Marta Vartíková, *Od Košíc po február* [*From Košice to February*] (Bratislava, 1968), p. 71. Jaroslav Nedvěd, "Cesta ke sloučení sociální demokracie s komunistickou stranou" ["The Road to the Merger of the Social Democratic and Communist Parties"], *Rozpravy Československé Akademie věd*, No. 8 (1968), 46–48.

41. Opat, *O novou demokracii*, pp. 162–66; Belda, *Na rozhraní*, p. 70; Vartíková, *Od Košíc*, p. 78.

42. Vartíková, *Od Košíc*, pp. 74–77.

43. Barto, *Riešenie*, pp. 138–47; Faltan, *Slovenská otázka*, pp. 216–17.

44. Hubert Ripka, *Le Coup de Prague: Une révolution préfabriquée* (Paris, 1949), p. 39.

45. Belda, *Na rozhraní*, p. 60.

46. Ibid., pp. 72–73; Opat, *O novou demokracii*, pp. 178–89.

47. The same factors operated against the communists, to a smaller extent, in Moravia. The communist share of the vote in Moravia was 34.5 percent as against 43.3 percent in Bohemia.

48. Belda, *Na rozhraní*, p. 74.

49. Vartíková, *Od Košíc*, p. 80; Jarošová and Jaroš, *Slovenské robotníctvo*, p. 157; Barto, *Riešenie*, p. 159.

50. Barto, *Riešenie*, p. 160; Belda, *Na rozhraní*, p. 80.

51. Belda, *Na rozhraní*, p. 83; Opat, *O novou demokracii*, pp. 193–95; Barto, *Riešenie*, pp. 170–71; Falt'an, *Slovenská otázka*, p. 222. For the Czecho-Slovak negotiations in the National Front, see the informative article by Miroslav Bouček and Miloslav Klimeš, "Národní fronta Čechů a Slováků v letech 1946–1948" ["The National Front of the Czech and Slovaks in the Years 1946–48"], *Sborník historický*, 20 (1973), 207–14.

52. Opat, *O novou demokracii*, pp. 135–36.

53. Gottwald on July 8, 1946, in presenting the "construction program" of his new government to the National Assembly. See Opat, *O novou demokracii*, pp. 197–200. Also in September, 1946, and on October 4, 1946.

54. Ibid., pp. 191–96; Belda, *Na rozhraní*, pp. 84–86. While claiming the premiership and a proportionate share of posts in the central government, the communists were extremely reluctant to accept the results of the elections in the Slovak National Council and the board of commissioners. It was not until August 7, after bitter wrangling between the KSS and the DS, that the DS was allowed to take 60 percent of the seats in the SNR and 9 out of 15 posts on the board of commissioners. The communists fought tooth and nail against relinquishing the commissariat of interior, which controlled the police. In the end they agreed to relinquish it, not to a DS member but to a nonparty expert, Gen. Mikuláš Ferjenčík. Moreover, contrary to the principle that the strongest party should get the chairmanship of the board, which Gottwald had invoked to claim the premiership, this important post was retained by the communist Husák. See Vartíková, *Od Košíc*, pp. 109–11; Jarošová and Jaroš, *Slovenské robotníctvo*, p. 163.

55. James F. Byrnes, *Speaking Frankly* (New York, 1947), pp. 143–44; Ripka, *Le Coup*, p. 41. In addition to the insult at the peace conference, the Americans were angered by a Czechoslovak deal with Rumania, under which Prague resold American goods to the Rumanians at a profit, and by the Czechoslovak failure to compensate American citizens for the loss of property in Czechoslovakia through nationalization. The American rebuff was a great blow to Masaryk, who had to explain it in a secret cabinet meeting on October 7. See Belda, *Na rozhraní*, pp. 120–21; U.S. Department of State, *Foreign Relations of the United States 1946*, Vol. VI: *Eastern Europe: The Soviet Union* (Washington, 1969), pp. 216, 220ff.

56. Belda, *Na rozhraní*, p. 95; Opat, *O novou demokracii*, p. 204.

57. Belda, *Na rozhraní*, pp. 172–73.

58. Jaroslav Opat, "K metodě studia a výkladu některých problémů v období 1945–1948" ["On the Method of Study and Explanation of Some Problems in the Period of 1945–1948"], *Příspěvky dějinám KSČ* (February, 1965), 65–83.

59. Belda, *Na rozhraní*, pp. 121–22; Opat, *O novou demokracii*, pp. 236–38.

60. Ripka, *Le Coup*, pp. 51–55. Apparently, the Czechoslovak acceptance of the invitation to go to Paris was in part a result of a misunderstanding brought about by Soviet inefficiency. Masaryk sought advance Soviet approval for accepting the invitation, but Bodrov, the Soviet chargé d'affaires in Prague, lacked instructions. Failing to get a reply from Moscow in time, the Czechoslovak government announced its acceptance—only to be told by Moscow that it must not go to Paris. See Belda, *Na rozhraní*, pp. 122–25. Masaryk, who clung to relations with the West, was crushed by the humiliation. For more information see Josef Belda et al., "K otázce účasti Československa na Marshallově plánu" ["On the Question of the Czechoslovak Participation at the Marshall Plan"], *Revue dějin socialismu*, VIII (1968), 81–100.

61. *For a Lasting Peace, for a People's Democracy*, November 10, 1947.

62. Eugenio Reale, who participated at the conference as the delegate of the Communist party of Italy, in Milorad Drachkovitch and Branko Lazitch, eds., *The Comintern: Historical Highlights* (New York, 1966), p. 260.

63. Vladimir Dedijer, *Tito* (New York, 1953), p. 292.

64. The minutes of E. Reale in Drachkovitch and Lazitch, *The Comintern*, p. 254; Jarošová and Jaroš, *Slovenské robotníctvo*, p. 232.

65. Conference of the Nine Communist Parties, p. 118, quoted in Korbel, *Communist Subversion*, p. 186.

66. Nedvěd, "Cesta ke sloučení," p. 56; Belda, *Na rozhraní*, pp. 154–67; Opat, *O novou demokracii*, pp. 242–45.

67. For the Slovak November crisis see Jarošová and Jaroš, *Slovenské robotníctvo*, pp. 221–52; Vartíková, *Od Košic*, pp. 147–62; Lettrich, *History*, pp. 249–51. For Gottwald's formula to solve the crisis, see Václav Král, ed., *Cestou k únoru* [*The Road to February*] (Prague, 1963), p. 270.

68. Nedvěd, "Cesta ke sloučení," pp. 58–59.

69. The KSČ raised demands for the nationalization of private trade and for new land reform. In February, 1948, it was defeated in an attempt to prevent an increase in the salaries of public servants. It continued to use the security apparatus to increase pressure, and managed to hush up an investigation of the attempt against the lives of three democratic ministers.

70. According to a confidential survey of public opinion taken by the communist-controlled Ministry of Information, the KSČ faced a loss of eight to ten percent in the next election. See Ripka, *Le Coup*, p. 190.

71. Miroslav Bouček, *Praha v únoru* [*Prague in February*] (Prague, 1963), pp. 25, 149; Karel Kaplan in *Historica* (Prague, 1963), V, 241.

72. The literature on the February crisis is quite extensive. Among the communist accounts and documentary collections are: Belda, *Na rozhraní*, pp. 223–62; Bouček, *Praha*, pp. 143–254, and *Únor 1948: Sborník doku-*

mentů [*February 1948: A Collection of Documents*] (Prague, 1958); Král, *Cestou*, pp. 329–410; Miroslav Bouček and Miloslav Klimeš, *Dramatické dnú února 1948* [*The Dramatic Days of February, 1948*] (Prague, 1973), *passim;* Jiři Veselý, *Prague 1948* (Paris, 1958), pp. 71–190, which is a French adaptation of his *Kronika únorových dnů* [*Chronicle of the February Days*] (Prague, 1958); and Alois Svoboda *et al., Jak to bylo v únoru* [*What Happened in February*] (Prague, 1949), *passim.* A Czech National Socialist account may be found in Ripka, *Le Coup*, pp. 201–316, of which there is an English translation, *Czechoslovakia Enslaved* (London, 1950), and a Social Democratic one in Bohumil Laušman, *Kdo byl vinen?* [*Who is to Blame?*] (Vienna, n.d.), pp. 108–54. President Beneš's side of the story is told in detail by the head of his chancellery, Jaromír Smutný, in "Únorový převrat 1948" ["February Revolution, 1948"], *Doklady a Rozpravy,* Nos. 12 (1953); 19 (1955); 21 (1955); 25 (1956); and 28 (1957); published by the Institute of Dr. Edvard Beneš in London. For Steinhardt's report of the February coup, see *Foreign Relations of the United States, 1948,* 9 vols. (Washington, 1974), IV, 738–756. Accounts by Western scholars may be found in Korbel, *Communist Subversion*, pp. 206–35, and Paul E. Zinner, *Communist Strategy and Tactics in Czechoslovakia, 1918–1948* (New York, 1963), pp. 204–16. The most recent analysis was given by Pavel Tigrid, "The Prague Coup of 1948: The Elegant Takeover," in Thomas T. Hammond, ed., *The Anatomy of Communist Takeovers* (New Haven and London, 1975), pp. 399–432. Among the numerous accounts by Western journalists, perhaps the best may be found in Dana Adams Schmidt, *Anatomy of a Satellite* (Boston, 1952), pp. 108–21.

73. Report of ČTK, the Czechoslovak News Agency, in Král, *Cestou*, p. 347. Steinhardt informed Czechoslovak officials that the United States would consider favorably an application for a credit of $25 million to purchase American cotton. See Schmidt, *Anatomy*, p. 110. Although Czechoslovakia experienced great economic difficulties at the time, the economic weapon was quite inadequate to affect the crisis.

74. According to Belda, *Na rozhraní*, p. 265, Zorin assured Gottwald that "the Soviet Union would not allow Western powers to interfere in the internal affairs of Czechoslovakia." Since, however, none of the Western powers intervened in the crisis, the Soviet Union did not have to do so either. Although the crisis had international repercussions, it was a purely internal one.

75. The purge involved some 28,000 persons. See Karel Kaplan, *Utváření generální linie výstavby socialismu v Československu* [*The Formation of the General Line of the Construction of Socialism in Czechoslovakia*] (Prague, 1966), p. 27.

76. Kaplan, *Historica*, V, 250ff.

77. For the Slovak side of the crisis see Vartíková, *Od Košíc*, pp. 181–84; Jarošová and Jaroš, *Slovenské robotníctvo*, pp. 265–67; Lettrich, *History*, pp. 259–60.

4

Daniel Yergin

Shattered Peace: The Origins of the Cold War and the National Security State

Daniel Yergin's recent study of cold-war origins is one of the most rewarding narrative syntheses since the stately work of Herbert Feis— Churchill-Roosevelt-Stalin *(Princeton, 1957);* Between War and Peace: The Potsdam Conference *(Princeton, 1960); and the lesser* From Trust to Terror *(New York: Norton, 1970)—and William H. McNeill—* America, Britain, and Russia: Their Cooperation and Conflict, 1941–46 *(New York: Oxford University Press, 1953). Yergin enjoyed the advantage of access to British and American documentary collections that were closed to McNeill and only partially available to Feis. On the other hand, the earlier authors still convey a solidity and massiveness that Yergin's focus on personality and anecdote cannot rival. Admittedly the very colorfulness of Yergin's narrative can be misleading. In other chapters of his book Yergin dissects the bureaucratic and not merely personal inputs to American policy: the long-ripening "Riga axioms" within the State Department that predisposed U.S. policy toward distrust of Moscow, or the pressure of the aviation industry and the Air Force for a remilitarized United States. Further historical work must now focus even more carefully on these organizational determinants of United States conduct.*

Yergin's political judgments are also nuanced. By his critical focus on American policy the author naturally conveys a revisionist stance. Nevertheless, he realizes that Soviet sources might suggest a different story, and he constantly stresses the repressiveness of Stalin's regime— in part perhaps to disarm orthodox critics, in part because he believes the Soviets might well have been repressive without being expansionist. The question remains whether a dictator who sought such oppressive

*security at home would really have remained tolerant of the ambiguity
of pluralist regimes on his borders. The story is still ex parte, although
it is illusory to believe that even if we someday have Soviet archives
open to us, questions of intention can be fully resolved.*

*Daniel Yergin is a researcher with the Harvard Center for
International Affairs and the Harvard Business School. In addition to
his historical work, he writes frequently on international economic and
political affairs. This selection, chapter 12 of* Shattered Peace, *"The
Margin of Safety," is reprinted with his permission and that of his
publisher, Houghton Mifflin Company.*

The Margin of Safety

JAMES RESTON: The only weakness in what was otherwise a magni-
    ficent statement of the President—namely, that he gave the im-
    pression, rightly or wrongly, that the people who were going to
    get help were the people who were in desperate straits and who
    had an armed minority at their border; whereas I would like to
    have seen him indicate that you can fight Communism in other
    ways—in economic ways.
JAMES FORRESTAL: The core of the thing is are you going to try to
    keep Germany a running boil with the pus exuding over the rest
    of Europe?

                                Telephone conversation, March 13, 1947 [1]

Even as U.S. policymakers were formulating the Truman Doctrine,
they saw before them in Western Europe an economic crisis with
momentous political ramifications. Their response took the form of a
policy that answered several questions at once—what to do about
Germany? what to do about Western Europe? what to do about the
Soviet Union? The goals were several as well—the economic revival
of Western Europe, the creation of an environment hospitable to
democracy and capitalism in Western Europe, the maintenance of the
balance of power on the European continent, and the "containment" of
the Soviet Union and communism. The industrial might of western
Germany was presented as essential for the recovery of its noncommunist neighbors. In this way, with its firm entrenchment in a Europe-
wide framework, a reconstituted West Germany would become politically acceptable throughout the rest of Western Europe.

The chosen instrument for achieving these various goals was American economic power. "It is necessary," Harry Truman reminded
members of the Associated Press in April 1947, "that we develop a
new realization of the size and strength of our economy." [2] The

realization involved a subordination of international economics to international politics, an essential feature in the rise of the national security state. Prior to 1947, economic matter (involving trade as well as reconstruction) and political questions were usually dropped into different boxes, although that separation had eroded somewhat by 1946.

Official thought on international economic matters, coming out of the Second World War, had been obsessed with preparing for a multilateral world—that is, an open international trading system, free of tariffs and other restrictions, and unhindered by bilateral trade agreements. Despite disagreement about the importance of foreign trade to the postwar American economy, many assumed that the trade barriers of the 1930s had helped pave the way to the Second World War, and they wanted to avoid a rerun. Dominating the planning was a curious kind of optimism about how easy it was going to be to pass through what was loosely referred to as the "post-war transition" and get on to the main business of constructing the new multilateral trading world.

This is not to say that American officials ignored the damage done by war. In his diary, for instance, Henry Stimson recorded his shock at the "powerful picture of the tough situation" that John McCloy brought back from a trip to Germany in April 1945—a scene of devastation that suggested itself as "worse than anything probably that ever happened in the world."

In general, however, the officials in Washington who managed policy at the conclusion of the war and immediately afterward tended to discount the pressing problems symbolized by the urban rubble, which, like graveyards, dotted the Continent. Those who worked abroad, in public and private capacities, took more seriously the effects of the wartime trauma and the depths of the postwar problems. In February 1946, Colonel Sosthenes Behn, founder of International Telephone and Telegraph, wandered into the offices of his New York bank, J. P. Morgan, "very blue about the foreign outlook." Behn said that he "liquidated every foreign property that he could as fast as he could." His hope—"to build up a big domestic company." [3] A couple of months later, E. F. Penrose, an American economics official based in London, was struck on returning to Washington by "the attitude of rather casual and easy optimism about European revival in many Washington circles." In 1946, the State Department put more attention and more staff to work on an international trade charter and tariff reduction than on relief and reconstruction. The Administration was relieved to be done with UNRRA, the United Nations relief organization, which was too independent of Washington and too controversial with many congressmen. Also, perhaps, a strong element of wishful thinking influenced the tendency to underestimate the task of reconstruction; for even before the war was over, officials had already concluded the postwar assistance programs would arouse considerable domestic opposition.[4]

At the end of 1945, an unexpectedly grave food crisis gave the first major signal that the "post-war transition" might prove much more treacherous than the blueprints had allowed. By early 1946, more than 125 million Europeans were subsisting on no more than 2000 calories a day; many of those millions, on no more than 1000— in grim contrast to the 3300 calories a day that was the average in the United States.[5]

In response, Truman, in the spring of 1946, sent Herbert Hoover on another of the former President's regular spring forays into foreign policy, this time to survey famine conditions abroad. After World War I, Hoover had proved himself not only an expert famine relief administrator in Europe, but also an excellent strategist in using food to contain communism, and he was welcomed back into policy councils with something like religious awe. Foreshadowing what was to become a common theme in the next year, he argued, both publicly and privately, not only in Washington but also as he toured abroad, that economic distress should be evaluated in terms of conflict with the Soviet Union. Like Forrestal, he even felt the need to warn the Pope that "Catholicism in Europe was in the gravest danger from the Communist invasion, the gates of which would be wide open from starvation." Hoover sketched a similar scene for Attlee, but was somewhat disappointed when the only response from the British Prime Minister was, "This has been very interesting" and "I shall be seeing you at lunch." [6]

The food crisis eased later in 1946, temporarily at least, and optimism quickly returned to American leaders. Industrial production picked up in Europe—for instance, by 1947, Holland had exceeded prewar averages—and officials on both sides of the Atlantic were sure that the worst was past. On October 5, 1946, Hugh Dalton noted that he and Will Clayton "are agreed that UNRRA must definitely stop, as arranged, in the next year, and that, apart from the Germans, only Italy, Austria and Greece should rank for further doles from either the U.S. or U.K." [7] Then came a crisis so serious that, in itself, it pushed the polarization between East and West to the point of virtual partition of Europe.

The crisis had been pending, brought on not only by the visible destruction—the dead and injured, the apartments burned out, the factories flattened, the railway bridges destroyed—but also by invisible devastation. Capital equipment was obsolete and worn out. The labor forces in Europe were exhausted, undernourished, and disorganized. Technical skills had been lost. Such reconstruction as had taken place created a great hunger for American goods, and so aggravated the problems. And then the weather—droughts in the summers of 1946 and 1947 and what has been called a Siberian winter in between—brought conditions to a crisis point. The weather, to be sure, was not the cause of this crisis, but rather, the precipitant.

For clarity's sake, we might see the picture in three panels. The first was the food and raw materials crisis that had been mounting through 1946. Western Europe was no longer able to obtain food stores from traditional sources in Eastern Europe and the Far East. In Western Europe, soil fertility had declined markedly, and the traditional market links between town and country had been sundered. European wheat production in 1947 fell to less than half of what it had been in 1938. British coal production in 1946 was 20 percent lower than it had been in 1938; in the western parts of Germany, the output of coal was only two-fifths of what it had been in 1938.

Second, the war had broken established habits and patterns of economic activity within Europe and between Europe and the rest of the world. The Europeans were not able to sell to former customers abroad. American efforts to penetrate the sterling bloc of the British Empire aggravated Britain's economic problems. The successful insistence by the U.S. that the British make the pound convertible in the summer of 1947 created an immediate, massive, and worldwide rush from pounds to dollars, and so made matters much worse. The most important of all the economic dislocations involved the collapse of Germany, which had formerly played a central role in Europe as both importer and exporter. Before the war, the three Western zones alone had been the source of one-fifth of all industrial production in Europe; in the immediate postwar years, production there barely reached a third of those prewar levels.[8]

But, in 1947, the heart of the problem was a financial crisis. Part of the problem was inflation—wholesale prices had risen 80 percent in France during 1946. Such inflation led to strikes and promoted instability. Even more important was the need to find a way to finance both the equipment necessary for reconstruction and the food and other raw materials that Europe needed to obtain from the United States. The trade balance between the United States and Europe was not at all in balance. In 1947, the United States exported to Europe almost seven times as much as it imported from Europe. This seemed to indicate a worsening trend, for U.S. imports from Europe had actually declined between 1946 and 1947, while the demand for U.S. exports—both manufactures and commodities—was increasing.

Meanwhile, inflation in the United States, which Washington started to see as a serious problem in March 1947, widened the gap. Wholesale prices in the United States rose 40 percent between June 1946 and September 1947. By the second quarter of 1947, the U.S. export surplus was running at a staggering annual rate of $12.5 billion.

How could Europe finance its vital purchases from the United States? Lend-lease had long since ended; UNRRA would cease in mid-1947; other credits were being drawn down. The foreign assets of the European countries were disappearing; and they had lost a very substantial part of the invisible earnings that had formerly flowed in from overseas investments, shipping, insurance, and so forth. They were unable to sell goods to traditional markets elsewhere in the world and indeed these former markets themselves were now lining up in competition with the Europeans for the product of the American machine.

The result became known as the "dollar shortage" or the "dollar gap." The only way the Europeans could continue to buy was if the U.S. financed the purchases in some fashion.[9]

"The dollar shortage is developing everywhere in the world," British Chancellor Hugh Dalton complained in the spring of 1947. "The Americans have half the total income of the world, but won't either spend it in buying other people's goods or lending it or giving it away on a sufficient scale. The Fund and the Bank still do nothing. How soon will this dollar shortage bring a general crisis?" [10]

When the Americans finally perceived the crisis, they responded with alacrity, driven at times by something akin to panic, especially as they measured the problem against what they perceived as Soviet intentions. "I am deeply disturbed by the present world picture, and its implications for our country," Will Clayton noted, a week before the Truman Doctrine speech. "The reins of world leadership are fast slipping from Britain's competent but now very weak hands. These reins will be picked up either by the United States or Russia." But the United States could not assume this leadership "unless the people of the United States are shocked into doing so." He was not suggesting that they be deceived, but only that they be led to see the "truth" as seen by Administration officials and as reported "in the cables which daily arrive at the State Department from all over the world. In every country in the Eastern Hemisphere and most of the countries of the Western Hemisphere, Russia is boring from within." The key lay in providing the dollars necessary to finance recovery and thus underwrite political stability.[11]

By this point, the Americans were consciously turning away from trying to make the Great Power consortium work. Dean Acheson made this point on April 18 (while Marshall was still in Moscow) when he explained that diplomacy and negotiations, what he called the first of the country's instruments for carrying out its foreign policy, had not succeeded in building "with the Soviet Union that mutual trust and confidence and cessation of expansionism which must be the foundation of political stability. We have concluded, therefore, that we msut use to an increasing extent our *second* instrument of foreign policy, namely, economic power, in order to call an effective halt to the Soviet Union's expansionism and political infiltration, and to create a basis for political stability and economic well-being." [12] In other words, Acheson was saying that the Rooseveltian approach had failed; containment, economic to begin with, was the appropriate course.

George Marshall arrived at a similar conclusion three days before Acheson's speech. As a result of his April 15 meeting with Stalin, the Secretary became convinced that the Russians were stalling, waiting for an easy victory in Europe. On his way home from Moscow, Marshall stopped for two hours at Tempelhof Airport in Berlin. There he instructed Clay to push economic revival in Bizonia. Back in Washington, the Secretary met a few journalists in an off-the-record session. "Marshall kept talking about Western Europe, especially France and Germany," James Reston noted.

Marshall ordered that more effort in the State Department be put into the staffwork for a new kind of aid program that would become known as the Marshall Plan. It was to be continental in scope (or at least half-continental), a point he had emphasized as early as February. And it was to cover the entire range of European economic problems. "We can no longer nibble at the problem and then nag the American people on the basis of recurring crises," observed Robert Lovett, who succeeded Acheson as Undersecretary in early summer. He added, "It is equally apparent that the Congress will not make funds available unless there is some reasonable expectation that the expenditure of these funds will produce more visible results; or alternatively, unless it can be shown that the failure to expend these funds will produce calamitous circumstances affecting our national security and our economic and social welfare." [13]

The Marshall Plan had two basic aims, which commingled and cannot really be separated—to halt a feared communist advance into Western Europe, and to stabilize an international economic environment favorable to capitalism. It was not much tied to any concerns about an impending American depression, which was what the Russians claimed at the time, and as some recent writers have argued. Such a case exaggerates both the importance and the general need that was felt for overseas markets. For instance, the export surplus of the United States with Europe in 1946 and 1947 accounted for just 2 percent of the U.S. gross national product. In fact, influential leaders like Harriman and Hoover explicitly supported increasing the output of the German steel industry so that the American steel industry would not become too dependent on the export market. The Council of Economic Advisers reported to President Truman in October that foreign aid, insofar as it financed exports, provided both "a temporary prop to the domestic market" and "an additional strain." [14]

As should be clear, the anticommunist consensus was, by this time, so wide that there was little resistance or debate about fundamental assumptions. One State Department official, for instance, described the "departmental frame of mind" as follows: "The failure to reach agreement on Germany at Moscow was due primarily to Soviet anticipation of continued deterioration in France, Italy and Western Germany plus hope for a U.S. depression. It was essential to improve the Western European situation in order to prevent further weakening in our bargaining power."

Here was a focus for the expansive doctrine of national security. Under George Kennan, the new Policy Planning Staff came to general agreement on May 15 "that the main problem in United States security today is to bring into acceptable relationship the economic distress abroad with the capacity and willingness of the United States to meet it effectively and speedily." American officials worked in an atmosphere of increasing tension. Ambassador Walter Bedell Smith, home on leave, told senior military intelligence officers in the War Department on May 16; "There are no limits to the Soviet objectives. Statements made by Lenin to the effect that a great struggle between Communism and capitalism will take place and that one or the other must go down are still being reiterated by Stalin." He added, "They have no inhibitions." Officials were more and more worried.[15]

Similar fears were becoming increasingly common outside government. Unless something were done soon to arrest the decline in confidence, businessmen would clearly make individual decisions that, in sum, would only speed Europe toward a collapse. "Everything I heard and read—and I hear and read a lot—points to the gravity of food, fuel, finance and communism impending in France," wrote Russell Leffingwell of the Morgan Bank in May. "It is a matter of great practical business importance to this bank. We cannot afford to have the Paris officers and directors living in an unreal Pollyanna dream, and we think it most important they should understand the gravity of the risks, and conduct their business accordingly."

No encouraging signs appeared in May. So short was the food supply in Germany and Austria that rations had fallen below the official level of 1550 calories—down to 1220 in some regions, even to 900 in others. "We do not see why you have to read *The New York Times* to know the Germans are close to starving," General Clay angrily cabled the War Department in May from Berlin. "The crisis is now, not in July."

The Americans feared that the Soviet Union would exploit the economic crisis to extend its political control over the rest of Europe.[16] But was this truly Moscow's goal? It seems unlikely. Certainly, the Truman Doctrine had been read and annotated very carefully in Moscow. Yet, despite its evangelical tone, its clear promise to use American economic power for explicit American political goals, and its establishment of American military power close to the Soviet periphery in Turkey, it was obviously understood by the Russians to be confined in operation chiefly to Greece, which was an area Stalin had deeded to the West. Stalin still seemed interested in maintaining the consortium, and his public statements represented that interest. If he could have at low cost pushed communism—or, to be more precise, extended *his* power—into Western Europe, no doubt he would have done exactly that. But he always had a tendency to exaggerate the strength of his enemies. Within the Soviet Union, where the balance of forces was in his favor, he had destroyed them; in international politics, where the balance was at best uncertain, he respected their power and tried to bluff and do business with them, and consolidate his own position, all at the same time. Perhaps he was more impressed by American power in the immediate postwar years than were the anxious American policymakers. Not only did the United States wield enormous economic strength, but its air power and the atomic bomb made up at least in the short term for the absence of a large American land army in Europe. He no doubt recognized that a major communist military or political assault in Western Europe would have generated an all-too-strong and unpredictable reaction in the United States. After all, the Americans had just intervened in Europe for the second time in less than three decades over the question of the balance of power on the Continent. Stalin presumably did not take too seriously the talk in the United States of preventive war, though no doubt he did take note of it. He also knew that, if circumstances changed, it could become a more immediate topic. In ordering the Yugoslavs to end their assistance in the Greek civil war, Stalin declared, as already noted, that Britain and the United States—"the United States, the most powerful state in the world"—would never permit their lines of communication in the Mediterranean to be broken. What he said about the American reaction to a communist victory in Greece could have been multiplied by ten for communist moves in France or Italy.[17]

Similarly, Stalin was not going to relinquish his sphere. The wartime Grand Alliance had been an international popular front. As its legacy and mirror, it had left behind national popular fronts, coalitions of communists and noncommunists. This was the case in Western Europe, in France and Italy, and also the case, although in far more difficult circumstances, in Eastern Europe, to varying degrees in Czechoslovakia, Hungary, even Poland. As the Grand Alliance fissured, such coalitions became anomalies, and coalition members on one side of the dividing line in Europe who were allied to forces on the other were regarded as fifth columnists, traitors-in-place. So strong was the memory of the Comintern that the Americans could not see clearly the advantages of dealing with national communist parties, of recognizing them as entities independent of Moscow, of using U.S. economic power to build a bridge across the chasm.

The worsening economic situation made the coalitions in Western Europe increasingly unstable.* Washington explained to the French and the Italians that economic aid was much more likely if (as the American ambassador in Italy put it), they "would find the means of correcting the present situation." Correction followed. The communists, though fighting hard to remain in the French and Italian governments, were pushed out of both in May 1947. A couple of days after the exclusion of the communists in France, John McCloy, the new president of the World Bank, announced a major loan to France.[18]

Stalin's answer came at the end of May—though it is still unclear whether this was a genuine response, a coincidence, or whether the Russians cynically used the changes in France and Italy as a pretext for their own purposes. In late 1945, under Soviet tutelage, the Hungarians had elected a noncommunist majority, with the leading role played by the Smallholders party. The country was governed by what the State Department privately called "a moderate coalition cabinet." The situation did not last. In February 1947, the former secretary-general of the Smallholders was arrested, allegedly confessed to espionage, and disappeared. Many in Hungary took as a very important signal the fact that his arrest had been carried out not by local security forces, but by the Red Army itself. In May, Premier Ferenc Nagy was impli-

---

* Of course, having communists in the Western European coalition governments did create problems. "We can't carry on a discussion between two Great Powers," Bevin had complained to Bidault, "with a third Great Power in the cupboard with a listening device."

cated in the "confession," chose exile, and the communists very much tightened their control over the Hungarian government. This was only the most obvious example of how the Soviets were now consolidating their hold over Eastern Europe in the context of international polarization. Poland, for instance, had been the first issue to seriously divide the members of the Grand Alliance, long before the war's end. In January 1947, it was resolved, in a fashion. That country had remained in a very unsettled domestic condition since the German defeat. As election day approached, the communists became ruthless against their opponents, the elections themselves were fraudulent, and the communist-dominated "Democratic Bloc" won an overwhelming majority in the parliament.

Polarization was having its influence in the West, as well, but there the now-excluded communist parties continued to function, protected by law. In Hungary, as elsewhere in Eastern Europe, terror was added to expulsion, with the consequent destruction not only of the noncommunist parties, but also of noncommunist politicians.

Most American officials saw the takeover in Hungary as further proof of Soviet expansionism. "You no doubt realize the extent to which this issue has rocked the Department," Harold Vedeler of the Central European Division wrote in August 1947 to Ambassador Steinhardt in Prague. "At the time the coup occurred many meetings and extended discussions were required before the Department was able to come to a conclusion on sending a note of protest rather than to take the matter to the Security Council at once." One of the reasons for not going to the Security Council was a desire to "concentrate on our Greek policy." Another was that if the Americans sought to have the Russians censured "for unilateral actions" in the Allied Control Council in Hungary, then "the Soviets might level counter charges against us concerning MacArthur's actions in Japan."

One could have viewed the events in Hungary in a less alarmist fashion—while not minimizing the internal consequences, still seeing it as a defensive, even conservative move on Stalin's part. Within the State Department some tried with no success to make that argument. "The Communist coup in Hungary is not 'a critical act of the struggle of Communism and Western Democracy for the control of Europe' but is rather a routine and anticipated move on the part of the USSR to plug an obvious gap in its security system," suggested H. Stuart Hughes, head of the Division of Research on Europe in the State Department. "It was not the democratic character of the Hungarian government that brought down upon it the wrath of the Soviet Union. It was its foreign policy of cultivating the favor of the Western democracies, particularly the United States. The Hungarian statesmen of the

Smallholders Party simply refused to do as the Czech leaders had done and to recognize the geographic and strategic realities that had placed their country within the Soviet sphere of influence and the consequent suicidal character of a pro-Western foreign policy." Hughes added that, if nothing more, "the Truman doctrine accelerated the process" of communization, for "the removal of the Communist ministers from the governments of France and Italy indicated that this doctrine was receiving a practical political interpretation in the West." [19]

As they devised this ambitious program of economic assistance for a prostrate polarized Europe, the Americans saw four challenges: first, to get the Europeans to create a cooperative plan that would move beyond relief to revitalization; second, to avoid the kind of criticism that had accumulated around the Truman Doctrine, of being too negative and too nakedly anticommunist; third, to keep the Russians out of the program; and, fourth, to get the Congress into the plan by winning its approval.

Marshall unveiled the concept in a speech at the Harvard Commencement on June 5, 1947. With his remarks, the State Department forestalled some of the sort of criticism that had hurt the Greek-Turkish program. Marshall sketched the picture of European collapse; called for a program of reconstruction, not relief; asked the Europeans to take the initiative; and invited all nations to participate, which meant that the Soviet Union was implicitly included in the invitation.[20]

The open invitation, however, was a ploy. The prospect that Russia might actually accept greatly alarmed the Americans, who had already written off the Economic Commission for Europe because of Soviet participation. But they had not wanted to bear the onus of excluding Russia from the proposed program. That would have created political problems in Western Europe. The U.S. might have been viewed as the power that had partitioned Europe. (Onus-shifting was one of the main goals of diplomacy and propaganda in these years, with each side trying to convince the international galleries that all blame for dividing the Continent lay with the other.) On the other hand, the Americans were hardly disposed to grant any aid to Russia for fear that it would try to immobilize any program it did join, and they were also convinced that Soviet participation would be the quickest way to assure congressional rejection. As Bohlen put it a few years later, they had taken "a hell of a big gamble" in not explicitly excluding Russia.

Their concern mounted when Molotov arrived in Paris at the end of June with upward of a hundred advisers, to join Bevin and Bidault in preliminary discussions on a European program. "I am deeply concerned about the next six months," Forrestal said on July 2, "and I've got one eye on what's going on in Paris and what I think will be the alternative if the result I hope eventuates from that—namely—that the Russians don't come in. I think the most disastrous thing would be if they did." [21] But the Americans could have been more confident than they were. The odds were in their favor. "In the discussion of any concrete proposals touching on American aid to Europe," read the internal instructions for the Russian group, "the Soviet delegation shall object in terms of aid that might prejudice the sovereignty of the European countries or infringe upon their economic independence." What that meant became evident when Molotov offered his own plan in the preliminary discussions: each country to draw up a list of its needs, and then ask the United States to come up with the requisite money. But it was clear to all the delegates in Paris that in exchange for aid the United States would insist on inspection, considerable disclosure, and cooperation, and that both the British and the French would agree to that approach, and that the Russians would not. As we shall see, the Russians were also concerned about the effect of such a program on their hold over Eastern Europe, and they realized that it would almost certainly deny them reparations from the Western zones of Germany. Moreover, in the American scheme the Russians might actually have been required to provide raw materials to Western Europe.

Molotov, according to Djilas, considered accepting an invitation to the follow-up planning conference, so that he could then stage a walkout, but was overruled by Moscow; and so, on July 2, Molotov and his delegation packed up and speedily departed Paris and the preliminary meeting, blasting American imperialism on the way out.[22]

The Americans had hoped, however, that some of the Eastern European countries would participate in the program. In this regard, the Marshall Plan was the last great effort, using the powerful and attractive magnetism of the American economy, to draw these countries out of the Soviet orbit. The effort represented a reversal. In 1946, Washington had very consciously restricted and tightened aid and refused to give credits in an ill-conceived attempt to force those countries to break formally with the Soviet Union on foreign policy issues.[23]

Responding to Marshall's speech, Poland indicated that it might attend the Europe-wide conference that was to open in Paris on July 12. Certainly Poland's needs were great. UNRRA had estimated that, after termination of its own program, Poland would require almost $300 million in relief in 1947 just to satisfy such basic needs as "the health and growth requirements of her children and mothers." In the middle of 1947, 80 percent of Warsaw remained in rubble; up to 30,000 corpses still lay buried beneath the ruins of the Warsaw Ghetto. Polish officials made clear that they wanted to trade with the West. And in fact Poland was still trying, under its communist leaders to pursue a path somewhat independent of Moscow. Wladyslaw Gomulka, secretary-general of the Polish party, was not following the Soviet model. He even went so far, in May 1947, as to declare that Marxism "does not give us any ready, universal indication or recipe which can be made use of with an identifiable result, without regard to time, place, and the existing conditions." [24] More obviously than Poland, Czechoslovakia was trying to maintain an independent course. Foreign Minister Jan Masaryk was a guest on the yacht of the Norwegian foreign minister when word came through that Molotov had agreed to go to Paris. "Never in my life have I seen a man so happy as Masaryk," remembered the Norwegian minister. [25]

After their Paris walk-out, the Russians would hardly allow the nations of Eastern Europe to participate in the American scheme. The Poles abruptly announced on July 9 that they would not attend the follow-up conference that was to open three days later. For the Czechs, matters were more complicated. They had already said that they would attend the second meeting. Masaryk and the communist premier Klement Gottwald, in Moscow on other business, were suddenly summoned to the Kremlin. Stalin and Molotov, expressing "surprise" at the Czech intention, indicated that they understood at least part of the purpose of the Marshall Plan; for they reportedly "emphasized their conviction that the real aim of the Marshall Plan and the Paris Conference is to create a western bloc and isolate the Soviet Union . . . Even if the loans should be granted sometime in the future by America they would not be without decisive limitations on the political and economic independence of the recipients." Thus, said the Soviet leaders, Czech participation would be interpreted "as an act specifically aimed against the USSR."

The Czechs renounced their acceptance. [26]

The most important reason for the Soviets' rejection of the plan would seem to have been their fear that it would disrupt their sphere in Eastern Europe. Second, they saw the Marshall Plan as an alternative to reparations—but an alternative that might be of no benefit to them. It was less important that American economists would poke around in Soviet production statistics. And because the Russians rejected the plan, so did the Eastern Europeans.

"Perhaps in view of the manner in which the incident dramatically revealed the real position of Czechoslovakia in international affairs, there could be detected a certain sympathy in the Department for this country, or at least the moderates, which had not been apparent since the summer of 1946," commented Harold Vedeler of Central European Affairs. But the Czech "trip to Canossa," as Vedeler called it, also created an odd kind of pleasure in American policy councils, in effect, further proof of malignant Soviet intentions. "Russians smoked out in their relations with satellite countries," Kennan noted to Marshall. "Maximum strain placed on those relations." The Americans did not see the Soviet reaction to the Marshall Plan as a defensive move by a country that could hardly compete with the United States economically, but rather as a further indication of aggressive designs. "The Czechoslovak reversal on the Paris Conference, on Soviet orders, is nothing less than a declaration of war by the Soviet Union on the immediate issue of the control of Europe," commented Ambassador Smith in Moscow. "The lines are drawn." [27]

The most important line on the European map had been drawn two years before, in 1945. It divided Germany between East and West. This line was supposed to be temporary, in pencil, as it were. But now, in 1947, it was about to be permanently inked in. For the Marshall Plan also provided a solution to the vexing problem of what to do about Germany. The basic question had remained unanswered. Were the Four Powers (but principally the United States and the Soviet Union) to cooperate in policing and punishing the former Reich, or were the occupation zones in the former Reich to become potential allies for one side or the other in the developing confrontation? For many months, American opinion on Germany had been shifting steadily away from favoring cooperation with the Russians. The failure to agree on common policies with the Russians and the expenses and difficulties of the occupation encouraged the trend. Moreover, as Europe failed to revive economically, the conviction grew in the West that Germany would have to play a central role in Western European reconstruction.[28]

In the autumn of 1946, Americans had taken a step toward partition when they amalgamated the British and American zones to form Bizonia. The initial emphasis was on economic problems alone. The Americans studiously avoided giving Bizonia a political coloration, because, explained General Clay in September 1946, "We believe it would widen the gap between west and east." [29] But by the end of 1946, Americans, at least those within policy councils, were tending to see Germany as a battleground between East and West. In December, former general John Hilldring, now Assistant Secretary of State for Occupied Territories, provided the double rationale for Bizonia: "It will serve the purpose of getting the United States government out of the red in three years in Germany, and it will give us a climate in which to plant our political ideas in Germany." He added, "We are fighting all totalitarian concepts in Germany, Nazism and Communism."

The break-up in April 1947 of the Moscow Council of Foreign

Ministers meeting with no progress on Germany provided the impetus for the Americans to take the next steps. As Clay noted in early April, "My three weeks at Moscow convinced me that nothing of import will come from this conference other than to bring the issues squarely on the table." [30]

We must recognize, however, that "success" at Moscow might well have disturbed the Americans more than failure, for many feared that any compromise that maintained Four-Power unity would open the door to Soviet domination of Germany and the rest of Europe. "The present zonal basis will continue, which, I think, is good," Dulles wrote to Vandenberg during the Moscow Council. "It is useful to have more time to consolidate the Western zones and not expose them yet to Communist penetration." [31] Upon Marshall's return from Moscow, the reorientation of U.S. policy speeded up. The Americans put more emphasis on raising the level of industry and restoring production in Germany, and thought more about the possibilities of a West German state.[32]

But the efforts to push economic recovery in Germany continued to encounter already familiar obstacles. While the overall thrust was clear, implementation created conflict and confusion between the State and War Departments. Clay frequently became so riled that he almost habitually announced his imminent resignation. An ongoing controversy between the British and Americans over the "level of industry" and socialism in the Ruhr coal mines hindered the development of Bizonia. Moreover, the very idea of economic recovery generated much resistance, for the future of Germany remained a volatile issue. The Russians, of course, remained adamant on the subject of reparations and obsessively fearful of a revivified Germany. But U.S. encouragement of German recovery also stirred much opposition in Western Europe, especially France. In addition, the Western Europeans wanted their reparations from Germany. "We have had a stop order in effect on reparations from our zone since May 1946," John Steelman, a senior White House adviser, informed the President in the spring of 1947. "As a result, we are getting a great deal of the blame for the inability of many western European nations to restore their capital goods structure. Moreover, much of the German plant is standing idle and some is rusting away."

The apprehension about German recovery was also widespread in the United States, and reached some who were close to the President, such as Edwin Pauley, Truman's reparations adviser. In March 1947, Herbert Hoover, returning from a survey of Europe for the Administration in one of his annual forays into foreign policy, wrote a report urging that German recovery be given the highest priority. Hoover's proposals outraged Pauley, who warned the President that they "would restore Germany to the same dominant position of industrial power which it held before the war . . . I cannot avoid looking into the future and contemplating the Germany which this plan would produce—a Germany not merely as powerful industrially as the Germany of Hitler, but *more* powerful because of the incredible advances of science." No one doubted, of course, that *something* had to be done about Germany —and quickly. "We are reaching a point," John Steelman told the President, "where almost any action would be an improvement." But he added, "There must be other approaches to these problems than the revival of a German colossus along the lines suggested by Mr. Hoover." [33]

The Marshall Plan was that other approach, an alternative solution to the German problem. It reduced the tension over German recovery by placing that nation at the center of a Continent-wide effort. Without Germany, it was argued, Europe could never recover, and the Americans made clear to jittery Europeans that success in the Marshall Plan depended upon an economically vital Germany. Aid from the United States would compensate the Western Europeans for the reparations they would not be getting from Germany. Meanwhile, economic recovery would keep most of Germany looking to the West, and so integrated into a Western system. Here, then, were the central and double aims of the Marshall Plan—economic recovery and economic containment. Here, also, was a solution to the German Question. But, while the American occupation authorities had a plan for the political fusion of Bizonia that they had informally discussed with the British by August 1947, they were reluctant to go the whole distance and commit themselves to the establishment of a separate government in Western Germany, at least until after the next Council of Foreign Ministers meeting.[34]

By the terms of Marshall's offer, the Europeans (albeit abetted by American "friendly aid in the drafting") were to draw up the actual plan themselves. This they did, though not without difficulty. There was a certain degree of suspicion of American intentions. The British believed that the U.S. was trying to interfere with the Labour Party's welfare state program, and they also thought Washington had aggravated England's financial problems. Galloping inflation in the U.S. had certainly compounded the dollar shortage. Britain was "being rooked" by the Americans, Dalton complained at the end of July. "We should tell them that we were going to *stop buying* and keep them guessing for how long . . . The result of this would be to bring prices down." The French opposed a concentration on German recovery for powerful emotional, as well as strategic, reasons. It was feared that this issue, highly explosive in French domestic politics, could topple the government. In addition, France had hopes of replacing German steel production with its own.

There was a good deal of conflict within the American government, as well. The State Department needed to convince the War Department to integrate Bizonia formally into the planning for the Marshall Plan. At the end of August, Charles Bonesteel, who had moved over from War to State, provided Undersecretary Lovett with a script for a conference meant to persuade top-level War Department officials that Bizonia should become part of the Marshall Plan. In Bonesteel's dialogue and stage directions, we again see how officials polished their own beliefs, rather than fabricating fake ones, to sell policies: "Our approach should be more educational, with a slight dictatorial flavor . . . Chip and yourself present the broad global picture, bringing out the two-world assumption and the need to work on a tighter organization of the Soviet world. The importance of treating Europe west of the Iron Curtain on a regional basis should then be emphasized." After advising that "the budgetary nettle" be firmly grasped, Bonesteel moved to his climax. "We should then put forward the requirement that the German economic matters be discussed at Paris . . . Emphasis should be laid on the security aspect of drawing more closely to us the nations of Western Europe now wavering between communism and us. Throughout the presentation the strategic and security aspects should be underlined and emphasized at every opportunity."

As the Marshall Plan discussions proceeded, there was also disagreement within the State Department. Washington became unhappy with the excessive zeal applied to tariff reductions by one of the American officials who was helping to provide "friendly aid" by sitting in on the negotiations among the Europeans. Will Clayton—"Doctrinaire Willie," as Dalton had taken to calling him—was, in Washington's view, giving rather too much attention to reducing trade barriers, and U.S. officials exerted pressure "to bring Mr. Clayton fully in line with the departmental position." [35]

In mid-September, the sixteen Western European nations completed a proposal—with provisions to increase production and exports, create financial stability, and provide for increased economic cooperation. They forwarded it to the United States, and asked for twenty billion dollars over the next four years to pay for imports from America.

Despite efforts to deflect possible criticism of the proposal in Europe and the United States, American policymakers thought of the Marshall Plan as "a Truman Doctrine in Action" (in George Elsey's words).

That is, it was a countermove to Soviet expansionism. "The problem is Russia," War Secretary Robert Patterson wrote to a newspaper publisher in June 1947. The "real menace," he said, was "the basic belief of the ruling group in the USSR that a communist state cannot exist in the company of democratic states." He also noted how he had shifted from the Yalta to the Riga outlook: "I thought during the war that the belief had been abandoned, but apparently it is still part of the creed. It means aggression, of course." [36]

What Patterson was expressing, of course, was the shared view of the men within the Executive who were making U.S. foreign policy. But now their common outlook was given formal, public, and even elegant statement. The prestigious journal *Foreign Affairs* published in its July issue an article entitled "The Sources of Soviet Conduct." Its author was a certain Mr. X. Appearing just as Molotov was sitting down in Paris with Bevin and Bidault to discuss Marshall's offer, the article undoubtedly strengthened the Kremlin's conviction that the Marshall Plan was primarily an anti-Soviet device. This Mr. X, author of what is arguably the single most famous magazine article in American history, was soon revealed to be none other than George Kennan—at this point head of the State Department's Policy Planning Staff and one of the major authors of the Marshall Plan. The article would forever link Kennan's name to the policy of containment.

The godfather of the article was James Forrestal, who for many, many months had been asking in one form or another that same question—whether the United States was facing a traditional nation-state or a militant religion. Forrestal personally had few doubts but that it was the latter. It will be recalled that he had commissioned an analysis on the subject by a Smith College professor, Edward Willett, who had explained Soviet foreign policy almost entirely in terms of ideology. Forrestal had been distributing Willett's various drafts to a decidedly mixed reaction. "I question the adequacy of an analysis of Russian foreign policy based mainly upon deductions from dogma," Robert Strausz-Hupe of the University of Pennsylvania informed Forrestal. Philip Mosely of Columbia University commented, "I cannot agree in drawing the conclusion that the Soviet government operates blindly on the basis of philosophical assumptions. It is only one element which enters into an immediate and concrete decision or into a program of, say, ten years of policy as sketched out for the future when they envision it." [37]

And, of course, Forrestal had sought the opinion of George Kennan, who, instead of commenting, presented at the end of January his own paper on "The Psychological Background of Soviet Foreign Policy." Virtually unchanged, it found its way as the Mr. X article into the July issue of *Foreign Affairs*.[38] Kennan had been asked to comment on a paper stressing the role of Soviet ideology, and this, as he himself said afterward, undoubtedly affected the thrust of his own piece. But Kennan was also continuing the line of argument of the Long Telegram as he here made the case that the United States was dealing not with a Great Power pursuing imperial goals, but principally with a messianic religion, an ideological force, for which coexistence was always a threat.

"Its political action," Kennan wrote, "is a fluid stream which moves constantly, wherever it is permitted to move, toward a given goal. Its main concern is to make sure that it has filled every nook and cranny available to it in the basin of world power. But if it finds unassailable barriers in its path, it accepts these philosophically and accommodates itself to them." The appropriate response, Kennan called "containment"—"the adroit and vigilant application of counterforce at a series of constantly shifting geographical and political points, corresponding to the shifts and maneuvers of Soviet Policy." He expressed some exultation over the challenge and "a certain gratitude to a Providence which, by providing the American people with this implacable challenge, has made their entire security as a nation dependent on their pulling themselves together and accepting the responsibilities of moral and political leadership that history plainly intended them to bear."

The article, reiterating the Riga outlook in a bipolar world, did express the outlook of the Truman Administration. It provided a name—"containment"—to describe this thrust in American foreign policy. But it should be noted that Kennan meant to admonish not only those whom he considered still blind to the inevitable challenge, but also those whose alarm had run wild. To that latter group, he was saying that the confrontation should not be seen in military terms, that hostilities need not be imminent, and that preventive war was unnecessary.

"The Sources of Soviet Conduct," by Mr. X, received wide attention. The article was quoted and cited, it seemed, almost everywhere in the American press. Both *Life* and *Reader's Digest* excerpted it. "I thought you might be interested in having a copy of the article by 'X' in the July issue of *Foreign Affairs* and have therefore arranged to get some reprints, one of which I enclose," a State Department official wrote to the American ambassador in Czechoslovakia. "I give you one guess on whom the author is . . . We leave it to you to make such distribution on a personal basis in your area as you may consider appropriate." [39]

By the summer of 1947, the "two-world assumption" had completely displaced any notions of cooperation. From Moscow, Ambassador

Smith described the Czech reversal on the Marshall Plan as a Soviet declaration of war for the control of Europe. It is probable in turn that the Russians saw the Marshall Plan as a declaration of war by the United States for control of Europe. Although clothed in generous language, it capped a process of reorientation for Washington, away from relief and reconstruction per se to relief, reconstruction, *and* anticommunism. American aid would no longer be used to create links and bridges, but rather to isolate communists. The Russians now assumed that the United States would use its great economic power for the specific goal of isolating the Soviet Union, and that American leaders had lost all interest in the Great Power consortium. The Marshall Plan precipitated a dramatic shift in Soviet foreign policy. That the Cezchs and even the Poles would consider participating in the Marshall Plan despite Soviet displeasures indicated to Stalin that a dangerous diversity existed within his sphere. This he would no longer tolerate in a changing international environment. For Stalin, spheres of influence would no longer mean a process of mutual accommodation but rather one of hostile confrontation.

In December 1947, Laurence Steinhardt, the American ambassador to Czechoslovakia, gave his own testimony as to the change that followed the Czech acceptance and then renunciation of the invitation to discuss the Marshall Plan: "It is no mere coincidence that the rather benign attitude of Moscow toward the Czech government suddenly hardened after the acceptance. By benign I mean that up to that time the Russians had not exercised much pressure on them. They had made a few suggestions here and there in connection with their political and commercial decisions, but not much more than other governments make to one another, and they had not, as far as we could see, directly interfered or given any orders." [40] Perhaps by December of 1947, U.S. policymakers were feeling some nostalgia for the ambiguity that had characterized the Czech position in 1946 and into 1947.

The first public reaction to the Marshall Plan by the Russians was a hastily improvised series of trade treaties with Eastern Europe, called, with some exaggeration, the Molotov Plan. This, however, was only the beginning of the Russian efforts to consolidate a new empire.

If there was any turning point in Soviet policy toward Eastern Europe and the West, it was the organizing conference of the Cominform—the Communist Information Bureau—held in September 1947 in a manor house that was now a sanitorium belonging to the Polish State Security Service. Not a lineal descendant of the Comintern, and of considerably more exclusive membership, the Cominform advertised itself as a coordinating body for national communist parties in the Soviet Union and Eastern Europe, along with those of France and

Italy. It was totally dominated by the Soviets, and was to be used to tighten the Soviet hold on Eastern Europe. It was also the mechanism for directing the Italian and French Communist parties to begin those disruptive activities in which, Washington thought, they were already engaged.

The Cominform was a device for restoring ideological unity to the communist parties, but this was ideology not in the service of Marx, but of the Soviet state. At the meeting in Poland, Andrei Zhdanov, already identified as a keeper of ideological purity in the USSR, proclaimed the division of the international system into two camps—that of "imperialist and anti-democratic forces" and that of "democratic and anti-imperialist forces." Curiously, he said that Soviet foreign policy continued to be based on the possibility of coexistence between capitalism and communism, but now the United States was creating a hostile bloc against the socialist states—that is, against the Soviet Union. The United States, he said, was an expansionist power, as evidenced by the network of military bases it was establishing around the world, and by the use of its economic power to create a sphere of influence over Western Europe and over Britain and its empire. There was some degree of truth in what Zhdanov said, although the Americans hardly saw it. Nor could the Russians admit that American policy was in part in response to a perceived threat of Soviet power and influence. Zhdanov was obviously deeply concerned about the revitalization of the Western zones in Germany and their integration into a Western political and economic system.

The Soviets were responding in kind, and with a vengeance, to the drawing together of such a Western bloc. The cynical Russians, joined by the enthusiastic Yugoslavs, denounced the French and Italian parties for their parliamentary reformist course, their popular-frontism —the very line approved in the last meeting of the Comintern in 1943, and, more important, mandated by Stalin himself during and immediately after the war. "While you are fighting to stay in the Government," Zhdanov now taunted the French communists, "they throw you out." He ridiculed the Italians: "You Italian comrades are bigger parliamentarians than de Gasperi himself. You are the biggest political party, and yet they throw you out of the Government." Jacques Duclos, the representative of the French Communist Party, went into shock; he sat by himself in the park swinging his legs, talking to no one. He literally cried in rage. The Italian and French parties left the meeting in Poland with their marching orders: to intensify the class struggle, to go over—as they did with disruptive strikes—into opposition against the Marshall Plan and American influence.

In Eastern Europe, political diversity was to come to a quick end.

Zhdanov criticized "national communism." This was an attack on Gomulka, who had defended a "Polish way to socialism," which was wide enough to accommodate the small entrepreneur and farmer. In fact, Gomulka had resisted the whole idea of a Cominform, but he was forced to accede to the Russian demand that the Cominform endorse collectivization (on the Soviet model) as the only appropriate path to socialism. In Berlin at the same time, East German communists were instructed that there was no longer a separate German road to socialism. The Cominform meeting marked the beginning of the Stalinist reign of terror in Eastern Europe, although the worst was yet to come. In the autumn of 1947, there was still a coalition in Czechoslovakia, although it seemed more and more like an archeological remnant, a relic of another time and spirit.[41]

Meanwhile, in Washington, the Truman Administration was very worried that Congress would not approve the Marshall Plan, even though the $20 billion proposed by the Europeans had been pared to $17 billion. Policymakers were sure that a congressional rejection would lead to the collapse of Europe. Budget-conscious Republicans, now in the majority on Capitol Hill, and highly suspicious of liberal "give-aways," were vocally resistant to the idea of further aid. They complained, as they added up the host of programs approved or pending, that (in the words of Representative John Taber) "there seem to be no grasp of any business principles in connection with this situation." There was also resistance on procedural grounds, a continuing resentment of the dramatic manner in which the Truman Doctrine was introduced, which had seemed to preclude any real debate.[42]

To deflect such criticism, the State Department drew Vandenberg deeply into the development of the Marshall Plan. A few years later Marshall would recall that he and the Michigan senator "couldn't have gotten much closer together unless I sat in Vandenberg's lap or he sat in mine." The Administration put considerable effort into selling the plan to Congress and the public. Hosts of special committees—some presidentially appointed, some congressional, some composed of leading laity like the now-retired Henry Stimson—studied the matter. All of them reported that the Marshall Plan was essential to the national security, and that it would help, not hurt, the United States economically. Even so, the winning of congressional approval was difficult.

An important point must be made here. As with the Truman Doctrine, the Executive was consciously trying to "educate," even manipulate, public opinion. But, again as with the Greek-Turkish aid, it was doing this in order to bring the public around to accepting its own worried world view. The arguments that the Administration used to present the issue to the public were congruent with the concerns expressed privately within policy councils. In their attempt to educate public opinion American leaders may have confused two things—the Soviet Union as the alleged perpetrator of economic distress in Europe, and the Soviet Union as likely beneficiary of that distress. But, then, that distinction was blurred in their own minds. When Marshall left Moscow in April 1947, he was convinced that the Soviet Union was deliberately retarding European recovery to achieve its own political goals.[43]

The sense of urgency among U.S. policymakers, high from the beginning, kept increasing, as it became more and more apparent that they had continued to underestimate the depth of the crisis. "At no time in my recollection have I ever seen a world situation which was moving so rapidly toward real trouble," wrote Undersecretary Lovett at the end of July, "and I have the feeling that this is the last clear shot that we will have in finding a solution." A few weeks later, Henry Ford II, as a member of a presidential air policy commission, went to see Lovett. "He was even more pessimistic than were the Joint Chiefs of Staff," Ford reported, "and felt that war could come at any time and that there were at least two crises a day in the State Department." The President himself was feeling the same way. "The British have turned out to be our problem children now," Truman wrote to his sister in August. "They've decided to go bankrupt and if they do that, it will end our prosperity and probably all the world's too. Then Uncle Joe Stalin can have his way. Looks like he may get it anyway." [44]

Bad news followed bad news in August and into September. The smallest wheat crop in France in 132 years. Extra rations distributed to Ruhr coal miners in a desperate bid to encourage higher production. Near-exhaustion of dollar reserves in France and Italy, while U.S. prices kept rising. Many European countries cutting back on the purchases of essential U.S. goods. And massive strikes—the communist parties in the West now clearly bent on a policy of opposition and disruption.[45]

The State Department's Policy Planning Staff summed up the situation: "The margin of safety in Europe, both from an economic and political viewpoint, is extremely thin." U.S. leaders concluded in early autumn 1947 that a Marshall Plan approved and appropriated by Congress in mid-1948 would be too late unless stopgap aid were provided immediately.[46]

At the end of September, Truman hosted a small group of congressmen in the Cabinet Room at the White House.

"I do hope that we can reach some decision on this and get things started," Truman said. "General Marshall has reviewed the trouble he is having with Russia in the United States, and Bob Lovett has given you the detailed picture. We'll either have to provide a program of interim aid relief until the Marshall program gets going, or the governments of France and Italy will fall, Austria too, and for all practical purposes Europe will be Communist. The Marshall Plan goes out of the window, and it's a question of how long we could stand up in such a situation. This is serious. I can't overemphasize how serious."

"I had hoped very much, Mr. President, there would be no special session of Congress," said Sam Rayburn. "Can't something be worked out?"

"It doesn't seem we can get the money any other way, Sam," replied Truman. "Congress has got to act."

"That is just the situation," added Lovett.

"Then the plan had better be well worked out, right down to the details, and everything ready so that we can get right to it the minute Congress meets," said Rayburn.

"Communism has started its campaign of aggression," said Charles Eaton, the Republican who was chairman of the House Foreign Affairs Committee. "We have already met the challenge in Greece and Turkey. We've got to stop Communism, and I'm ready to work with Senator Vandenberg."

But Majority Leader Charles Halleck had a word of caution: "Mr. President, you must realize there is a growing resistance to these programs. I have been out in the hustings, and I know. The people don't like it."

On October 15, Clark Clifford summarized the reasons for calling a special session of Congress: "Two most important issues today are high prices and aid to Europe. They are inevitably bound together. The situation in each instance is getting worse . . . In France the subway and bus strike is spreading and we can expect serious trouble. The President must have a plan. It must be thought through now so it can be quietly set in motion." [47] On October 23, Truman announced that he was calling the special session. The campaign for foreign aid continued. "The people can never understand why the President does not use his supposedly great power to make 'em behave," Truman wrote to his sister on November 14. "Well all the President is, is a glorified public relations man who spends his time flattering, kissing and kicking people to get them to do what they are supposed to do anyway." Three days later, he presented to a joint session of Congress his proposal for almost $600 million in interim aid for France, Italy, and Austria. A month later, after more debate and more flattering, kissing, and kicking, he was able to sign the bills providing the emergency assistance.[48]

Between Truman's message and the approval of interim aid, there occurred the last act, the anticlimax, of the Yalta approach—the London Council of Foreign Ministers meeting. As in Moscow the preceding spring, the issue again was how to proceed on a German peace settlement and what to do—or not do—about reparations. No optimism remained; polarization had gone too far. The Americans, British, and French all thought in advance that this Council would almost certainly fail, that they would not be able to work out a German settlement with the Russians, and that therefore they should go ahead and consolidate the Western zones. The Russians, for their part, expected to face a united Western front, which was planning to establish a Trizonia, and they were extremely bitter about the steps toward fusion that had already taken place.[49]

In October, looking ahead to the Council, Robert Murphy laid out Administration thinking on Germany. "We have maintained the position until there is either a break-down of the Four-Power relationship in Germany, or a solution of it, that we would not admit having established a political structure." However, if the London meeting did not lead to a resolution, "shortly thereafter we would be obliged to develop a political organization in Western Germany." He added, "Naturally, this is a serious step." The United States would be accused of splitting Germany, but Murphy was not too much concerned about this. "We will have to meet that charge when we get to it and we are prepared to do so."

He did foresee one danger—Berlin—"an island in the heart of the Soviet zone." The Russians, he explained, "could easily make our lives unbearable and we would eventually have to leave Berlin. But we have no intention of doing so."

There was something paradoxical in the American stance. Expecting failure in London, the Americans, along with the British, were at work on the foundations of a new West German state as an alternative to a Four-Power occupation. But such preparations in themselves were sure to increase Soviet suspicion and obstructionism and thus would guarantee the very failure that the Americans and British were convinced was at hand. On balance, however, it must also be said that the deterioration of the Four-Power occupation had proceeded apace, day by day, over many months. By the time of the London meeting, the Americans had had just about enough of any effort toward a Four-Power German settlement. Indeed, they feared it.* [50]

So, there were charges and countercharges at the London meeting, which opened on November 25, 1947, but little of substance—save for what happened when the meeting ended. France left no doubt that it now belonged to the Western bloc; indeed, the French even encouraged secret meetings during the London Council among the three Western foreign ministers to discuss other possible solutions to the German question.

Knowing that he was isolated, Molotov responded with unyielding intransigence and acid propaganda. In 1933, it may be recalled, William Bullitt had marveled at what he called Molotov's "magnificent forehead" and was reminded of a "first-rate French scientist, great poise, kindliness and intelligence." But now all that Westerners noticed on Molotov's forehead was a bump that swelled when he felt pressured.[51] He was certainly under such stress in London, as he tried to find some way to stop the movement toward unification in the Western zone. But his violent language only strengthened the determination of the Western powers to proceed.

The two sides debated back and forth on reparations. The Russians still sought reparations valued at ten billion dollars, to be delivered by 1965. To this, the British were somewhat more responsive than the Americans, perhaps because they were more sensitive to the war ravages of the Nazis. But both nations rejected any compromise with the Russians on this issue. The State Department believed that Congress would not vote aid for Europe were the Soviet Union to receive German reparations.

On December 3, Bevin told Harold Nicolson about his strenuous efforts, the day before, to have a real heart-to-heart talk in his own flat with Molotov.

"You cannot look on me as an enemy of Russia," Bevin had said to the Soviet foreign minister. "Why, when our Government was trying

---

* On November 6, Marshall told the Cabinet that all he expected from the Russians at the next Council of Foreign Ministers meeting were "various ruses . . . to try to get us out of western Germany under arrangements which would leave that country defenseless against communist penetration." He explained, "The world situation is still dominated by the Russian effort in the post-hostilities period to extend their virtual domination over all, or as much as possible, of the European land mass." He said that the Americans would resist the Soviet moves at the foreign ministers meeting and instead "see that [Germany] is better integrated into Western Europe" and press the other Western European countries to so accept Western Germany.

to stamp out your Revolution, who was it that stopped it? It was I, Ernest Bevin. I called out the transport workers and they refused to load the ships. I wanted you to have your Revolution in your own way and without interference. Now again I am speaking as a friend. You are playing a very dangerous game. And I can't make out why. You don't really believe that any American wants to go to war with you—or, at least, no responsible American. We most certainly do not want to. But you are playing with fire, Mr. Molotov . . . If war comes between you and America in the East, then we may be able to remain neutral. But if war comes between you and America in the West, then we shall be on America's side. Make no mistake about that. That would be the end of Russia and of your Revolution. So please stop sticking out your neck in this way and tell me what you are after. What do you want?"

"I want a unified Germany," replied Molotov.

That was virtually all Bevin could get out of him.[52]

But a bit of explication is needed. A "unified" Germany meant treating Germany as an economic unit so that the Russians could obtain reparations from the Western zones. It also meant preventing the birth of a strong, Western-oriented West Germany.

Meanwhile, strikes, in part led by the communists to protest the Marshall Plan, were spreading in France. With Marshall's permission, John Foster Dulles left London on December 4 for a firsthand survey of the French situation. He brought back an alarming report—utilities running only intermittently in Paris, his own train rerouted because tracks had been blown up, industry at a standstill. The impression was widespread that Europe was rolling toward the precipice while the conference dragged on. *New York Times* correspondent C. L. Sulzberger wrote in his diary that he had come to Brussels "mainly to organize an emergency system in case the strike wave shuts off communications with New York; or even worse, in case it becomes a real political menace and a Communist bid to take over in Europe . . . am also distributing large chunks of money to correspondents in France, Belgium, Italy, Spain so they can get out their families if necessary, amid chaos." [53]

By December 6, Bevin and Marshall were privately planning how to bring about a breakdown in the Council.

"We ought," said Bevin, "to force the debate on the main outstanding economic questions and also possibly indicate our requirements for the political organization of Germany in a way to bring out that the Soviet objective was a Communist-controlled Germany."

"Quite frankly," replied Marshall, "what would be popular in the U.S would be that I should break off and tell the Russians to go to the devil." But he feared that such popular approval would not last. "It might be wise to indicate the differences on matters of real substance and to suggest that unless agreement could be had on them we would have to proceed—always making it clear, however, that we were not permanently breaking. It was important, of course, to choose our ground carefully and to time it to the best possible advantage."

Marshall, who had no intention of sitting through a long conference, concluded that the meeting could serve no further use. On December 11, he reported to Washington: "It is plainly evident that Molotov is not only playing for time but is consistently, almost desperately, endeavoring to reach agreements which really would be an embarrassment to us in the next four to six months rather than true evidence of getting together."

"We are all with you," Truman wired Marshall.[54]

During the weekend of December 13 and 14, the American delegation reached the decision to end the session. And so at the seventeenth session on Monday, December 15, after a last debate on reparations, Marshall called for adjournment. "No real progress could be made because of Soviet obstructionism," he said.

Denying responsibility for the impasse, Molotov accused Marshall of seeking adjournment "in order to give the U.S. a free hand to do as it pleased in its zone of Germany."

The Council, said Bidault, "should adjourn rather than further aggravate relations between the Four Powers." On that, at least, the foreign ministers could agree, and adjourn they did, without fixing a date for another meeting.

There was a certain relief in the break-up. "The Russians had at last run against a solid front," said Marshall three days later, with some satisfaction. But the ministers also recognized the gravity of the situation. Bidault privately worried that there might be a rupture in French-Soviet diplomatic relations, and that a coup was imminent in Czechoslovakia.[55]

The Council led to two specific outcomes. First, the Western powers agreed among themselves to move further toward the creation of a new West German political state, although trying to avoid, as Robert Murphy put it, "unseemly haste." There would be one more try at a united Germany, and if that did not work, then Bizonia would become the basis of this new state, along with, it was hoped, the French zone. They committed themselves to a German currency reform, an economic move to counter inflation, but also of great political significance if done without the Russians. The Western countries would carry it out by themselves if necessary, although Clay believed that it was not "absolutely impossible" to get the Russians to go along on a new currency.

Second, Bevin and Marshall decided that some kind of Western alliance was required. "The issue," Bevin said, "was where power was going to rest." He elaborated: "We must devise some western democratic system comprising the Americans, ourselves, France, Italy, etc. and of course the Dominions. This would not be a formal alliance, but an understanding backed by power, money and resolute action. It would be a sort of spiritual federation of the west."

There was no choice, Marshall replied. Events had to be taken "at the flood stream." [56]

Just before the Council session had opened, Edwin Pauley, occupying what was by then the largely ceremonial post of special adviser on reparations, had written to Marshall: "The forthcoming CFM meeting will be one of transcendental significance. It will constitute one of the Great Divides of American policy in this era."

Pauley was right. The London Council marked the end of the approach to postwar relations with the Soviet Union that Roosevelt had so optimistically, yet tentatively, outlined in the midst of the war. Such an approach had failed, ending in a dismal parody of diplomacy. We might be more precise and say that the Yalta axioms had died some months earlier, at Moscow in the spring of 1947. At London, they were buried. The Americans now looked in other directions.

Nations try to live less dangerously, to find some security, and so the Americans responded in kind to what they feared—to the threat of war by preparing themselves for war. The aging Admiral Leahy expressed the consensus among U.S. leaders when he wrote, the day after the break-up—in the course of noting in his diary that the impasse on Germany had resulted from Soviet insistence on reparations—that the consortium was finished. "No proposal was made by any of the Foreign Ministers for another meeting and it appears now that some other method of arranging a peace in Europe must be found." One step, he said, was a separate treaty with a Western-oriented West Germany, although "the Soviet Government would offer violent objection to such, even to the extent of using military power if necessary." Indeed, he feared that Russia would decide "to start its 'inevitable' war without delay." There was no choice in Leahy's mind— American foreign policy had to be militarized.

"In view of the very menacing situation that confronts western civilization," wrote the admiral, "I believe that the United States should begin a partial mobilization of forces of defense without any delay." [57]

Notes

1. Telephone transcript, March 13, 1947, Joseph M. Jones papers, Harry S. Truman Presidential Library, Independence, Mo.
2. *Harry S. Truman Public Papers: 1947,* p. 212. Also see Elsey to Freeland, May 11, 1967, George Elsey papers, Truman Library.
3. Colonel Behn in Wasson to Lamont, February 25, 1946, Thomas Lamont papers, Baker Library, Harvard University. Henry Stimson diary, Yale University, April 19, July 25, 1945. For another eyewitness reaction to Europe's dislocation, see Lane to Dewey, August 14, 1945, Lane to Durbrow, August 3, 1945, Arthur Bliss Lane papers, Yale University. The studies of multilateral planning are many, for instance, Richard Gardner, *Sterling-Dollar Diplomacy* (Oxford, 1956), and Richard M. Freeland, *The Truman Doctrine and the Origins of McCarthyism* (New York, 1972).
4. E. F. Penrose, *Economic Planning for Peace* (Princeton, 1953), pp. 321–33; Edward Mason oral history, Truman Library, pp. 29–31. For the concern on U.S. public opinion and international relief, Lubin to Hopkins, January 6, 1944, and report to Lubin by Cantril and Lambert, November 15, 1943, Post-War Planning file, Harry Hopkins papers, Franklin D. Roosevelt Presidential Library, Hyde Park, N.Y.
5. War Council minutes, November 7, 1945, Box 23, Robert Patterson papers, Library of Congress; Penrose, *Economic Planning,* p. 320; Francis Williams, *Twilight of Empire: Memoirs of Prime Minister Clement Attlee* (New York, 1962), p. 136; Harry Truman, *Year of Decisions* (Garden City, 1955), p. 236; Byrnes quoted in *FRUS, 1946,* I, p. 1441; Clayton-Wallace telephone conversation, April 15, 1946, Wallace papers, University of Iowa.
6. John Morton Blum, *The Price of Vision: The Diary of Henry A. Wallace* (Boston, 1973), p. 554; memo on world trip, May 7, 1947, Gibson memorandum, February 21, 1947, Box 220, Herbert Hoover papers, Herbert Hoover Presidential Library, West Branch, Iowa. War Council minutes, May 16, 1946, Box 23, Patterson papers.
7. Hugh Dalton diary, October 5, 1946, London School of Economics.
8. United Nations, *Economic Report: World Economic Situation 1945–47* (New York, 1948), pp. 123–25; Ingvar Svennilson, *Growth and Stagnation in the European Economy* (Geneva, 1954), pp. 253, 246; United Nations, *A Survey of the Economic Situation and Prospects of Europe* (Geneva, 1948), p. 5. Also see Richard Mayne, *The Recovery of Europe, 1945–1973* (Rev. ed., New York, 1973), pp. 117–18, and *Business Week,* August 2, 1947.
9. United Nations, *Situation and Prospects of Europe,* pp. 53–55, 62–74, 144; Harry Bayard Price, *The Marshall Plan and Its Meaning* (Ithaca: Cornell University Press, 1955), pp. 29–32; Dirk Stikker, *Men of Responsibility* (New York, 1966), pp. 163–65; Nourse to Truman, May 7, 19, October 18, 1948, Nourse papers; "Some Aspects of Foreign Aid Program," October 18, 1948, Salant papers, both in Truman Library.
10. "Overseas Deficit," May 2, 1947, III–4, miscellaneous papers, Dalton

papers. Also see memorandum to Mr. Rowen for Prime Minister, July 29, 1947, Attlee papers, University College, Oxford, England.

11. Frederick J. Dobney, *Selected Papers of Will Clayton* (Baltimore: Johns Hopkins Press, 1971), p. 198; Cleveland to Jones, July 2, 1947, Jones papers. Also see Salant to Clark, May 12, 1947, Salant papers. *FRUS, 1947*, III, pp. 210–11. Freeland argues (*Truman Doctrine*, p. 154) that plans for aiding Europe had been deferred for domestic political reasons. On the contrary, policymakers did not recognize the economic problems until the winter and spring of 1946–47.

12. Acheson speech, April 18, 1947, Box 1, Jones papers.

13. Bohlen and Marshall interviews in Harry Price oral history collection; Gimbel, *The American Occupation of Germany: Politics and the Military, 1945–49* (Stanford, 1968), pp. 123, 150; Lovett to Lamont, July 31, 1947, Lamont papers; James Reston notes, vol. 1, Black Book, Krock papers. For Marshall's early emphasis upon Europe-wide approach, see Marshall to Bowles, February 17, 1947, Bowles papers, Yale University. Kennan, in charge of drawing up the program as head of the Policy Planning Staff, had been keenly interested in a Europe-wide approach for some time. In 1942, he had suggested, "We endeavor to take over the whole system of control which the Germans have set up for the administration of European economy, preserving the apparatus, putting people of our own into the key positions to run it, and that we then apply this system to the execution of whatever policies we may adopt for continental Europe, in the immediate postwar period." Two years later he observed that European integration, in the form of some kind of federation, seemed to be the best solution to the problem of Germany and "the only way out of this labyrinth of conflict which is Europe today." Kennan to Burleigh, June 18, 1942, remarks to staff at Lisbon, June 1944, Kennan papers, Princeton University.

14. United Nations, *Situation and Prospects of Europe*, p. 61; Council of Economic Advisers, "Third Quarter Review," October 1, 1947, Nourse papers; Harriman and Hoover cited in Forrestal diary, April 9, 1947, pp. 1566–67, Princeton University. The Kolkos mistakenly argue: "As a capitalist nation unable to expand its internal market by redistributing its national income to absorb the surplus, the United States would soon plunge again into the depression that only World War II brought to an end. The alternative was to export dollars, primarily through grants rather than loans" *The Limits of Power: The World and United States Foreign Policy, 1945–54* (New York: Harper & Row, 1972).

15. *FRUS, 1947*, II, p. 240, III, p. 220; Dobney, *Clayton*, p. 202. Smith talk in F.P.M. to Peterson, May 16, 1947, ASW 091 Russia, RG 107, Modern Military records, National Archives. "I agree with the general object of the Marshall Plan to help maintain the Western European countries in their battle against Communism," Taft wrote on November 28, 1947, to Harry Bannister, Box 786, Robert A. Taft papers, Library of Congress.

16. Leffingwell to Lamont, May 21, 1947, Lamont papers; Jean Edward

Smith, ed.; *The Papers of General Lucius D. Clay: Germany 1945–49*, 2 vols. (Bloomington: Indiana University Press, 1974), pp. 356, 361; Keyes to Hoover, May 21, 1947, Hoover papers.

17. Djilas, *Conversations with Stalin* (London: Pelican, 1969), p. 141.

18. Dalton diary, September 10, 1946; *FRUS, 1947*, III, p. 894.

19. Kolko, *Limits of Power*, pp. 212–15; Hugh Seton-Watson, *The East European Revolution* (New York: Praeger, 1956), pp. 190–202; Vedeler to Steinhardt, August 12, 1947, Box 55, Steinhardt papers, Library of Congress; Hughes to Booth, June 11, 1947, H. Stuart Hughes papers. For "moderate coalition," "Secret Summary for Secretary," June 2, 1947, with Marshall to Truman, June 2, 1947, Box 180, President's secretary's file, Truman papers.

20. *FRUS, 1947*, III, pp. 224–25, 237–38; memorandum on June 5, 1947, speech, Jones papers.

21. Marshall and Bohlen interviews, Price oral history collection; Forrestal conversations with Ploesser, July 2, 1947, Box 92, Forrestal papers. For the writing off of the Economic Commission for Europe, see George Kennan, "Problems of U.S. Foreign Policy," Lecture, Washington, D.C., May 6, 1947.

22. B. Ponomaryov, *History of Soviet Foreign Policy, 1945–70* (Moscow: Progress, 1974), p. 163; Bohlen interview in Price oral history collection; Price, *Marshall Plan*, pp. 26–29; Djilas, *Conversations*, pp. 99–100.

23. *FRUS, 1947*, III, p. 235; Hickerson to Acheson, April 11, 1947, Hickerson to Labouisse, April 5, 1947, Winiewicz-Thompson conversation, April 3, 1947, Box 3, Hickerson files, State Department papers, National Archives; Thomas Paterson, *Soviet-American Confrontation* (Baltimore: The Johns Hopkins University Press, 1973), pp. 210–11; Robert Elson, "New Strategy in Foreign Policy," *Fortune*, December 1947, p. 222.

24. *FRUS, 1947*, III, pp. 260–61; notes on Poland, September 10, 1947, Christian Herter papers, Howard University; Pate to Lane, March 21, 1947, with UNRRA memo, Lane papers. Gomulka quoted in Nicholas Bethell, *Gomulka* (London: Penguin, 1952), p. 135; Karel Jech, ed., *The Czechoslovak Economy, 1945–48* (Prague: State Pedagogical Publishing House, 1968), p. 54. For the initially keen Polish interest in the Marshall Plan, also see Eugen Loebl, *Sentenced & Tried: The Stalinist Purges in Czechoslovakia* (London: Elek, 1969), p. 25.

25. Interview with Halvard Lange, Price oral history collection.

26. *FRUS, 1947*, III, pp. 318–22; Ripka, *Czechoslovakia Enslaved* (London: Victor Gollancz, 1950), pp. 56–71; Jech, *Czechoslovak Economy*, pp. 55–56.

27. Vedeler to Steinhardt, August 12, 1947, Box 55, Steinhardt papers; *FRUS, 1947*, III, pp. 335, 327.

28. Eisenhower to Clay, March 1, 1946, Clay folder, Eisenhower papers, Eisenhower Library, Abilene, Kansas.

29. Clay to Warburg, September 21, 1946, Box 26, James F. Warburg papers, John F. Kennedy Presidential Library, Waltham, Mass. War Council minutes, November 7, 1946, Box 23, Patterson papers.

30. John Hilldring, Lecture, Washington, D.C., December 5, 1946; Clay to Dodge, December 23, 1946, Joseph Dodge papers, Detroit Public Library; Clay to Hoover, April 7, 1947, Hoover papers.

31. Memorandum of Hoover-McNeil conversation, February 20, 1947, Hoover papers; Dulles to Vandenberg, March 29, 1947, John Foster Dulles papers, Princeton University.

32. Forrestal diary, April 28, 1947, pp. 1600–1601; Hoover to Taber, May 26, 1947, John Taber papers, Cornell University.

33. Smith, *Clay Papers,* pp. 387–91, 345, 372, 375, 412–13; Clay to Hoover, June 8, 1947, Hoover papers; Gimbel, *American Occupation,* pp. 156–58, 170; Forrestal diary, May 17, 1947, p. 1618; Pauley to Truman, April 15, 1947, Steelman to Truman, n.d., Box 133, President's secretary's file, Truman papers, Truman Library. For Hoover's report, see Gimbel, *The Origins of the Marshall Plan* (Stanford: Stanford University Press, 1976), pp. 182–84. Bizonia clearly posed a policy dilemma for the British. For their effort to balance off their heavy financial burden in Germany against the fears that the U.S. would undercut their plans for socialization of heavy industry in the Ruhr, see CAB 128/6, pp. 45, 126–28, Cabinet papers.

34. Royall to Taber, August 8, 1947, Taber papers; Smith, *Clay Papers,* p. 416; Gimbel, *American Occupation,* p. 195. In his excellent new study, *The Origins of the Marshall Plan,* John Gimbel argues that the "American economic dilemma in Germany" provided "the primary motivation for the Marshall Plan" (p. 279). Only by linking Germany to an overall Western European recovery could the U.S. overcome French resistance to a re-vivified Germany. He convincingly documents that, contrary to later memories, the Four-Power occupation broke down because of French obstruction-ism—not the Soviets'. See pp. 33–34, 48–49, 85–97, 112, 127–31, 138–39. In effect, he rightly says that the history of the German occupation in 1945 and 1946 was rewritten in 1947 and thereafter. He gives serious attention to the reparations issue and the role of "hidden reparations" from the Western zones. He also puts emphasis on the continuing clash between the State Department, worried about France and the rest of Western Europe, and Clay and the War Department, anxious to get out of the occupation business by getting Germany back onto its feet. Despite my agreement with his thesis that the Marshall Plan provided a "solution" to the German problem, as well as the considerable skill and care with which he makes his argument, I find his focus too narrow. The Marshall Plan was an effort to cope with the "problem" of Europe, which had three dimen-sions—Germany, the Western European economy, and the Soviet Union. Gimbel is right that an incorrect interpretative framework—what I have called the Riga axioms—was applied to Germany. Nevertheless, the fears and misperceptions of the Soviet Union among U.S. policymakers were very genuine. Second, their alarm about the German economy was more than matched by their alarm about what was happening in the economy of the rest of Western Europe, and he pays practically no attention to the latter. Finally, in developing his State-War controversy, he overlooks the significance of the close personal relationship between Byrnes and Clay.

And it is not surprising that he finds no "plan" in the spring and summer of 1947. What existed—and from this emerged the plan—was a perception of crisis, a sense of danger and responsibility, and some general intentions and some thoughts about the need for a comprehensive response. All this said, Gimbel's book is a major addition to the literature, and is important for directing attention to the way in which the Marshall Plan was meant to provide a solution for Germany. But neither in the minds of its originators nor in fact was the plan separated from the confrontation with the Soviet Union.

35. Dalton diary, July 30, June 26, 1947; Bonesteel to Lovett, August 27, 1947, 740.00119 Control (Germany) 8–2747, State Department papers, National Archives; for "friendly aid" and Clayton, *FRUS, 1947*, III, pp. 223–30, 370; for France, Gimbel, *Marshall Plan*, pp. 252–54. On June 23, General Albert Wedemeyer, in reporting on a trip to Europe the previous month, observed that he had noted "restrained anti-American feeling" in Britain. "Lew Douglas the ambassador confirmed this. It is understandable—no people feel friendly toward creditors and may look to us as Shylocks. Life is very austere." Wedemeyer added, however, "There can be no doubt about the almost universal British desire to remain close to America in a political, economic and military sense." Attached to memo by Humelsine, July 15, 1947, FW 740.00119 Control (Germany) 7–749, State Department papers. The disastrous five weeks between July 15, when the British made the pound convertible in accord with the Anglo-American loan agreement, and August 20, when Britain suspended convertibility, fueled British antagonism. See R. Gardner, *Sterling-Dollar Diplomacy*, pp. 306–25, 337–42.

36. Elsey quoted in Paterson, *Soviet-American Confrontation*, p. 207; Patterson to Hoyt, June 23, 1947, Patterson papers.

37. Forrestal to Lippmann, January 7, 1946, Mosely to Forrestal, October 14, 1947, Box 70, Strausz-Hupe to Forrestal, March 14, 1946, Box 71, Forrestal papers; Forrestal diary, October 15, 1946, p. 1301.

38. Kennan, "Psychological Background," Box 18, O'Connor memo, October 7, 1946, Box 68, Forrestal papers; Kennan, *Memoirs 1925–50* (Boston: Atlantic Little-Brown, 1967), pp. 373–76.

39. George Kennan, "The Sources of Soviet Conduct," *Foreign Affairs*, July 1947; Riddleberger to Steinhardt, August 29, 1947, Box 55, Steinhardt papers.

40. Vandenberg to Roberts, August 12, 1947, Arthur Vandenberg papers, University of Michigan; Laurence Steinhardt, Lecture, Washington, D.C., December 1947.

41. See Vladimir Dedijer, *Tito Speaks* (London: Weidenfeld & Nicolson, 1954), pp. 302–6; Bethell, *Gomulka*, pp. 135–38, 146–47; Djilas, *Conversations*, pp. 99–101; Marshall D. Shulman, *Stalin's Foreign Policy Reappraised* (Cambridge, Mass.: Harvard University Press, 1963), pp. 14–17, 84; Alexander Werth, *Russia: The Post-War Years* (New York: Taplinger, 1971), pp. 294–326; A. I. Sobolev, *Outline History of the Communist International* (Moscow: Progress, 1970), pp. 512–15; Adam Ulam, *The Rivals*

(New York: Viking, 1971), pp. 131–34; for the German communists, see
Wolfgang Leonhard, *Child of the Revolution* (Chicago: Henry Regnery,
1958), pp. 458–61; for a Western survey of the Polish road, John Scott,
"Report on Poland," June 1, 1947, Box 55, Steinhardt papers.

42. *FRUS, 1947*, III, pp. 350–51; Taber to Hoover, May 21, 1947,
Hoover papers; Taft to Bannister, November 28, 1947, Box 786, Taft
papers; Hinshaw to Aldrich, October 27, 1947, Box 82, Winthrop Aldrich
papers, Harvard University.

43. Marshall interview in Price oral history collection; Vandenberg to
Roberts, August 12, 1947, Arthur Vandenberg papers.

44. Forrestal diary, July 26, 1947, p. 1751; Lovett to Lamont, July 31,
1947, Lamont papers; Ford to Johnston, Air Policy Commission papers,
Truman Library; Margaret Truman, *Harry S. Truman* (New York: Morrow,
1973), p. 352.

45. Southard to Snyder, August 12, 1947, Snyder papers; "Notes on Boat
Trip Coming Over" and London, September 3, 1947, Herter papers;
Lovett to Taber, September 21, 1947, Taber papers; *Business Week*, August
9, 1947, p. 86, September 6, 1947, p. 102.

46. *FRUS, 1947*, III, pp. 344–46, 361, 470–71, 475–76; Leahy diary,
September 29, 1947, Library of Congress; Margaret Truman, *Truman*, p.
354.

47. For the dialogue, McNaughton file to Bermingham, October 4, 1947,
Frank McNaughton papers, Truman Library; memorandum, October 15,
1947, Box 4, Clark Clifford papers, Truman Library.

48. Truman, *Truman*, p. 356; *Truman: Public Papers, 1947*, pp. 475–76,
492–98; Leahy diary, November 17, 1947.

49. *FRUS, 1947*, II, pp. 684, 680, 687, 713.

50. Robert Murphy, "The Current Situation in Germany," Lecture,
Washington, D.C., October 1947; Smith, *Clay Papers*, pp. 351, 440, 448,
458–60, 463–64, 491; Marshall's presentation with Humelsine to Secretary
of Agriculture, November 12, 1947, 711.61/11–1247, secret file, State Department papers, National Archives.

51. *FRUS, 1947*, II, pp. 732, 738, 749, 756; *FR:USSR*, pp. 57–60; Dean
Acheson, *Present at the Creation* (New York: Norton, 1970), p. 313.

52. *FRUS, 1947*, II, pp. 731, 757, 759, 817–18; Harold Nicolson, *Diaries
and Letters, 1945–62* (London: Fontana, 1971), pp. 107–8.

53. John Foster Dulles, *War or Peace* (New York: Macmillan, 1950),
pp. 106–7; C. L. Sulzberger, *A Long Row of Candles* (New York: Macmillan, 1969), p. 373.

54. *FRUS, 1947*, II, pp. 751–73, 764–65. On Marshall's lack of patience,
see John Hickerson interview, Dulles oral history interviews, Princeton
University.

55. *FRUS, 1947*, II, pp. 769–72, 826, 812.

56. Ibid., pp. 819, 823, 827, 815–17. Smith, *Clay*, pp. 501–2 (misdated).

57. Pauley in *FRUS, 1947*, II, p. 715, Clay to Patterson, December 23,
1947, Box 30, Patterson papers; Leahy diary, December 16, 1947.

5

John Gimbel

The Origins of the Marshall Plan

*John Gimbel's prior works on Germany (see Introduction) have
consistently argued that postwar occupation arrangements broke down,
not because of Soviet intransigence but because of French resistance.
The conventional history written in the light of the Cold War and
buttressed by the recollections of General Lucius Clay, head of the
U.S. military government, maintained that Germany became a Soviet-
American battleground when the Russians refused to follow through
on agreements for administering all four occupation zones as one
economic unit. Carefully reexamining the documents, Gimbel found
the French to be the major impediment to Allied cooperation on
Germany. Only as Soviet-American cooperation chilled over other
issues did American policymakers choose to soft-pedal disagreement
with the French and displace the confrontation upon the Russians.*

In his new study, The Origins of the Marshall Plan, *Gimbel resumes
this argument and takes up again another earlier theme: namely, the
bureaucratic conflicts between the U.S. State Department and the War
Department (supporting Clay). The War Department was entrusted
with administering our occupation zone and had to win the needed
funding from Congress. It wished to minimize the tax burden involved
in supporting the ravaged German economy, hence it moved consistently
to allow the Germans to rebuild their industry. The State Department
was sensitive to Germany's neighbors, still battered from 1940–45,
if not 1914–18, and worked to slow up German reconstruction. In his
new book, Gimbel suggests the Marshall Plan was designed to reconcile
all these conflicting priorities.*

Gimbel is probably the leading expert on the huge archives left by

*the United States Office of Military Government in Germany (OMGUS).
He has valuably demonstrated that while the German question became
central to the Cold War, it was not at the root of the antagonism.
Nevertheless, my own evaluation is that Gimbel's account may
excessively polarize historical issues. He argues strongly in his recent
study that the Marshall Plan of 1947 was no plan at all—granted, but
the word "plan" need not be taken so literally. And by the time the
initiative emerged fully clad in 1948 as the European Recovery
Program—to which the name Marshall Plan is also commonly ascribed—
it certainly had scope and coherence. Likewise, the fact that the French
were the major early irritant in Germany need not exclude a growing
dispute with the Soviets. In the fall of 1946 John Kenneth Galbraith
caught the complexity of the problem when he wrote, "In the last
analysis unification of Germany will depend not on France but on
Russia. The French opposition so far has, in a measure, served as a
cover for Russian intentions." **

My reservations, however, should not detract from the significance
of Gimbel's work in demythologizing the German issue. For this
selection I have chosen chapter 19, "Germany and the Marshall Plan,"
and portions of chapter 20, "Of Myths and Realities," from* The
Origins of the Marshall Plan. *They are reprinted with the permission
of the author and publisher, Stanford University Press, and the trustees
of the Leland Stanford Junior University.*

Germany and the Marshall Plan

The complicated negotiations with Britain, France, and the Army
on the bizonal level of industry and the Ruhr coal-management plan
finally convinced the State Department that it would eventually have to
assume administrative responsibility for the policies it wanted implemented from the American base in Germany. Faced with the financial
responsibilities that accompanied administrative responsibilities in Germany, the State Department moved toward a position it had prevented
the Army from taking for more than two years: it became more
critical of France's aims and objectives regarding Germany and the
future of Europe, and it finally concluded that France's territorial and
economic demands were, in fact, incompatible with any program
that would have Germany achieve a viable economy in the future.

---

* John Kenneth Galbraith, *Recovery in Europe*, National Planning Association Pamphlet No. 53 (October 1946), p. 31.

Though much has been written about the continuing influence of a Morgenthau-plan mentality on American policy in Germany, the issues were much more complex than that.[1] Riddleberger had, in fact, outlined the American dilemma in Europe as early as November 24, 1945, when he discussed the pitfalls of a policy that would try to destroy Germany's industrial war potential on the one hand and prevent the creation of a "soup kitchen" economy on the other.[2] Essentially, the problem was and remained one of achieving balance, moderation, and a "golden mean," which—as I have shown—the French would not discuss, much less consider; which the State Department would not further unless France was satisfied; and which the Army would not pursue, in part because it wanted to promote sufficient economic recovery to make a case for relief from the civil-political responsibilities of the occupation and in part because it was out of sympathy with the State Department's broader politico-economic mission in Europe.*

Late in April 1947, when Marshall learned from Clay and from his own advisers what the political and economic consequences of his and Bevin's Moscow decisions on Germany were likely to be, he instructed Kennan and the PPS to initiate studies that would, in effect, look toward a balanced solution of Europe's economic problems, rather than toward the unilateral rehabilitation of the bizone which the Army, the British, Herbert Hoover, and the Eightieth Congress seemed to prefer. As noted previously, the PPS divided the problem, recommending a

---

* Interestingly, the Russians made specific proposals that would have had the effect of achieving a balance between reparations, exports, and imports, and German consumption, and they did so repeatedly—at Potsdam, during the Clay-Sokolovsky discussions in Berlin late in 1946, and at the Moscow CFM in 1947. See *FRUS*, 1945, Potsdam II, 810, for the Soviet proposal of July 23, 1945, which said: "In working out the economic balance of Germany the necessary means must be provided for payment for imports approved by the Control Council. In case the means are insufficient to pay simultaneously on reparations account and for approved imports, all kinds of deliveries (internal consumption, exports, reparations) have to be proportionally reduced." See *FRUS*, 1945, Potsdam II, 276–81, for a discussion of the Russian proposal, and Clay to War Dept., for Echols, Oct. 11, 1946, RG 165, file WDSCA 387.6, Sec. IV, Box 351, NA, for the Russian proposal in the fall of 1946, a proposal that Clay considered to be "a reasonable basis for discussion." Clay's judgment that the Soviet proposal violated neither the Potsdam Agreement nor the level-of-industry plan may be found in Clay to War Dept., for Noce, Jan. 22, 1947, RG 165, file WDSCA 387.6, Sec. VIII, Box 354, NA. See SecState to the President and ActgSecState, March 19, 1947, *FRUS*, 1947, II, 264, for the statement that at Moscow Molotov "insisted that German industry must be set at a level to insure her internal needs, payments of imports, and reparations."

limited German recovery program (the Coal for Europe plan) and a long-term European program to be developed by the Europeans themselves, albeit with American "friendly aid in the drafting." [3] Both recommendations were essential elements of the Marshall Plan, the first one to pacify the Army and the second one to pacify the Europeans and the State Department.

The Marshall Plan emerged issue by issue during 1947, but in conformity with the PPS's two major recommendations and with remarkable clarity and consistency. A limited amount of general German economic recovery would have to occur as an essential component of the Coal for Europe program, and perhaps to satisfy the Army, the British, the Congress, and the American public. But Germany's recovery would have to be controlled in such a way as to satisfy the political interests of Bidault and to ensure the prior recovery of Germany's neighbors and provide for their security. [4] In the interests of better control, neither the American Army, nor the British, nor the German Socialists would be permitted a free hand in the Ruhr and the Rhineland. Furthermore, the announcement of German recovery programs, such as those provided for by the Bevin-Marshall decisions in Moscow and detailed in the Clay-Robertson level-of-industry plan, would have to be coordinated with the long-term program for European recovery; their implementation would have to be delayed until the Europeans agreed upon a common recovery plan, and—if necessary —those aspects of the German recovery program that were ready for implementation before the common plan could be developed would have to be kept under wraps until it was politically opportune to reveal them to Germany's neighbors or to make them public.

As Kennan's committee had recommended, the German-recovery phase of the PPS report (the Coal for Europe program) went forward immediately, even while the long-term program was still very much in its embryo and developmental states, and long before the Americans had a clear conception of the general European plan. That condition produced the events and situations already described: the British-American coal talks, the wrangling over the coal-management plan and socialization, the dispute about the export price of coal, and the conflict between Berlin and Washington on the bizonal level-of-industry plan. The condition also confronted the State Department with the task of reconciling its limited German recovery program—which was moving ahead more rapidly than the general European recovery program—with its own priorities and with France's demands for security, territory, coal, a decimated German economy, and a decentralized German political structure. The latter remains to be described.

Early in June 1947 the State Department urged OMGUS to proceed rapidly with the British to develop a coal-production program in Germany. Later in June the Committee of Three asked Clay and Murphy to report on what was needed to permit the German economy to contribute actively to European recovery and to bizonal self-sufficiency.[5] On July 2, 1947, the State Department instructed Clay to make sure that the level of industry being planned for the bizone would provide for a self-supporting German economy, but also to make sure that substantial reparations deliveries from Germany would occur, even though doing the latter might be at the expense of Germany's future standard of living.[6] One day later the Committee of Three combined these and other instructions and adopted a policy statement on Germany and the Marshall Plan:

1. The United States would make known publicly its willingness to have its zone of Germany collaborate in the European recovery program, but no initiative was to come from Berlin even though "the occupied area must be represented when European recovery plans are being prepared."

2. If the restoration of European international commercial relations required an increase in American expenditures in Germany, or if such restoration would set back German self-sufficiency, American expenditures in Germany would be increased, or the German economy would be compensated by provision of American relief monies to the country or countries benefiting from Germany's trade so as to enable them to pay Germany.

3. The American commander in Europe would consult with European countries and international organizations regarding German production and trade and ensure that emphasis was given to the export of German goods needed by the European countries for their economic recovery and rehabilitation.

4. Transactions of a substantial nature, or those which resulted in trade exchanges between Germany and other European countries—but not in conformity with the three preceding principles—were to be referred to Washington for decision.[7]

According to Petersen, who sent the policy statement to Clay on July 10, 1947, paragraph 2 was a frank admission that United States policies and programs in the interests of general European recovery might delay a self-sustaining German economy and require an increase in funds for Germany or for other countries so they could pay Germany for her exports.[8] That paragraph was, in fact, a hasty and uncoordinated reversal of previous policy, and when it was grafted onto the draft of JCS directive 1779 on July 11, 1947, it stood there in flat contradiction of another section of the same directive, which stated that the United States would "not agree to finance the payment of reparation by Germany to other United Nations by increasing its financial outlay in Germany or by postponing the achievement of a self-sustaining German economy." [9]

The flow, the content, and the contradictions of the policy instructions and directives that went from Washington to Berlin in June and July 1947 testify to the State Department's attempt to reconcile the irreconcilable: German recovery to self-sufficiency and France's demands for coal, security, and economic advantage. Matthews, who had worried similarly to McCloy in 1945, warned Lovett on July 11, 1947, that "conversations looking toward the level of increase in German industry are about to result in an agreement between the British and ourselves with benefit to the economy of Germany," that German coal exports would be reduced, and that unless France received compensating benefits the French government would face serious political problems.[10] On the same day, Clayton and Caffery heard from Ramadier and Bidault that France had not changed its German policies and demands, and that if France could not be accommodated there would be no Marshall Plan. They advised Marshall immediately to use "extreme care . . . in dealing with this matter." [11]

Neither extreme care, nor caution, nor attempts at rational argument or persuasion were enough to allay France's fears, and Bidault's warnings of impending doom for France, the Marshall Plan, and Europe increased with multiplier effect as he received more and more information about the British-American plans for the bizone. Bevin, who was in Paris, warned that publication of the level-of-industry plan "would be a tragic mistake." The Army ordered Clay to hold up everything for the time being. Harriman, who "found Bidault in a hysterical condition," tried to convince him of the absolute necessity for a new level of industry in the bizone and claimed "that the point had been reached where measures had to be taken." But Bidault had already told him he was "very alarmed about developments in Germany," and he warned that "he would be compelled to protest" if the Americans went ahead with their plans.[12]

Marshall finally capitulated and advised Bidault on July 21, 1947, that no further action on German recovery plans would be taken until "the French Government has had a reasonable opportunity to discuss these questions with the United States and United Kingdom Governments." [13] Marshall had been influenced by a personal plea from Bidault, by official demands from the French government, by suggestions from Bevin, and by advice from Kennan to hold tripartite talks and use the occasion to "place squarely before the French the choice between a rise in German production or no European recovery financed by the U.S." [14] Marshall's sensitivity to the political tightrope on which he was walking is revealed most clearly in a memorandum he wrote to Secretary of Agriculture Anderson on July 22, 1947. Anderson had been in Europe from July 1 to 14, 1947. Upon his return he wrote a report for Truman and asked the State Department for advice on its possible publication. In reply, Marshall assured Anderson that he had been "tremendously impressed" with Anderson's report to the cabinet, but that recent French reactions to the level-of-industry plan for Germany had "produced a very delicate situation, particularly with regard to the development of the meetings of the sixteen nations in Paris." Under the circumstances, Marshall said, the publication of Anderson's report would be unwise "for the reason that it stresses the economic reconstruction of Germany virtually to the exclusion of any mention of our interest in the reconstruction of the liberated areas—which is the basis of the Paris conference." In other words, Marshall liked the report but feared that its publication would "add fuel to the flames now raging by reason of the agreement negotiated between General Clay and General Robertson." [15]

TRIPARTITE TALKS ON GERMANY AND THE MARSHALL PLAN

As noted previously, Marshall agreed to discussions on Germany with the French for political reasons, and he did so before the Americans and British had agreed on what they would discuss. What the two powers finally discussed with France is conveniently summarized in the State Department's instructions of August 12, 1947, to Ambassador Douglas, who was the American delegate and the chairman of the London tripartite discussions. The French were to be given every opportunity to make a full statement, but Douglas was to "make it clear that in the absence of a fusion of the French zone with the US and UK zones, the US and UK are responsible for and will take final decision on all matters regarding the bizonal areas." Douglas was to defend the Clay-Robertson plan vigorously against modification, but "if in your judgment there is a genuine threat to the success of the European economic plan or if democracy in France will be threatened unless changes are made," the issue was to be referred to Washington for further instructions. Douglas was to discuss neither the resumption of reparations nor the rate of reactivation of Germany industry. If the French raised the Ruhr management issue, Douglas was to tell them that "acceptance" was not involved, but that the matter could be discussed in the CFM scheduled for November. If France raised the question of the French zone's union with bizonia, Douglas was to make clear that the United States desired such union, but that it would not hold up the new level-of-industry plan pending a French proposal and its discussion. If France wanted to discuss the Saar, Douglas was to say that he had no instructions and that the matter was being dealt with through diplomatic channels.[16]

As Clay had predicted in July, the French made clear in London that their major objection to the bizonal level-of-industry plan was that it threatened the Monnet Plan's projected steel production figure of 12 million tons per year. At issue were France's plans to replace German steel production with French steel production, ostensibly to ensure permanently France's economic and political security. The French said they could not accept the plan in the absence of a prior agreement that made certain Germany would have to export "sufficient coal and coke to insure that German steel production will not absorb so much German coal as to hamper the steel production of other countries, particularly French Monnet plan." [17] Before the London talks were over, the United States instructed Douglas to advise the French of American willingness to discuss the matter and to "give sympathetic consideration" to the proposal for a Ruhr authority which would assure "that access to production of the Ruhr shall not in the future . . . be subject to the will of Germany." According to Douglas, the British were prepared to cause trouble on the issue, and he therefore decided to take a chance and try to get France to approve the final communiqué without using the policy statement.[18] He hardly needed to do so, since he, Clayton, and Caffery had already told Bidault on August 19, 1947, that they had instructions to postpone further informal discussion with the French on the question of an international board for the Ruhr, but that they "were authorized to say . . . that at some more appropriate time we would be glad to give sympathetic consideration to the French position on the Ruhr." [19] Although Bidault was disappointed, "even" chagrined, and threatened once again that "no French Government, neither the present one nor any succeeding one, could ever agree to a revised level of industry for Germany, without some assurances as to French security and access by Europe to the products of the Ruhr," he finally became reconciled—particularly after the three Americans said they would recommend that discussions be held on the issues immediately after the London tripartite talks.[20]

The political considerations that were so important to the decision to hold the tripartite talks on Germany also dictated the content and the emphasis of the final communiqué. The communiqué covered up disagreements, played down the many issues that had not been resolved, and failed to make clear that France continued to object to the level-of-industry plan and its implications.[21] The talks and the communiqué nevertheless gave both sides what they wanted: Bidault got the political leverage he said consultations would give him to forestall political crisis and to remain in control in France. The British and Americans could now publish the Clay-Robertson bizonal level-of-industry plan and use it officially as the basis for Germany's contribution to the Marshall Plan for European economic recovery.

The issues that were not agreed upon during the London tripartite talks were the subjects of continuing discussions and negotiations in Berlin, Paris, London, and Washington throughout 1947 and on into 1948. For example, the military governments in Berlin negotiated agreements on the Saar, coal, coke, and the Moscow sliding scale for German coal exports.[22] In Paris, Clayton, Caffery, and Douglas—seconded by Kennan and Charles H. Bonesteel (a colonel on the War Department General Staff, on assignment with the State Department)—initiated informal talks with the French on the international board for the Ruhr, thus laying the basis for the final agreement on a Ruhr coal and steel authority, which came out of the London six-power talks of 1948.[23]

Interesting and significant though the continuing negotiations are, they are beyond the scope of this study. Once the Americans had reasonable assurances that the French would not (could not, since they had been consulted) *openly* and *publicly* protest the Ruhr coal-management plan, the price of export coal, and the Clay-Robertson level-of-industry plan, they concentrated on giving "friendly aid" to the CEEC in Paris on the form, structure, technicalities, and nature of the European recovery program. In the end, they made sure that the German decisions that Marshall and Bevin had made in Moscow would be implemented.

Germany and the CEEC

A convincing body of evidence now available makes clear that the Americans conceived and developed the Marshall Plan as a method for resolving the United States economic dilemma of the German occupation. There are, for example, Marshall's and Dulles's reports on the Moscow CFM; [24] the PPS's report of May 23, 1947, with its emphasis on German coal for Europe; and the SWNCC message of June 19, 1947, to Clay, which said that "any program of European reconstruction must necessarily take Germany into account." There is a record of Clayton's remarks to Bevin and the British cabinet members that "a radical change is needed in approaching the German coal problem as *sine qua non* to any consideration of the over-all European problem." Finally, there is the Committee of Three's policy decision of July 2, 1947, which said that "the occupied area must be represented when European recovery plans are being prepared." [25]

Kennan's recommendation that the Europeans themselves develop the long-term program of European recovery, together with the political decision to have them do so despite Clayton's vigorous protests that *"the United States must run this show,"* and the continuing public posture taken by Marshall and others that the United States would limit its role to "friendly aid," all made it difficult for the Americans to get the kind of German program they wanted and needed. Interestingly, Molotov seems to have sensed that there was more to the Marshall invitation than met the eye, for he asked Bevin and Bidault in Paris whether they had additional information from the Americans.[26] Though I have no way to demonstrate the conclusion, Molotov's performance at Paris late in June and early in July 1947 makes sense if one assumes that the Soviets detected either duplicity or a political-economic trap in the Marshall Plan. Why else would Molotov ask, as the first order of business, whether Bevin and Bidault had "inside" information from the United States or whether they had made any "deals" among themselves? Why would he ask the two unanswerable questions he proposed they send to Washington: How much money was the United States prepared to spend on European recovery, and would the Congress vote to approve the credits? Perhaps Molotov knew from Russia's own experience with economic planning that the grand plan implied by Marshall's invitation was impossible to achieve—either because the capitalistic economic systems would refuse to stand still for that, or because the various nations would not attempt the encroachments on their national sovereignty implied in the program, or because of the sheer *technical* impossibility of constructing the economic input-output tables that would be required for the task. Since its economic objectives were either unbelievable or impossible to achieve, Molotov's assumption that the Marshall Plan was essentially a political program, not unlike the imperialism that Marxist-Leninists were inclined to see, has a certain logic.

Molotov's departure from Paris on July 3, 1947, undoubtedly helped to narrow the range of political disagreement after that, but it did not pave the way for the kind of German-based European recovery program the Americans had in mind. On July 20, 1947, Caffery reported on the first week of the CEEC's Marshall Plan talks in Paris, concluding that the "French, of course, have not abandoned outwardly their . . . 'pastoral' approach to [the] German problem and contend that security lies in 'pulling heavy industrial teeth' of Germany." [27] On August 6, 1947, after a three-day round of discussions on the progress of the CEEC and on the latest PPS paper (of July 23, 1947), Clayton, Caffery, Douglas, Murphy, and Paul H. Nitze (the Deputy Director of the Office of International Trade Policy, State Department) recommended formally that it was time to give "friendly aid" to the Paris conference. The recommendation produced considerable discussion in Washington and Paris on how to give "friendly aid" without facing charges of dictation and on how to develop a "united front" in Washington to ensure against contradictory "friendly aid" from the War Department and the State Department.[28] On August 14, 1947, the State Department sent guidelines to Paris for Clayton's and Caffery's use in "informal talks with appropriate committee chairmen and others."

These guidelines were vague and cautious on details, but firm on principles that would require effective German participation in European recovery. The guidelines said the participating countries were paying too little attention to Marshall's call for self-help and mutual aid. "An itemized bill summing up prospective deficits against a background of present policies and arrangements will definitely not be sufficient." The Americans expected the production programs of participating countries to be based not only on their own needs, but also on fulfilling the needs of the other participating countries. Apparently to ensure that Germany would be included as a full participating country, the guidelines concluded by stating that "further aid can be given [regarding the] role of western Germany." [29] The importance of the latter emerged in future exchanges.

Clayton and Caffery reported on August 20, 1947, on their "friendly aid" in Paris, noting—as one example of a fundamental problem—that the combined steel-production figures submitted by the bizone and France would require more coke than would be available anywhere.[30] Douglas believed that the "French must be persuaded to abandon [their] present position that original Monnet plan must be accepted practically unchanged no matter what the cost to US or to general recovery," and he thought the United States would have to be represented in Paris to defend the bizonal production plans against the competing demands of the Monnet Plan. Though the United States need not take the lead, Douglas said, "neither should we hang back." [31]

Meanwhile, in Washington, further discussion within the State Department produced the consensus "that sufficient friendly aid is not being given." Two days later, Lovett cabled Marshall (who was attending an inter-American conference on peace and security at Petropolis, Brazil) that the CEEC was scheduled to produce a report within a week, and that the news was all bad. The CEEC was going to come out with sixteen shopping lists that would require an unreasonably large grant of American aid and that would in the end fail to establish European self-sufficiency by 1951. Lovett said the conference had gone ahead despite Clayton's and Caffery's instructions of August 14. The United States had "pointed out [the] necessity for primary emphasis on efficient utilization of existing capacity rather than on capital development," but "adequate results have not ensued." According to Lovett, "the time has now arrived for us to give some indications that the present plan is not acceptable and to do so promptly." He recommended that Clayton and Caffery be instructed to press for a European plan based upon self-help and mutual aid rather than on long-term capital improvements in the individual nations. They should "emphasize the breaking of specific bottlenecks well known to them and to us." [32]

Lovett talked about shopping lists, costs, and principles, but he also alluded to the fundamental issues at stake. The "specific bottlenecks well known to them and to us" referred to the Ruhr and the Rhineland, to the PPS's Coal for Europe program, and to the limited rehabilitation of transportation and of steel and machinery production that was needed in Germany to implement the coal-recovery program. Lovett's insistence on self-help and mutual aid rather than on long-term capital improvements referred to the conflicting demands for coal, coke, steel, manpower, and other factors of production between the Monnet Plan and the Clay-Robertson bizonal level-of-industry plan. Finally, his note that the Americans wanted "primary emphasis on efficient utilization of existing capacity rather than on capital development" meant that the Americans had opted for the Clay-Robertson plan for Germany rather than the Monnet Plan for France; for European recovery that would include substantial German recovery rather than for European recovery that would, in the first instance, benefit France. It was well known that the greatest source in Europe of idle or underutilized capital equipment—on which the Americans wanted to put "primary emphasis"—was in Germany. The Harriman Committee, for example, referred to that knowledge when it observed that "over-all production in some European countries has shown remarkable recovery, [but] it is still true that Europe's total production, *especially when Germany is taken into account,* is well below prewar levels, with the critical item of coal a prime example." [33] Marshall himself referred to it in a speech he made to the Chicago Council on Foreign Relations on November 18, 1947: "The truth is that far from being accorded a preference over any Allied country, German recovery has lagged so far behind that of the other countries of Europe as to retard the whole effort for European recovery. At the present time industrial production in Western Germany is less than one-half that of pre-war." [34]

Armed with a State Department policy statement of August 26, 1947, and assisted by Charles H. Bonesteel and Kennan (who supplied additional, oral instructions "relating to general political situation"), the Americans in Paris, with Marshall's approval, told the CEEC what they wanted. The fundamental objectives of the program were "to move entire area" toward a "working economy independent of abnormal outside support." To do that "participants must . . . foster European recovery as a whole, and . . . make national contributions to this common goal." In order to maximize self-help and mutual aid, the "program must . . . concentrate initially on elimination of bottle-necks and [on] other opportunities for greatest immediate recovery at lowest cost in scarce resources," and—as if to nail down the German contribution firmly—the "program must be directed primarily toward short-run recovery rather than long-run development; full use of existing or readily repairable capacity and restoration of normal domestic and intra-European intercourse therefore have priority . . ." Clayton and his colleagues in Paris translated their instructions into seven "conditions," which they presented to the leadership of the CEEC on August 30, 1947. The "condition" providing specifically for Germany's recovery stated that "long-run development projects should not be allowed to interfere with the reactivation of the most efficient existing productive facilities. The latter must have first priority." [35]

AMERICAN STRATEGY AND THE CEEC

The State Department's strategy was to dovetail German rehabilitation with the general European recovery program and to present to the United States Congress a single foreign-aid package. To do that, it sought acceptance in Paris of a set of broad, general principles that would permit implementation of the level-of-industry plan for the bizone and allow a rate of reactivation of German industry that would also be acceptable to the Army, the British, the Congress, and ultimately the American public. The strategy, to be followed on three fronts, was outlined in detail by Charles Bonesteel in a memorandum of August 27, 1947, to Robert Lovett.

In Paris, "the United States will state to the participating countries that it is our intent to meet their views with regard to bizonal matters in so far as is possible, consistent with our responsibilities as the military governors. This intention to be based clearly on the assumption that the Paris conferees give assurances of an equal intent with regard to their national programs, and further demonstrate this intent by their actions at Paris. The demonstration of their intent requires, in effect, that discussions of the German zones are part of a broader discussion of all national programs."

In London, Douglas would consult with the British to get them to agree to the proposed discussions in Paris.

In Washington, the difficult assignment of satisfying the Army would go to Lovett, Bohlen, and Saltzman, who would meet with Royall, Eisenhower, Draper, Lauris Norstad (the Director, Plans and Operations Division), "and no others," if that could be arranged. According to Bonesteel, the State Department approach to the Army should be "educational, with a slight dictatorial flavor." Lovett and Bohlen could "present the broad global picture, bringing out the two-world assumption" and emphasizing the need to counterbalance the "Soviet world" and to treat "Europe west of the Iron Curtain on a regional basis." With respect to budget and finances, the State Department might assure the Army that it was committed to obtaining "considerably greater sums for Germany as part of the regional program." Last, the Army should be told of "the requirement that the German economic matters be discussed at Paris," emphasizing the "security aspect of drawing more closely to us the nations of Western Europe now wavering between communism and us." [36]

Implementing the Strategy

The Army. The State Department's grand strategy proved difficult to implement, even though the Army and the Harriman Committee (the President's Committee on Foreign Aid) fell into line readily. The Army accepted the strategy and agreed to discussions in the CEEC regarding integration of the bizone into the European recovery program. Clay accepted the decision taken in Washington, but he apparently did so on the assumption that he was leaving, for he later made clear that "no self-respecting man would continue to operate with the degree of interference he had experienced" and that he "would not be willing to continue under these conditions for another year." [37]

The Harriman Committee. Convincing the Harriman Committee was easy. Harriman had endorsed Herbert Hoover's report on Germany in March 1947, and he had been promoting Hoover's recommendations since then. After Truman created the Committee in June 1947, Harriman arranged for it to hear reports from Marshall, Kennan (on the political background of the Marshall Plan), Eisenhower (on economic stability and national security), and others.[38] The records of an August

15 meeting of the subcommittee for economic and financial analysis
—whose membership included Calvin B. Hoover, former Chairman of
the German Standard-of-Living Board in Berlin—reveal a strong bias
in favor of stimulating coal production in the Ruhr and Rhineland,
increasing the bizonal level of industry, and (in the interests of speedy
European recovery) reactivating plants that were in excess of those
needed by the German economy under the level-of-industry plan.[39] On
September 10 and 11, 1947, the full Harriman Committee heard
speeches and reports by several government functionaries, including
Kennan, Bonesteel, and Lovett. Lovett reviewed the developments in
Paris, summarized the State Department's August 14 guidelines, "which
will not be compromised," and described the Clayton-Kennan-Bone-
steel attempt to get the technical experts in Paris to modify the requirements for American aid. He concluded that the current CEEC documents and reports could not be translated into a workable program,
and he observed that "the Department of State desires that the work
to date not be considered as constituting a program." [40]

The message the Harriman Committee got on September 10 and 11,
1947, is described in a letter of September 12, from Owen D. Young,
the chairman of the subcommittee on economic and financial analysis,
to Harriman. It said, in part:

> I share fully the apprehension of the State Department that if we
> fail to meet the present food and fuel emergency which faces the
> German people and if we fail to help them develop promptly a long
> range program of rehabilitation, which will enable them to support
> themselves, there is grave danger that western Germany will become
> communistic and will be taken over by Russia. If Russia could sup-
> plement her present vast resources of raw materials and manpower
> with the creative, productive and organizing capacity of the German
> people, she would become shortly the most powerful nation in the
> world. The result very likely would be that all of Western Europe
> would be forced to accept a communistic program. The United States
> would then be faced with a menace which would make the Hitler
> threat in perspective look like child's play.[41]

It is needless to push the point further, for the published report
of the Harriman Committee is filled with statements and allusions at-
testing to the Committee's acceptance of the State Department's strategy
and policy. There is, for example, the statement that "the amount of
aid allotted to Germany may have to be higher than was set at Paris."
Further: "In the opinion of the Committee . . . it is the policies
pursued in Germany by our own Government wihch are of all-
importance to the success of any aid program." In addition: "It cannot
be too strongly emphasized that the producing and purchasing power

of Germany, and, through Germany, the producing and purchasing power of all Central Europe, is indispensable to the recovery of Western Europe." Finally, there is the entire section entitled "Report on the Special Position of the Bizone." [42]

The British. The British initially rejected Washington's proposal to have the CEEC discuss the integration of the bizone into the European recovery program, and the Americans eventually had to seek Britain's support by roundabout means. Perhaps the British agreed with Murphy, who warned on September 8, 1947, that if Germany were discussed in the CEEC the European countries would try to obtain indirect financing from the United States through Germany.[43] Upon hearing of the British rejection, Marshall cabled Douglas to impress upon Bevin the seriousness with which he regarded the British opposition. Marshall noted that "the force of US pressure" to get a cooperative, regional approach at the expense of national programs such as the Monnet Plan "is seriously weakened if the one European area in which the US has direct responsibility abstains." He argued that Germany had not been adequately included in the CEEC reports, and he noted as evidence that the bizone's CEEC questionnaire had reported that mining-machinery production would reach about $1,000 million in 1951, but that the CEEC experts had planned for *only* $13 million in mining-machinery exports from Germany between 1948 and 1951. Further, he noted, the CEEC reports contemplated *no* net steel exports from Germany after 1947.[44]

Douglas was unable to turn Bevin and the British around. Harried by problems in Paris, confronted with the CEEC delegates' resistance to excessive American "friendly aid," and warned by Bevin that direct United States interference would delay the CEEC reports, Douglas asked the State Department to go more slowly. On September 12, 1947, he reported that he had not brought up the bizonal-inclusion question with the British because of the other difficulties he and Clayton were having in Paris. He and Clayton suggested that it might be "more appropriate to ask for the inclusion of the bizonal areas when the conference is reconvened after the submission of the 'provisional' or 'first report.' " [45] Five days later Douglas repeated his advice, saying that the United States could press for inclusion of the bizonal areas after the first CEEC report had been received by the United States government "and when, should it be necessary, the conference is reconvened for the purpose of modifying the first report or preparing a second." [46] In the end, Britain accepted the State Department's strategy and policy on Germany during the broader negotiations in the CEEC and in Washington.

The CEEC. Irony of ironies—in view of what had happened since

1945—as the Marshall Plan talks progressed in 1947, the State Department began to press actively for German recovery over the objections of the liberated countries. It apparently did so roughly in correspondence to its accumulating knowledge of the costs of a European recovery program unless something more was done in Germany than to implement Kennan's Coal for Europe program. Late in August 1947, after Clayton and others had reviewed the draft CEEC reports being prepared in Paris, Clayton advised Sir Oliver Franks, the President of the CEEC in Bevin's absence, that the $28.2 billion Marshall Plan aid figure that was emerging "was out of the question." He reported to Washington that he was "convinced there is no other way to deal with this situation than to impose certain necessary conditions." [47] The State Department responded with a flurry of activity, much of which mocked the concept of "friendly aid."

On August 26, 1947, the State Department sent Clayton and Caffery a policy statement listing certain fundamental objectives and conditions, which have been summarized previously. It also outlined a procedure for informal and formal American review of the CEEC reports with respect to "both general policy matters and technical questions." It said Germany was to be "covered fully into program" with the revised bizonal level-of-industry plan as the basis. The latter might be changed in the interests of general European recovery as "recommended by conference on same basis that conference makes similar recommendations for changes in Monnet or other national plans." [48] On August 30, 1947, Clayton and Caffery presented the American "conditions" to the Executive Committee of the CEEC. They told the Committee that the preliminary materials and reports they had examined were "disappointing," that the $29.2 billion preliminary aid figure was "much too large." They insisted that the CEEC had to develop a common, regional approach rather than simply add up the uncoordinated national requests. Significantly, the Americans illustrated their arguments from the example of coal and steel, remarking that the CEEC report on steel assumed that all existing steel plants in the sixteen nations would operate at full capacity from 1948 on, even though there was insufficient coal and transportation for this purpose. Confronted with the "conditions," and advised of Clayton's opinion that the existing conclusions of the CEEC "might, if formally advanced, prejudice the success of the entire Marshall program," the Executive Committee gave up "any idea of completing the report by September 1." [49]

A MISSIONARY'S REPORT

Kennan and Bonesteel—who had been present when the "conditions" were discussed with the CEEC Executive Committee in Paris—reported independently to Lovett. They endorsed the official Clayton-Caffery-Douglas "suggestion that the time has come to present our views to [the] governments directly," [50] and Kennan filed a personal, fascinating analysis of the reasons for the failure of the Paris Conference to develop a satisfactory European recovery program.

Kennan concluded that the United States "must not look to the people in Paris to accomplish the impossible. . . . No bold or original approach to Europe's problems will be forthcoming. . . . Worst of all: the report will not fulfill all of the essential requirements listed by Mr. Clayton . . . on August 30." None of the CEEC delegates was a strong political figure at home, Kennan said, and none could afford to "take extensive liberties with the anxious reservations of the home governments." Furthermore, since the Russians were not present, "the gathering has reverted, with a certain sense of emotional release, to the pattern of old-world courtesy and cordiality in which many of the participants were reared and for which they have instinctively longed throughout the rigors of a post-war diplomacy dominated by the Russian presence." That condition had "practically ruled out any critical examination of the other fellow's figures—particularly as most of the delegates must have lively doubts as to the entire validity of some of their own, and cannot be eager to enter a name calling contest between pot and kettle." At bottom, however, the CEEC delegates' difficulties were compounded by three basic problems and conditions, none of which "can be corrected within the brief period of grace which still remains." Britain's sociopolitical sickness was one of the basic problems. Another was the failure to integrate Germany into the European program. The third was the general political weakness of the participating governments.

According to Kennan, Marshall's Harvard speech had put the European nations to a test, which they had failed. The United States could let things ride, "receive a report which will not really be satisfactory, review it and reject it in due course, making no further effort to aid." Another alternative—"the one we should adopt"—would be for the United States to "make efforts to have the report presented in such a way as to avoid any impression of finality; let it come to us on the understanding that it will be used only as a basis of further discussion; try to whittle it down as much as possible by negotiation; then give it final consideration in the Executive Branch of our Government and decide unilaterally what we finally wish to present to Congress. This would mean that we would listen to all that the Europeans had to say, but in the end we would not *ask* them, we would just *tell* them what they would get." That, according to Kennan, was "what some of the more far-sighted of the Europeans hope we will do." [51]

Three days after Kennan's report, and on Caffery's renewed request for "vigorous and direct representations" to the governments concerned, Lovett sent a circular telegram to the American representatives accredited to the CEEC nations. He instructed them to see the respective foreign ministers or prime ministers as soon as possible and to say that the CEEC plan had "numerous deficiencies" that would make it "unacceptable" to the State Department, "undoubtedly evoke strong criticism" in the United States, and "endanger" the entire program. The amount of aid to be requested was too high, Lovett continued, and the "whole program shows little more than lip service to principles of European self help and mutual help." The telegram summarized the American "conditions," generally went on in the same uncompromising way, and closed with the information that the State Department was trying to get the British to agree to an American proposal to discuss the bizonal plans in the CEEC and integrate Germany into the recovery program. [52]

A footnote in *Foreign Relations* states that "replies from the American missions indicated that these views received sympathetic consideration by the various foreign ministers." But if the British response is indicative, and if Bevin's conclusions are accurate, the footnote is a pure fabrication. Bevin, Sir Edmund Hall-Patch, and Roger M. Makins told Douglas that the seven "essentials" were not new to them, that it was impossible to postpone the scheduled date for the CEEC's report in order to meet the American demands, that the participating countries had already cooperated as much as was possible, and that "any effort to press further would . . . so impair national sovereignty that many countries would rebel." In reporting these things to Washington, Douglas noted that "in view of the foregoing, it would have been futile to press for a decision" on CEEC discussion of the bizone and its integration into the general plan. [53]

The American effort to have the CEEC report delayed and revised failed also. The Executive Committee told Clayton and his colleagues on September 10, 1947, that "to meet entirely the US conception of a program would require a change in the terms of reference and this would mean a new conference." There was, in fact, "no possibility of the present Conference agreeing on an integrated plan." The most the Executive Committee would agree to do was to label the CEEC's report as "provisional," with the understanding that they would go to Washington—along with selected technical experts—to review the program there. [54]

While Marshall tried to arouse British sympathy for the American approach and expressed a veiled threat to take unilateral action regarding the bizone, Clayton and his colleagues tried again to move the Executive Committee in Paris. They finally reached an understanding to delay the CEEC's report for about a week and to let American technical experts work *directly* with the CEEC technical committees in Paris to improve the report. Meanwhile, the Americans and the Executive Committee would continue to discuss what further actions would be taken after the provisional report was issued. At this point Bevin asked Douglas to advise Marshall of his earnest "hope that the United States Government, having made its views known, will now allow the Conference to work upon them and complete its report in an atmosphere of calm and without any feeling of external pressure." It is also the point at which Clayton and Douglas decided not to push the question of German discussions in the CEEC and to advise Washington that "it would be more appropriate to ask for the inclusion of the bizonal areas when the conference is reconvened after the submission of the 'provisional' or 'first report' and press for inclusion during the remaining 8 days of the present phase of the work of the conference." [55]

The final result of all these things was the adoption of a procedure remarkably similar to the one Kennan had outlined on September 4, 1947. The CEEC issued a "first report" on September 22, 1947, and sent it to Washington as the European plan called for in the Harvard speech. In Washington the Advisory Steering Committee on European Economic Recovery reviewed the report. The committee had been established late in August when the decision to offer more "friendly aid" was made. It met for the first time on September 9, 1947, under tight secrecy and security rules. At one time it seems to have had about a third of the personnel of the State, Commerce, and Treasury Departments working for it.[56] The Advisory Steering Committee coordinated the CEEC reports with the Harriman Committee and other groups, and it finally met with the CEEC Executive Committee and selected technical experts in Washington in October and November to work out the outlines of the proposal that would be presented by the administration to the Congress.[57]

According to Ernest H. Van Der Beugel, a Dutch foreign affairs expert who participated in the Washington meetings, the discussions in Washington were largely technical but highly informative to the Europeans for what they revealed about the way the American system worked. The Americans, he said, used the Europeans as "part of a team charged with the difficult task of making the Paris Report as attractive as possible for the presentation to Congress." In the process, Van Der Beugel continued, "there was an inclination on the part of the Administration to change accents, to color presentations, to minimize some problems and overemphasize others, to hide existing shortcomings and to applaud practically non-existing achievements, in its efforts to win Congressional approval. . . . The aim was Congressional approval for a program created solely for the benefit of the Europeans. It was no wonder . . . that [the Europeans] had some difficulty, not only in adjusting . . . to this situation, but suddenly becoming part of this process." [58]

What the administration did—in fact needed to do—is perhaps illustrated best by quoting portions of an exchange between Vandenberg and Marshall during the Senate Foreign Relations Committee hearings on the European recovery program. According to Vandenberg, the first question he wanted to ask Marshall was also the one he considered to be most basic—too important to be left to Royall, who would appear before the Committee later for the Army.

> *Vandenberg:* What I want to ask you is for your comment as to whether there is any dependable hope for this program without a restabilization and integration of western Germany into the program.
> *Marshall:* The inclusion, or integration, of western Germany into the program is essential. Coal alone provides one of the great essentials to the recovery program, and Germany is a major source of coal. I merely say that it is essential that western Germany be considered an integral part of the program.
> *Vandenberg:* That does not quite go far enough. . . . I would think that it was just as essential that we had a rather definite and hopeful program for the stabilization of western Germany without too long a delay as it is to have a program for any of the rest of these countries, and to whatever extent you are able to make the statement I should like your comment as to the progress that is being made in that direction, and what the prospects are.

Marshall talked then in rather vague and general terms about coal, about conversations with the French, about administrative reorganization in Germany, and other things.

> *Vandenberg:* To get down to the bare bones of the thing, would it be fair to say that within the limitations of whatever four-power agreements are binding upon us, we are no longer proposing to await decisions of the Council of Foreign Ministers in respect to the mutual integration of the three other zones . . . and that we are now proceeding . . . without waiting for programs from the Council of Foreign Ministers, always intending . . . to leave our programs open to any who wish to subscribe?
> *Marshall:* That is correct, Senator. We are going ahead exactly on that basis. [59]

Of Myths and Realities

The background and origins of the Marshall Plan for European economic recovery described in this study suggest that neither the official and orthodox interpretations of its inception and purposes nor the ones offered by the revisionists are complete and credible.

CONTAINMENT

It would be ridiculous indeed to deny that the doctrine of containment and the hope for a Communist rollback were features of the discussion and debate on the European recovery program.[60] Kennan's chairmanship of the PPS would have been an anomaly if it had been otherwise. But Kennan and the PPS actually recommended on May 23, 1947, that "immediate measures be taken to straighten out public opinion on some implications of the President's message on Greece and Turkey." The PPS did not see "communist activities as the root of the difficulties of western Europe," and it wanted "to clarify what the press has unfortunately come to identify as the 'Truman Doctrine,' and to remove in particular two damaging impressions which are current in large sections of American public opinion." The two impressions were, first, "that the United States approach to world problems is a defensive reaction to communist pressure and that the effort to restore sound economic conditions in other countries is only a by-product of this reaction and not something we would be interested in doing if there were no communist menace," and second, "that the Truman Doctrine is a blank check to give economic and military aid to any area in the world where the communists show signs of being successful." [61]

But, as it turned out, there was no containing the doctrine of containment, to which Kennan himself contributed with his article in *Foreign Affairs*.[62] The State Department could not carry out the PPS's recommendation, because to do so effectively would have required a forthright discussion of German recovery, which was so essential to the Marshall Plan. As I have shown, a forthright discussion of the German problem aroused Bidault and threatened the political stability of France. Closer to home in the State Department, a forthright discussion of Germany would have called into question the "official" explanations for the difficulties in Germany since 1945. It would have called into question Byrnes's explanations of his failures in the CFM and of the origins of the bizone. It would have called into question the State Department's interpretation of Clay's reparations suspension, and it would inevitably have opened the subject of "hidden reparations." It would have called into question Marshall's explanations of the failure of the Moscow CFM, and it would have challenged the credibility of other pronouncements, releases, and statements—all of which were public knowledge. In a sense, Kennan, Acheson, Matthews, Cohen, Bohlen, and others in the State Department lived to reap the fruits of their own suspicions and of the various tests they had devised and used to frustrate the Russians and keep Clay and the Army off France's back in 1945 and 1946.

An effort to contain the doctrine of containment in 1947 and 1948 would also have flown in the face of a broad spectrum of opinion in the newly elected Eightieth Congress, where the State Department's wartime and immediate postwar stewardship was already under attack for "appeasement" of Russia. Scaring hell out of the Congress and the American people and emphasizing the Communist menace to promote the Greece-Turkey aid bill had paid off, as Joseph Jones pointed out so clearly.[63] In any case, the State Department took a pragmatic approach, rather than follow the PPS's recommendation to correct the anti-Communist emphasis of the Truman Doctrine. It chose to ride the Marshall Plan home safely on the high tide of anti-Communist rhetoric and opinion (which it had helped to further), rather than to risk the plan's defeat and the consequent rehabilitation of Germany by the Army and the Congress on the advice and recommendations of Herbert Hoover—or according to some other "bright and unworkable ideas," as Marshall put it.[64] Naturally, the flow of events themselves contributed to the State Department's option. How would it have been able to abandon the anti-Communist line and reconcile that with Molotov's behavior in Paris in June and July 1947; with the Soviet Union's pressure on Poland and Czechoslovakia not to participate in the Marshall Plan; with the creation of the Cominform in October 1947; and with the coup in Czechoslovakia in 1948?

OPEN-DOOR DIPLOMACY

It would be futile to deny that the concepts that have been described as characteristic of the diplomacy of the open door influenced and guided American policymakers in the inception, discussion, debate, and passage of the European recovery program. But to conclude, as William A. Williams did for example, that "the problem was to coerce the Russians, help western Europe, and thereby establish the reality of an open door system throughout the world" is to ignore the evidence and resort to a secular devil-theory of historical causation designed, perhaps, to bolster those already converted and to spread the gospel among the gullible and the naive.[65] Politicians, along with other mortals, never stand naked of the robes of the past as they make their way toward decisions; they do not go from day to day and issue to issue with an ideological blank slate. In other words, unless one expects miraculous conversions or a revolution, one can hardly expect the policymakers of 1947 to have forgotten or rejected Cordell Hull, Woodrow Wilson, and a host of others as they moved toward resolution of one of the major postwar problems with which they were faced: making peace with Germany and reconstructing war-torn Europe.

In any case, if published analyses and public rhetoric are reliable, there is little doubt that the American policymaking establishment was imbued with, permeated by, and committed to the private-enterprise economic system. American leaders wanted to create and preserve the forms of political and social organization and the patterns of international trade (multilateralism) most conducive to the free-enterprise economic system. They wanted an interlocking, worldwide system of production and consumption, and they apparently believed that that was the most efficient, effective, and just foundation for peace, prosperity, and a rising standard of living for all.[66] The "conditions" laid down by the Americans in Paris late in August 1947 included demands that the participating countries undertake internal financial and monetary reforms, stabilization of currencies, the establishment of proper rates of exchange, as well as "steps to facilitate the greatest practicable interchange of goods and services among themselves, adopting definite measures directed toward the progressive reduction and eventual elimination of barriers to trade within the area, in accordance with the principles of the ITO Charter." [67] The American determination to achieve these and other objectives in Europe helps to explain the progressive shift from the *invitation* of June 1947 to the *dictation* of October 1947: the progressive shift from letting the Europeans draft their own recovery program, to "friendly aid in the drafting," to Clayton's personal missionary work in the capitals of Europe in June and July, to the more stringent (but informal) advice and requirements of mid-August, to the presentation of "conditions" and "essentials" to the CEEC in Paris late in August and to the governments themselves early in September, and finally to the outright intervention in the development of the CEEC's program in September, October, and November. But, as I have shown in the analysis, the progressive shift from the *invitation* of June to the *dictation* of October was also heavily influenced and conditioned by the immediate objective of ensuring Germany's rehabilitation, which was to be dovetailed with the larger European program. In fact, it can be argued that the attempt to resolve the German dilemma was the occasion for calling forth the principles of the open door, rather than the reverse.

Significantly, Kennan—who had insisted in May (over the fierce protests of Clayton) that the Europeans themselves draft the plan—was the one who marshaled the major arguments in September for United States dictation of the final program of European recovery. In the end, he said, the United States should not ask the Europeans, but should just tell them what they would get. Kennan's reversal suggests that there was no clear "open door" plan when Marshall spoke in June, and it supports the idea that bureaucratic tinkering to solve the economic dilemma in Germany gave rise to the Marshall Plan. . . .

MARSHALL'S PLAN

Current interpretations of the Marshall Plan are all predicated, in some respect or other, on the assumption that there existed a rational plan or policy for European recovery in June 1947. But Marshall later denied that he had a plan at the time, and my study has demonstrated that his statements were accurate. When he spoke at Harvard on June 5, 1947, Marshall had no plan for European recovery, for containment, for creating a multilateral trade world, for promoting the open door in Europe, for forestalling a postwar American depression. He had a practical problem that he thought would have to be resolved, for its own sake and before someone with "all kinds of bright and unworkable ideas" tried to do it. With that in mind, the origins of the Marshall Plan may be reviewed.

Faced with the post-Potsdam impasse in Germany caused by France's actions, and appalled at the high cost of the occupation in appropriated dollars, the Army and Clay maneuvered for two years to try to bring France around. But the State Department refused either to apply sanctions against France or to admit publicly that France was indeed the major problem in Germany. Instead, State Department functionaries expressed suspicions about Russian intentions and long-range objectives, and they did so despite the Army's protests, despite the Army's evidence that the Russians were cooperating in Berlin to fulfill the terms of the Potsdam Agreement. Eventually, the State Department devised tests of Russian intentions, and finally its officials asserted openly that Russia had violated the Potsdam Agreement and other things. Meanwhile, the Russians went their own way in their zone. The British, who agreed with the Army on the need to reduce occupation costs in Germany, threatened several times to adopt unilateral policies in their zone. In July 1946 Bevin outlined a British plan to promote a self-sufficient economy in the British zone, which included the Ruhr. Searching for an alternative to Britain's plan for unilateral action in the Ruhr, Byrnes invited all the occupation powers to join their zones with the American zone in economic unity. Britain eventually accepted Byrnes's invitation, but France and Russia did not. Britain and the American Army expected zonal union to result in substantial reductions in the financial burdens of the occupation, and the two military governments developed a three-year plan to make the bizone economically self-supporting by 1949. But the State Department, which made policy for the United States in Germany, would not agree to economic policies in bizonal Germany that impinged on its plans for rehabilitating liberated Europe first. Neither would the State Department accept bizonal policies and practices that threatened France's political stability or left France's expectations for German coal exports unfulfilled.

Early in 1947 the Army and the British got an ally. The Republican leaders of the newly elected Eightieth Congress were determined to cut costs and to wrest power from the Executive Branch, from the Democratic administration. Some of them were prepared to conduct an investigation into the causes of the "failure" in Germany; some were prepared to review the State Department's wartime and postwar stewardship of American foreign policy; many of them were spoiling for a political showdown with the party of the New Deal. The combination of Congress's inclination to intervene in the German occupation, the Army's restlessness, the CFM's failure to make progress on a German settlement in Moscow, a British decision to increase German production, and Marshall's steady hand in the State Department finally broke the post-Potsdam impasse and inspired the Marshall Plan.

At the Moscow CFM in April 1947, Marshall agreed privately with Bevin to reorganize the British and American zones, to raise the German level of industry, and to make the two zones economically self-sustaining by 1949. Marshall was relatively new to his job at the time. He was burdened with the normal demands of bringing order to the shambles of policy left by Byrnes, who reportedly had carried the State Department around the world in his briefcase. Marshall's well-developed sense of procedure, order, and harmony was heavily taxed by the Greece-Turkey aid bill, the Austrian treaty, the Truman Doctrine, and the CFM in Moscow. He was pushed and pulled by advice from the State Department, the War Department, Dulles, and OMGUS; by France's demands for coal and other concessions; by Britain's initiatives to reduce Britain's dollar costs in Germany; and by Herbert Hoover's "independent" actions regarding German policy. But he was also mindful of the political currents in the United States that had brought forth the Eightieth Congress, pledged to economy in government; to reducing the power of the Executive Branch; to fighting communism at home and abroad; to turning around the diplomacy that had produced Yalta, Potsdam, the changes in Eastern Europe, and the "failure" in Germany. Instinctively sensing that the Moscow decisions on Germany would cause trouble, Marshall prevailed upon Bevin to agree to a six-week delay, in announcing them. Upon further reflection, and after consultations with Dulles, Clay, and his State Department advisers, he concluded that the Moscow decisions on Germany were politically dangerous and economically unwise. Although they might solve the German problem, they would do so at economic and political costs that his own department would not accept, and that would be virtually impossible to justify to potential critics who would charge the United States with rehabilitating its recently defeated enemy ahead of its friends and allies. The Moscow decisions on Germany threatened to cause political disaster in France. They would certainly bring heavy criticism from France, from Russia, from German hard-liners in the United States (such as Henry Morgenthau and the Society for the Prevention of World War III), from the liberal press in the United States (such as *PM* and the *New Republic*), and from leftists and Communists everywhere. Marshall decided that his commitment to Bevin would have to be modified, and that the Army's, Hoover's, and the Congress's plans for German recovery would have to be headed off.

True to his training and experience—and perhaps to his instincts as well—Marshall called for the equivalent of military staff studies on his problems. Immediately upon his return from the Moscow CFM he instructed Kennan to activate the Policy Planning Staff in the State Department and to prepare the studies that eventually became the basis for the Marshall Plan. Kennan and the PPS tried to resolve Marshall's post-Moscow dilemma by recommending a short-term program (Coal for Europe) that would do in Germany much of what he and Bevin had already decided in Moscow to do, and a long-term program of European economic recovery to be developed by the Europeans themselves. The short-term program would be merged with the long-term program and thus diffuse domestic criticism of Germany's recovery and help to ensure against the economic and political disaster that a "Germany first" program threatened to call forth, particularly in France, but not exclusively there. The PPS proposal of May 23, 1947, was in fact a plan to implement and gain acceptance for the German decisions that Marshall and Bevin had already made; decisions that raised the specter of a restored Germany equipped with the manpower, the resources, and the technical facilities that Germans had used with such profound effect in the past.

As Marshall said over and over, and as I have demonstrated, there was no "Marshall Plan" in June 1947. When Clayton went to Europe for consultations late in June, he had specific instructions about a

German-based Coal for Europe program and about socialization, but he had only very general and vague conceptions of what was to become the European recovery program. What he did in the capitals of Europe with respect to the latter eventually caused much concern in the State Department. The minutes of a round of discussions in the State Department in August 1947 show a "consensus that Mr. Clayton, while generally aware of departmental thinking with regard to the 'Plan,' holds fundamental divergent views on some aspects." The minutes also make clear that "a comprehensive departmental position has not been officially approved," and they show that "the time has come to firm up the overall departmental position." [68] The upshot was a formal policy statement, which was sent to Clayton and Caffery on August 26, 1947, nearly three months after the Harvard speech. But the "plan" was still incomplete, for Kennan and Bonesteel were dispatched to Paris personally to deliver oral instructions and policies regarding the "general political situation." [69] In short, what existed in the summer and fall of 1947 were the Bevin-Marshall decisions taken at the Moscow CFM, decisions that raised a spectrum of actual and potential domestic and foreign problems that would have to be resolved, defused, and—if necessary—kept from the arena of public discussion and debate, at least for a time.

Perhaps typical of the system that gave rise to it, the Marshall Plan was actually a series of pragmatic bureaucratic decisions, maneuvers, compromises, and actions. Typically also, contemporaries, commentators, and historians have construed the entire series as a plan for purposes of communication and rationalization (and maybe for other reasons). The questions that bureaucrats struggled with included the following: How could they sell a European recovery program to the American public and to an American Congress publicly committed to economy and reduced government spending? How could they explain a new foreign aid program to members of Congress who had already criticized wartime lend-lease and postwar United Nations (UNRRA) aid? How could they reconcile the fundamental differences between the Army and the State Department regarding the purposes, objectives, and length of the American presence in Europe? How could they reconcile the demands of France for German coal to implement the Monnet Plan and the demands of the American and British military governments for coal to provide a self-sufficient German economy? How could they increase coal production in the Ruhr and prevent the British and the German Social Democrats from alienating the American Congress and others by nationalizing the German coal industry? How could they reconcile the conflicting demands of the victorious powers for German reparations and of the military governments for a

German industrial base with which to achieve self-sufficiency for the bizone? How could they reconcile the conflicting demands of Germany's neighbors for cheap German imports and of the military governments for sufficient German export proceeds with which to pay for needed food and raw materials imports, and for previous outlays for such imports?

The series of pragmatic bureaucratic decisions and compromises that became the Marshall Plan included the decisions to do something about German recovery. Neither the Army, nor the British, nor the Congress would settle for less. It included the maneuvers to prevent socialization or nationalization in the Ruhr, and perhaps in all of Germany. Neither the Army, nor Forrestal, nor the Congress would settle for less. It included the actions and maneuvers to restore France and maintain Bidault in power—at least to prevent a leftist United Front in France, and definitely to forestall Communist ascendancy there. Neither the French government nor the State Department would settle for less. It included actions to rehabilitate the liberated nations and Germany's neighbors other than France, some of whom (especially Belgium, Luxembourg, and the Netherlands) were sympathetic to the economic rehabilitation of Germany while mindful of the need for continued security. It included a decision to reduce Germany's economic potential for war by resuming dismantling and reparations, a decision that was in turn countered by actions to rehabilitate Germany's coal, steel, transport, and other industries in the interests of short-term, speedy, and less costly European recovery, and of creating or promoting the eventual formation of a Western European economic and perhaps political union. The series included maneuvers to satisfy France's demands for coal, coke, security, and territory, but there were also actions that forestalled complete satisfaction of France's demands. It included compromises to satisfy Congressional demands for economy and an end to foreign aid, but there were also requests for billions of dollars of foreign assistance that somehow had to be made acceptable to the Congress. To satisfy the Congress and the public, the Truman administration talked about the advantages of multilateral trade and the free flow of goods which foreign aid would stimulate. It talked about the immediate effects of bad crops in Europe; about the hardships caused by the blizzards and the hard winter of 1946–47. It talked about the Marshall Plan as a one-shot deal,[70] as an experiment in pump priming, as a means to forestall a postwar recession, as a humanitarian act, as an economic effort that would reduce the need for military preparedness, as a measure for ensuring access to strategic resources, and as a hard-headed venture in the promotion of peace and security.[71] But the State Department also resorted to a practice it had used with effect before: it described and analyzed "the broad global picture" by emphasizing "the two-world assumption," the need to counterbalance the "Soviet World," and the desirability of "treating Europe west of the Iron Curtain on a regional basis." [72]

Interestingly, Bidault's and Molotov's actions in 1947 show that both France and Russia understood the primary motivation for the Marshall Plan to have been the American economic dilemma in Germany. Typically, the French would not even discuss Germany at first. When Bidault learned from Clayton and Harriman about the plans the Americans had for increasing coal production in the Ruhr and raising the level of industry of the bizone, he threatened to sabotage the Paris Marshall Plan talks and warned that if he did so there would be no Europe. As I have shown, Bidault and the French eventually bowed to the inevitable, but only after they realized that the State Department was as determined in 1947 to solve the German problem as the Army had been in 1945 and 1946. Unlike the Army, however, the State Department gave Bidault an opportunity to compromise and retreat without loss of face and power. As a result, the French modified their demands for separation of the Ruhr and Rhineland from Germany, and they agreed to negotiate on reparations, restitutions, and other economic questions arising from French annexation of the Saar. In turn, the State Department advised France that the United States supported in principle some form of international board that would control and allocate the basic production of the Ruhr. Molotov—also typically—protested the Marshall Plan procedures, probably for substantive reasons. He objected to making decisions on Germany outside the organized Council of Foreign Ministers. The State Department never gave *him* an opportunity to retreat gracefully or politically, and he apparently tried to find out what the Americans had promised Bidault and Bevin as a *quid pro quo* for their support of the Marshall Plan. He asked Bidault and Bevin directly whether they had inside information on the plan, he warned them of the serious consequences of any independent actions they might take in concert with the Americans, and then he left the Paris talks on the Marshall Plan early in July 1947. He interpreted Marshall's initiative in terms of the Marxist-Leninist dialectic, and, after he left Paris, he apparently contributed to the decisions in Moscow to establish the Cominform, to implement the so-called "Molotov Plan," and to organize and mobilize the vanguard that would lead mankind into the future.

Notes

1. See Lucius D. Clay, *Decision in Germany* (Garden City, N.Y., 1950),

p. 109, for a comment on the lingering sentiment in the United States for a "scorched earth" policy.

2. James W. Riddleberger, "United States Policy on the Treatment of Germany," State Dept. *Bulletin,* XIII (Nov. 25, 1945), 841–49.

3. Kennan to Acheson, May 23, 1947 *FRUS (Foreign Relations of the United States),* 1947, III, 223–30. [PPS: Policy Planning Staff.]

4. See Memorandum of Conversation, Ernest Lindley *(Newsweek)* and Mr. Williamson and Mr. Fuller, Aug. 11, 1947, RG 59, file 740.00119 Control (Germany)/8–1147, NA (National Archives, Washington), for the statement that "the Department was confronted with the necessity of rebuilding [the] German economy in such a manner as not to jeopardize the interests of European and world security."

5. War Dept., from SecWar, SecState, and SecNavy, to Clay, June 19, 1947, RG 107, file ASW 091 Germany, Book 2, Box 26, NA.

6. War Dept. to OMGUS, July 2, 1947, RG 107, file ASW 091 Germany, Book 2, Box 26, NA.

7. Minutes, Meeting of SecState, SecWar, and SecNavy, July 3, 1947, War Dept. Papers, SecWar, Office of Special Assistant, 334, Committee of Three, Jan. 1947– , NA.

8. Petersen to Clay, July 10, 1947, RG 107, file ASW 091 Germany, Book 2, Box 26, NA.

9. See JCS 1779, V, 18c and V, 16c, in U.S. Dept. of State, *Germany, 1947–1949,* Pub. 3556 (Washington, 1950), pp. 37–38.

10. Memorandum, Matthews to Lovett, July 11, 1947, *FRUS,* 1947, III, 717–22.

11. Caffery to SecState, July 11, 1947, *FRUS,* 1947, II, 983–86.

12. BrEmbassy to SecState, *Aide-Mémoire,* July 15, 1947, *FRUS,* 1947, II, 986–87, and note 16; Petersen to Clay, July 15, 1947, RG 107, file ASW 091 Germany, Book 2, Box 26, NA; Caffery to SecState, July 17, 1947, as noted in *FRUS,* 1947, II, 997, note 29; Caffery to SecState, July 20, 1947, *ibid.,* 997–99.

13. SecState to Bidault, July 21, 1947, *FRUS,* 1947, II, 1003–4.

14. Memorandum, by Director of PPS (Kennan), July 18?, 1947, *FRUS,* 1947, III, 332–33.

15. Clinton Anderson to Truman, July 18, 1947, Anderson Files (Germany Trip), Box 8, Truman Library; Marshall to Anderson, July 22, 1947, *FRUS,* 1947, II, 1154, note 56, 1156–57.

16. Marshall to Douglas, Aug. 12, 1947, *FRUS,* 1947, II, 1027–29.

17. Douglas to Lovett, Aug. 22, 1947, *FRUS,* 1947, II, 1047–49.

18. ActgSecState to AmEmbassy, London, Aug. 27, 1947, *FRUS,* 1947, II, 1063–64; Douglas to SecState, Aug. 27, 1947, *ibid.,* 1064–66. The record shows, however, that Douglas advised the French delegate (Massigli) informally of the U.S. position, which Douglas and his colleagues had passed on to Bidault in Paris on Aug. 19, 1947.

19. See Memorandum, Hickerson to Lovett, Aug. 23, 1947, *FRUS,* 1947, 1050–54, for a judgment that the American and British unwillingness to discuss with the French an international board for the Ruhr was a "negative

policy," and a prediction that "a serious crisis will be precipitated if we insist on the . . . negative position."

20. Caffery to SecState, Aug. 19, 1947, *FRUS*, 1947, II, 1041–42. But see Memorandum of Bonnet-Lovett Conversation, Aug. 21, 1947, *ibid.*, 1046–47, for the record of Bonnet's efforts to get a commitment on a Ruhr authority from Lovett.

21. The communiqué is in U.S. Dept. of State, *Germany, 1947–1949*, pp. 356–59. See also AmEmbassy, London, to SecState, Aug. 27, 1947, War Dept. Papers, file WDSCA 014 Germany, Sec. XXV, NA, and Hickerson to James C. H. Bonbright, Aug. 30, 1947, RG 59, Hickerson Papers, folder B, Box 4, NA, for the observation that "your clients [the French] behaved badly but I suppose no more badly than usual."

22. Murphy to Douglas, Sept. 5, 1947, *FRUS*, 1947, II, 1089–90; Murphy to Hickerson, Oct. 1, 1947, *ibid.*, 1096–98; OMGUS, from Clay, to TAG, for Noce, Sept. 30, 1947, RG 165, file WDSCA 463.3, Sec. VI, NA; OMGUS, from Wilkinson, to C/S, U.S. Army, for Clay, Oct. 10, 1947, *ibid.;* Draper to Clay, Nov. 22, 1947, *FRUS*, 1947, II, 725–26; OMGUS, from Hays, to Draper, CC 2392, Nov. 24, 1947, War Dept. Papers, file SAOUS 463.3 Germany, NA; CC 2510, Dec. 6, 1947, *ibid.;* Memorandum, William C. Baker, CAD, to Chief, CAD, Dec. 10, 1947, War Dept. Papers, file CSCAD 014 Germany, Sec. 29, NA.

23. See Douglas to Lovett, Sept. 2, 1947, *FRUS*, 1947, II, 1068–69; Caffery to SecState, Sept. 16, 1947, *ibid.*, 1072, and note 40; Memorandum of Marshall-Bidault Conversation, Nov. 28, 1947, *ibid.*, 739, note 74; *ibid.*, 1097; and John Gimbel, *The American Occupation of Germany* (Stanford, Calif., 1968), pp. 198ff, 208–9.

24. Marshall, Report on Moscow CFM, April 28, 1947, U.S. Dept. of State, *Germany, 1947–1949*, pp. 57–63; Dulles, Report on Moscow Conference, April 30, 1947, *Vital Speeches*, XIII (May 15, 1947), 450–53. Dulles said that "as we studied the problem of Germany in its European setting, we became more and more convinced that there is no economic solution along purely national lines." [CFM: Council of Foreign Ministers.]

25. War Dept., from SecWar, SecState, SecNavy, to Clay, June 19, 1947, RG 107, file ASW 091 Germany, Book 2, Box 26, NA; Clayton to SecState, June 25, 1947, *FRUS*, 1947, II, 932–33; Minutes, Meeting of SecState, SecWar, and SecNavy, July 3, 1947, War Dept. Papers, SecWar, Office of Special Assistant, file 334, Committee of Three, Jan. 1947–, NA. [SWNCC: State, War, Navy Coordinating Committee.]

26. Clayton, "The European Crisis," *FRUS*, 1947, III, 230–32; Caffery to SecState, June 28, 1947, *ibid.*, 297–99; Douglas to Marshall, June 28, 1947, RG 59, file 840.50 Recovery/6-2847, NA. [CEEC: Committee on European Economic Cooperation.]

27. Caffery to SecState, July 20, 1947, *FRUS*, 1947, III, 333–35. See Caffery to SecState, July 27, 1947, *ibid.*, 338–39; July 29, 1947, *ibid.*, 339–41, for further reports of French objection to German recovery.

28. Hickerson, Memorandum, Aug. 11, 1947, *FRUS*, 1947, III, 351–55,

said: "The United States must present a united front when talking to other powers. It would be undesirable to have two independent groups of U.S. representatives, one representing our interests in the over-all European recovery and the other representing our interests in Germany alone." Naturally, Hickerson thought the State Department should do it. See also SecState to AmEmbassy, Paris, Aug. 11, 1947, *ibid.*, 350–51; Caffery to SecState, Aug. 12, 1947, *ibid.*, 355–56; Memorandum Prepared by PPS, Aug. 14, 1947, *ibid.*, 360–63.

29. Lovett to Clayton and Caffery, Aug. 14, 1947, *FRUS,* 1947, III, 356–60.

30. Caffery to SecState, Aug. 20, 1947, *FRUS,* 1947, III, 364–67.

31. Douglas to SecState, Aug. 21, 1947, *FRUS,* 1947, III, 368–69.

32. Minutes of Meeting on Marshall "Plan," Aug. 22, 1947, *FRUS,* 1947, III, 369–72; Lovett to SecState, Aug. 24, 1947, *ibid.,* 372–75.

33. The President's Committee on Foreign Aid, *European Recovery and American Aid* (Washington, 1947), pp. 22–23 (emphasis added). For statistics on the comparative lag in German production see *ibid.,* p. 117; U.S. Congress, Senate, Committee on Foreign Relations, 80th Cong., 2d Sess., *Hearings . . . on United States Assistance to European Economic Recovery* (Washington, 1948), pp. 249–50; and Bert F. Hoselitz, "Four Reports on Economic Aid to Europe," *The Journal of Political Economy,* LVI (April 1948), 112–13.

34. Marshall, "Problems of European Revival and German and Austrian Peace Settlements," Nov. 18, 1947, in U.S. Dept. of State, *Germany, 1947– 1949,* p. 13.

35. *FRUS,* 1947, III, 375, note 5; Lovett to Clayton and Caffery, Aug. 26, 1947, *ibid.,* 383–91; Clayton to SecState, Aug. 31, 1947, *ibid.,* 391–96.

36. C. H. Bonesteel to Lovett, Subj: Discussion of Bizonal Economic Plans at Paris Conference, Aug. 27, 1947, RG 59, file 740.00119 Control (Germany)/8-2747, NA.

37. War Dept., from Noce, to OMGUS, Sept. 3, 1947, RG 165, file WDSCA 334 EECE, Sec. II, Box 319, NA; SecState to Douglas, Sept. 5, 1947, *FRUS,* 1947, III, 409–10; Memorandum of Conversation, Lovett, Saltzman, Draper, Clay, and Gordon Gray, Oct. 18, 1947, RG 59, file 740.00119 Control (Germany)/10-1847, NA.

38. ActgSecState to SecState, March 20, 1947, *FRUS,* 1947, II, 394–95; Meeting of the Non-Partisan Committee of Nineteen Distinguished Citizens, July 23, 1947, Records of the President's Committee on Foreign Aid, 1947, file PCFA—Minutes & Meetings, Box 1, Truman Library.

39. Minutes of the Meeting of the Subcommittee on Economic and Financial Analysis in Hanover, N.H., Aug. 15, 1947, Records of the President's Committee on Foreign Aid, 1947, file Subcommittee—Economic and Financial Analysis, Box 6, Truman Library. Calvin Hoover, it will be recalled, had been the Chairman of the OMGUS German Standard-of-Living Board in 1945 and had left Germany disappointed and unhappy with existing policy and with Germany's economic prospects for the future.

40. Minutes of the President's Committee of Nineteen on Foreign Aid,

Sept. 10–11, 1947, Records of the PCFA, 1947, file PCFA—Minutes & Meetings, Box 1, Truman Library; Notes for Press Conference, 9/11/47, *ibid.;* Interdepartmental Committee on Marshall Plan, Minutes, Sept. 9, 1947, Clifford Papers, file ERP—ECA Miscellaneous, Truman Library.

41. Owen D. Young to Harriman, Sept. 12, 1947, Records of the PCFA, 1947, file Member—Owen D. Young, Box 2, Truman Library.

42. The President's Committee on Foreign Aid, *European Recóvery and American Aid,* pp. 3, 7, 33–34, 117–22, and *passim.*

43. SecState to Douglas, Sept. 5, 1947, *FRUS,* 1947, III, 409–10; Sept. 8, 1947, *ibid.,* 410, note 2, and 418–19.

44. SecState to Douglas, Sept. 8, 1947, *FRUS,* 1947, III, 418–19.

45. Douglas to SecState, cable number 4950, Sept. 12, 1947, *FRUS,* 1947, III, 428–29; cable number 4951, Sept. 12, 1947, *ibid.,* 429–30.

46. Douglas to SecState, Sept. 17, 1947, RG 59, file 840.50 Recovery/9-1747, NA.

47. Clayton to Lovett, Aug. 25, 1947, *FRUS,* 1947, III, 377–79.

48. Lovett to Clayton and Caffery, Aug. 26, 1947, *FRUS,* 1947, III, 383–89.

49. Clayton to Lovett, Aug. 31, 1947, *FRUS,* 1947, III, 391–96.

50. Lovett to Marshall, Aug. 31, 1947, *FRUS,* 1947, III, 396–97.

51. Kennan, Situation with Respect to European Recovery Program, Sept. 4, 1947, *FRUS,* 1947, III, 397–405.

52. Caffery, from Dept. Economic Advisers, to Lovett and others, Sept. 5, 1947, *FRUS,* 1947, III, 405–8; ActgSecState, Circular Telegram to Representatives Accredited to CEEC Nations and Murphy, Sept. 7, 1947, *ibid.,* 412–15.

53. *FRUS,* 1947, III, 415, note 3; Douglas to SecState, Sept. 9, 1947, *ibid.,* 420.

54. Caffery to SecState, Sept. 11, 1947, *FRUS,* 1947, III, 421–23.

55. Caffery to SecState, Sept 12, 1947, *FRUS,* 1947, III, 425–28; Douglas to SecState, cable number 4950, Sept. 12, 1947, *ibid.,* 428–29; cable number 4951, Sept. 12, 1947, *ibid.,* 429–30. See also Douglas to SecState, Sept. 17, 1947, *ibid.,* 435, for a repetition of the advice to press for inclusion of the bizone *only after* the first report had been received.

56. Editorial Note, *FRUS,* 1947, III, 439–41; SecState to AmEmbassy, London, Nov. 5, 1947, RG 59, file 840.50 Recovery/11-547, NA; Frank A. Southard to Secretary Snyder, Oct. 3, 1947, Snyder Papers, file Congress —Interim Aid Program, 1947–48, folder 1, Truman Library; U.S. Congress, Senate, *Congressional Record,* 80th Cong., 2d Sess., March 11, 1948, pp. 2528–31.

57. Record of a Meeting Between Members of the Advisory Steering Committee and the CEEC Delegation, Nov. 4, 1947, *FRUS,* 1947, III, 463–70.

58. Ernst H. Van Der Beugel, *From Marshall Aid to Atlantic Partnership: European Integration as a Concern of American Foreign Policy* (Amsterdam, 1966), esp. pp. 77–93. See also Arthur Krock, in *New York Times,* Oct. 5, 1947, DNC Clippings, Box 24, Truman Library; Sir Hubert

Henderson, "The European Economic Report," *International Affairs*, XXIV (Jan. 1948), 19–29; and Michael Straight, "The Betrayal of the Original Concept," *The New Republic*, 118 (Jan. 12, 1948), 9–11.

59. U.S. Congress, Senate, Committee on Foreign Relations, 80th Cong., 2d Sess., *Hearings . . . on . . . European Economic Recovery*, Jan. 8, 1948, pp. 11–12.

60. See, for example, U.S. Congress, House, Committee on Foreign Affairs, 80th Cong., 1st Sess., *Hearings . . . on European Interim Aid . . .* (Washington, 1947), pp. 121–22, for a discussion on Nov. 13, 1947, about using an economic pistol on the Russians and forcing a change in the Soviet Union, as well as the prospects of a successful program to roll back Communism behind the iron curtain.

61. Kennan to Acheson, May 23, 1947, *FRUS*, 1947, III, 223–30.

62. George F. Kennan, [Mr. X], "The Sources of Soviet Conduct," *Foreign Affairs*, XXV (July 1947), 566–82.

63. Joseph M. Jones, *The Fifteen Weeks* (New York, 1955), esp. pp. 138–40, 150–51, 175–76.

64. See George F. Kennan, *Memoirs, 1925–1950* (Boston, 1967), pp. 325–26; Jones, pp. 223–24.

65. William A. Williams, *The Tragedy of American Diplomacy*, rev. & enlarged ed. (New York, 1962), p. 268.

66. See, for example, Thomas C. Blaisdell, "The Foreign Aid Program and United States Commercial Policy," *Proceedings of the Academy of Political Science*, XXIII (Jan. 1950), 397–407.

67. Caffery to SecState, Aug. 31, 1947, *FRUS*, 1947, III, 391–96.

68. Minutes of Meeting on Marshall "Plan," Aug. 22, 1947, *FRUS*, 1947, III, 370.

69. Lovett to Clayton and Caffery, Aug. 26, 1947, *FRUS*, 1947, III, 383–89.

70. U.S. Congress, Senate, Committee on Foreign Relations, 80th Cong., 2d Sess., *Hearings . . . on . . . European Economic Recovery*, Jan. 8, 1948, esp. p. 4.

71. See, for example, Marshall's and Lovett's remarks, respectively, in U.S. Congress, House, Committee on Foreign Affairs, 80th Cong., 1st Sess., *Emergency Foreign Aid. Hearings . . .* , Nov. 10, 1947, esp. p. 3; Nov. 12, 1947, esp. p. 44.

72. C. H. Bonesteel to Lovett, Memorandum, Subj: Discussion of Bizonal Economic Plans at Paris Conference, Aug. 27, 1947, RG 59, file 740.00119 Control (Germany)/8-2747, NA.

6

Hadley Arkes

Bureaucracy, the Marshall Plan, and the National Interest

The following selection is the work of a political scientist and is included here for a purpose different from that for which it was written. Arkes' book is an effort to discuss the origins and administrative structure of the European Recovery Program—with its managing body, the Economic Cooperation Administration (ECA)—to make an argument about political philosophy. For Arkes the evolution of the Marshall Plan as an administrative entity represented a healthy application of national interest. By national interest the author does not mean the geopolitical requirements of a state, but its very regime, i.e., its constitutional order and the core values that support its political and economic system. At each stage of its development, Arkes argues, the Marshall Plan forced American policymakers to articulate what they believed their country should be trying to achieve in light of its basic regime and values. Even more specifically it forced Congress to confront a problem that was both administrative and political, to take full acount of the consequences of its legislation in terms of an ongoing program and not merely to design a scheme for aid that would then escape its responsibility. In short, the Marshall Plan was allegedly a process of education for Americans. Although it was not unselfish, it was nonetheless elevating by virtue of its incentive for civic reflection.

I have chosen Arkes' chapter 14, "Theory and Coercion in the ECA," to illustrate another aspect of the program. Through the material in this segment the student can think about what political intervention in Europe was likely to accompany economic aid. Americans sought to make a distinction between political intervention and economic advising and Arkes documents their effort. Still, the

*distinction was often naive, and as the chapter shows, they often failed
to concede how much political influence was exerted. Nor, I would
argue, does this selection even get into the major intervention behind
the Marshall Plan. The program itself was based on winning the
cooperation of those politicians, businessmen, and labor leaders abroad
who believed in economic growth and were prepared to subordinate
any aspirations for redistributing power within a capitalist system. The
very process of offering aid and inviting Europeans to work out its
application tended to bring into coalition socialists and centrists and
conservatives in Europe and exclude the communists, as Yergin's earlier
chapter also suggests. Thus political intervention was not really
necessary once the European Recovery Program had been put into
place and started functioning. The major political exclusion had already
taken place. Arkes' discussion, however, remains a careful examination
of how United States officials sought to work out economic aid as a
problem in itself and not merely as an anticommunist measure. In their
day-to-day operations Americans involved in the European Recovery
Program saw their efforts as a politically neutral crusade on behalf of
productivity and technology and growth, and the crusading vigor they
demonstrated in this cause is worth recollecting. The passage is reprinted
with the permission of the author and Princeton University Press.*

Theory and Coercion in the ECA

I

To say that the ECA was not running the economies of the Marshall
Plan nations was not to say, however, that the agency had no important influence on the internal decisions of the ERP countries. The manipulation of aid that could represent some 3 to 5 percent of a national
budget would inevitably have some bearing on the choices available
to the national governments. But the "intervention" in this case had a
remote quality that was far more characteristic of the ECA. It inhered
a continuous pressure on the Marshall Plan countries for basic investment (as opposed to consumption), and this pressure in turn emanated
from the antibureaucratic features of the ECA—more specifically,
from the basic commitment of the ECA to cut back its program with
each successive year.

What we have called the "debureaucratization" features of the ECA
referred to the preferences for a decentralized agency that would complete its temporary assignment on schedule and leave no bureaucratic
vestiges behind. There was an attendant theory here, also, which sug-

gested that the prospect of a permanent foreign assistance program might undermine the ends of the Marshall Plan. Principally, it was feared that the Europeans would have less incentive to make hard domestic decisions if they thought American aid would always be available as a crutch. As the program wore on, this theory acquired a force of its own, and the debureaucratization theme assumed the weight of a primary commitment or an independent policy value.

When rumors arose in 1949 that the United States might continue the Marshall Plan after 1952, Hoffman declared: "I can think of nothing that will interfere more with achieving the aims of this act than to have the impression get out that this act will be extended. I think this particular activity must end on June 30, 1952." Senator Connally thought the "virility" would be taken out of the program, and Hoffman agreed that "the immediate effect would be to damp the efforts of the people who are really trying to make a success of it. They might slow up." [1] To a surprising degree, this question arose repeatedly in the Congressional hearings, as though Congressmen had to be assured again and again. The ECA reiterated the theme in its official reports, and the executives in the agency continued to affirm the theory.[2]

But what were the *operational* commitments of debureaucratization, and on what basis could we say that this feature achieved the status of an independent or primary value in the program? Here it is possible to identify at least two important empirical standards for the debureaucratization theme: (1) the basing of aid on 1938 consumption levels, and (2) the presumption in favor of standard annual reductions in the country programs of 15 to 25 percent.

Hoffman told the Senate Appropriations Committee in 1950 that the ECA had an "informal" understanding with the Marshall Plan countries that the United States would not underwrite programs that allowed *per capita* consumption to rise above the figures of 1938.[3] For the precise implications of that decision one has to go back a bit further, to the ECA's first annual report, *Recovery Progress and United States Aid*. To arrive at some consistent standard for the allocation of aid, the ECA needed a reliable forecast of investment and consumption in each country. The policy was to finance only that very basic capital investment that a country could not finance for itself, either with its own export production or with diversions from present consumption. But these tests, it was admitted, "could not be applied with precision," and so the ECA was faced with one of those "two-handed" matters of judgment. On the one hand, if standards of living rose above 1938 levels, American financing might simply be used to support more consumption. On the other hand, if consumption were repressed and goods were diverted from the home market into the export trade, there was the danger of a domestic inflation that could wipe out the previous gains and ultimately raise the cost of those export goods themselves. Thus, either alternative had its pitfalls. What the ECA was forced to do was adopt some stable preference in the form of a working rule of thumb:

> There is no easy criterion by which to judge the adequacy of living standards or rates of investment. Nevertheless, wherever there was an indication of an excessive use of resources, actual or proposed, in one of these major categories, the inference was drawn that fewer were needed, that the country could export more or import less, and that the requested volume of ECA aid was larger than necessary.[4]

That is, if living standards rose to such a level that the country seemed able to support more investment, it was *presumed* that it could indeed finance that investment, and that American aid could be diminished. Now, in taking the 1938 figures as the standard, Hoffman had a more precise test. By gearing American aid to the prewar levels of consumption, the ECA hoped to reduce the possibility that Marshall aid would be used to finance the importation of such goods as automobiles, furs, oranges, and bubble gum.

With production rising in the ERP countries, the 1938 standard provided some reasonably intelligible grounds for the future reductions in aid. But in 1949 Hoffman and ECA took an even more drastic step, and here they added a second empirical commitment to their pledge of debureaucratization. It was decided to give the British a 25 percent cut in aid, and lower the allocations to all the other ERP countries by 15 percent. Thomas Finletter, the head of the ECA mission in Britain, thought that "the British themselves took the initiative in whittling down the figure," and so he told the Senate Foreign Relations Committee. But he was apparently misinformed, and Hoffman stepped in to correct the record.

> MR. HOFFMAN. . . . I think I can add a little light on this. In July, when I first met Mr. Stafford Cripps [the British Chancellor of the Exchequer], we were talking about the second year's program. I told him I thought it should be understood that the Americans were very insistent that the second year's program be less than the first year's program, and he asked what amount of cut I had in mind.
>
> "Well," I said, "I think that as it is to be a 4-year program, it would be a good thing to aim at a 25-percent cut."
>
> What figure he had in mind up to that time I do not know. He came out with a 24-percent cut.

SENATOR TYDINGS. What did he say in response to your suggestions?
MR. HOFFMAN. He said, "That is a very drastic downward revision."
     I said, "Nothing less than a marked revision will convince the
Americans that the Europeans are really serious." [5]

The decision was not based on an analysis of projects or a calculation of dollar balances. It flowed exclusively from the presumption in
favor of debureaucratization, and it was now the chief operational expression of that commitment. In the next year the British formula was
applied across the board, and as Hoffman reported, "instead of asking
each country to submit a program for the coming fiscal year based
upon its needs for dollars, we asked each country to submit a program
based on the assumption of a 25 percent reduction from the aid it will
have received in fiscal 1950. . . ." [6]

If Hoffman was able to afford frankness in 1950, it was because
the steps had already been taken that subordinated the balance of
payments and the dollar theories. When the ECA introduced condi-
tional aid (with "drawing rights") what it did, in effect, was replace
the balance of payments as a guideline for aid. From that time forward
the amount of assistance that any country would receive would not
depend on its overall balance of payments deficit, but on its deficit with
the dollar area; and in the latter part of 1949, the ECA freed itself
from the dollar theory as well. It was felt that the system, as it stood,
provided little incentive for the ERP nations to correct their deficits,
for the larger the deficit, the greater was the claim, supposedly, for
American aid. Therefore the arrangement posed a fundamental
dilemma. If Marshall aid rose or fell in response to fluctuations in the
balance of payments, then it might grow larger in succeeding years
rather than smaller, and there could be no assurance at all that it
would end by 1952. Yet, if the dollar theory was abandoned, what
would one use for standards?

What the ECA finally did was to take the 1949 allocations as a base.
From that point it would progressively reduce the allocations with each
succeeding year as it moved toward 1952. Henceforth, as Howard Ellis
commented, "the incurring of a larger deficit would not establish a
presumption in favor of increased aid." [7] The state of the balance of
payments or dollar reserves, then, would not be allowed to determine
the life or magnitude of the Marshall Plan. Instead, it was the duration of the ECA that would determine the size of the program. Debureaucratization had now achieved the dominance of an independent
policy commitment; it was Marshall aid itself that was thrust into a
dependent position as a function of the administrative schedule.

As if to firm up that relation as unalterable, the commitment to debureaucratization began to shape now the kind of social science the ECA would use. Conventionally, our discussion of theory in the social sciences follows the categories of prescriptive and descriptive, ethical and empirical. But it is possible that there is variant between the two that might be called a "contingent" theory. That is to say, we may find ourselves in a situation where either one of two descriptive theories, or two sets of empirical assumptions may be equally valid, and yet there may be no means of deciding between them on empirical grounds. There is of course the old question, for example, whether the glass is half full or half empty, or whether the dominant pattern in society is one of conflict or cooperation.

For certain refined purposes of theory-building we might conditionally adopt one assumption rather than another. We might assume, for instance, that conflict is the dominant characteristic of social life, and we might go on from there to draw out some propositions about the management of conflict or the transformation of conflict in an industrial society. The kind of theory I have in mind here would be something like that, but it would also have certain slight differences. It would begin by recognizing that any one of several descriptive theories may be equally accurate or inaccurate, and we would forswear at the outset any effort to decide the issue on empirical terms. Instead, we would choose an "appropriate" descriptive theory on the basis of some intervening value judgment or consideration of policy.

Strange as it might appear on the surface, something of this nature seemed to be at work in the ECA. As we noted earlier, the ECA was faced with some staggering problems in managing its own empirical subject matter. To estimate the balance of payments for the OEEC countries, the economists in the ECA had to forecast the precise direction and volume of trade in various commodities, and the approximate proportions of investment in all the member countries. The result, as they realized, was highly problematic. But even so, there was always something else coming along to throw off the estimates—like the maneuvering that took place before the British devalued in the fall of 1949, or the inventory buildups and the rush for raw materials that followed the outbreak of the Korean war. And yet, admitting all these difficulties, the ECA still had to distribute aid, and it had to find some minimally rational standards by which to do it.

The strategy finally adopted was to construct models based on the most favorable assumptions. Before putting all the estimates together and proceeding "from the diagnosis to an estimate of aid . . . it was necessary *first* to assume that the country in question would achieve self-support status as rapidly as could reasonably be expected, and *then* to forecast what its balance of payments would be." [8] In the early period there seemed to be nothing rigid in this posture. No one's model was better than anyone else's, so it was as reasonable to use an optimistic model as a conservative one. Besides, the ECA seemed to imply that the model was largely hypothetical anyway, and the specific model chosen was far less important than the fact that some model—any model—was used. But it became evident after a while that the commitment to the model was much harder than anyone might have supposed—that it was a reflection, in fact, of the basic commitment to end the program by 1952. Thus, when a sharp difference arose between the ECA and the OEEC in estimating the Europeans' deficit on current account, and it was suggested that the figures of the ECA might have been unrealistic, the ECA tended to dismiss the criticism, not for being wrong so much as irrelevant. The justification of the ECA surely must have been one of the oddest statements that the people at the OEEC had ever encountered. As the Marshall Plan agency "explained,"

> The ECA has throughout adopted favorable assumptions on economic trends in the participating countries. It believes that the reduction in the over-all deficit on current account in 1948/49 from the level of about $6.04 billion forecast by OEEC to a level of about $5.07 billion, or a reduction by one-sixth, is possible of attainment while maintaining, though not improving, living standards. *It is very important that the over-all deficit be steadily reduced for this is the measure of the ability of the participants to move progressively toward self-support.*[9]

To translate, the OEEC figures suggested that the ECA might be wrong in its empirical estimates. The ECA replied that it could not be wrong, because these were the only estimates that were consistent with its premises: The figures simply had to be correct if the ECA was to reduce the program progressively. Since there was no question that the ECA was going out of business by 1952, there could be no question about the estimates either. If one happened to believe, in addition, that the Europeans would act decisively only if the Marshall Plan was certain to end by 1952, then the lower allocations could also present a self-fulfilling prophecy. If the Europeans believed it, they would have to become more active on their own behalf, and they might even achieve those projected improvements in the balance of payments. If the choice of the more ambitious estimates would actually succeed in prodding the Europeans and bringing about the desired end, then who was to say that these estimates were not, in the final analysis, the most accurate of all?

And happily enough, the dollar deficit of the OEEC nations did decline, dropping from $8.5 billion in 1947 to $1 billion in 1950. In

1951 Richard Bissell could tell a joint Senate committee that the problem of the European dollar deficit with the United States "has largely ceased to exist." [10] By that time, of course, Korea had superseded the questions of debureaucratization and the dollar deficit. Military production was on the rise, and American soldiers were coming to Europe with dollars. The Marshall Plan would be put in the service of the rearmament program, and the ECA itself would end on December 31, 1951, instead of June 30, 1952. The foreign aid program would be continued but with a different emphasis, as reflected in the title of the successor organization, the Mutual Security Agency. But in 1949 and early 1950 it was the commitment to debureaucratization that was still dominant. Hoffman could still tell Senator Fulbright—with no trace of apology—that the program would end by 1952, even though several of the ERP countries could not hope to be fully self-supporting by that time.[11] The ECA could go steadily on its way, then, making annual reductions of 25 percent. In 1950, however, Senator McCarran and the watchdog committee began to catch on to what was happening. They recognized that the ECA was using only a rule of thumb in making its reductions, and that the allocations had lost much of their foundation in economic fact. McCarran's reaction was in part a lecture to the ECA, but in part, also, an exercise in his own expanding recognition of what should have been evident to him for some time:

> When people were near starvation you could calculate requirements for calories, translate them into dollars, and feel some confidence that you had the answer. When factories were idle you could make an estimate of the quantities of copper, coal, and machinery to get them into operation, and you were proved correct if the result was that the factories got into operation. . . . [But] today those objectives have been reached and . . . the problem of determining how much money it is necessary for us to supply . . . is much more difficult.[12]

If the estimates lost their relation to precise standards, McCarran could be forgiven for wondering why Europe needed 25 percent less aid, rather than 50 or 40 or 15 percent.[13] The ECA could respond only by reciting the old slogan of a "cure rather than a palliative," but by this date it failed to convince anyone. The fact was that the ECA was now disarmed; it had no defense beyond the bare logic of its promise to end the program by 1952. If that seemed to make little sense as a basis for allocating aid to Europe, what sense did it make, after all, as a rule governing the size and resources of the agency itself? The ECA was pressed to show consistent decreases in administrative expenses and personnel; and yet the functions of the agency were not decreasing, but enlarging. Congress had been adding programs rather than deleting them, and in 1950, when the ECA was planning sharp cuts in administrative expenses, it was scheduled to increase its efforts in technical assistance, information, and end-use checking. Also, conditions had changed since that early period when the ECA was shipping large bulk commodities such as wheat. At that time the average ECA voucher was for $143,000. But now that it was shipping items like machine tools, which came in smaller packages, its average transaction was only $12,000 to $13,000. The overall value of American assistance had declined, but the volume of transactions had actually multiplied.[14] In short, the ECA had more to do, not less. Neither the reduction in the ECA nor the drop in the assignments of aid had any relation, then, to the substantive needs of European recovery. They had their origin in another value, and a prior commitment.

This was a logic that might have baffled Alice and the White Queen, but it had its uses. Hoffman was determined to convert the squeeze on resources into a form of pressure on the ERP countries. And in some respects it was a rather apt method for an agency like the ECA that disclaimed any intention of interfering in the decisions of the ERP countries, and which lacked the leverage for major interventions anyway. Thus Hoffman could say, with sincerity, that questions of nationalization were matters exclusively for the local government. Nor did he think it proper, for example, that the United States should refuse textile machinery to Britain for fear of competition.[15] But the concern for economic rationality could also give him the basis for some fine distinctions:

> I have had this [matter of nationalization] out with the British. I have said, so far as we are concerned what they do with their economy is their business, and what we do with our dollars is our business and if they start playing ducks and drakes with their economy to such a point that they cannot recover and our investment is not worth while, we are going to hold up the investment. . . .[16]

How the British happened to regulate the butchers and the bankers, Hoffman insisted, was no concern of the ECA. However, "they should not use our dollars to engage in social experimentation . . . [but] only for essential imports needed for recovery, and that has been the test." With that line of reasoning he could feel perfectly justified in cutting British aid if he suspected them of social experimentation, while at the same time he could find nothing inconsistent with his professions of noninterference. When more cotton goods began to appear on the consumer market in Britain, Hoffman found it appropriate to cut the British cotton imports by $60 million. Was the government entering the field of housing construction? Then $25 million might be shaved off the Marshall Plan exports of lumber.[17] And this was all compatible with the presumption in favor of basic investment. If the local government could divert funds to consumption, then Marshall aid could be eliminated proportionately. It was not surprising, therefore, that the British Labour Government found some difficulty in maintaining the pace of its social welfare programs. After the first year of the Labour Government, government consumption took 26.2 percent of the resources available for domestic use. By 1948 that figure had been reduced to 18.2 percent. With cuts in the programs for housing, health, and education, that figure was being pushed steadily downward. Projecting the trend, the proportion was expected to decline to 16.8 percent by 1952;[18] and as a result, in part, of these restrictions on welfare and consumption, the British managed to keep investment close to the ECA's target figure of 20 percent of the gross national product.

Still, if influence was to be exerted, it *was* more fitting for an agency with a pluralist orientation that its interventions remain more subtle and indirect. If it had to interfere at all, it was more appropriate for the ECA to do that by arranging incentives rather than dictating policies. Perhaps the ECA staff expressed it best in its first annual report:

> We are not seeking to impose on other countries any specific economic pattern. The degree to which other governments find it necessary and desirable to exercise direct controls over economic processes is a matter for them to decide. The United States is simply following a common-sense policy which will, if it is successful, reduce the insistent economic pressures that compel governments to ration, to control, and to regulate. . . .[19]

Thus, even where there were conscious goals for directing the Europeans, the ECA was still wedded to a liberal position, and even the irony of its intervention was characteristic: The most effective tool of coercion it had—the pressure of a continuing cutback in program funds—was a product of its own weakness as an agency.

II

We speculated earlier that several themes in the intellectual origins of the Marshall Plan might have converged to create an operating presumption in favor of deemphasizing political considerations. That is, the ECA was to concentrate on economic criteria; it would not (according to our hypothesis) attribute political motives where some other construction was possible, and it would not bring disagreements immediately to the level of overt political contest. Among the various themes these decision rules might have summarized were the following:

—that the ECA would represent a peculiar expertise for dealing with operations of a "business-like" nature, that it possessed a distinct legitimacy based on the perspectives of business management and economic rationality;

—that the preference for "a cure rather than a palliative" in Europe prescribed a full rein for the criteria of economic rationality;

—that nothing more had been decided on the national interest in Europe than the approval of an *economic* aid program—and by implication, if there were any larger political decisions to be made, they were to be reserved for another time and settled on their own terms, rather than simply precipitated by the decisions of the ECA;

—that the United States should confine its intrusions overseas by concentrating on the problem of reconstruction and avoiding, as much as possible, any involvement in domestic political decisions; and it should observe these limitations because, for one thing, it was more proper, but also because interventions would tend to confirm the propaganda of the Communists.

Unquestionably, the decisions of the ECA in cutting aid allotments could seriously restrict the policy choices open to the Europeans, and Paul Hoffman was one of the first to acknowledge that. Yet, as the passages above make equally clear, he saw nothing in the record that might have contradicted his own frequent insistence that the ECA would avoid any meddling in the internal decisions of the ERP countries. What removed the contradiction for him, apparently, was the belief that the ECA was doing something fundamentally different from political work. The agency was concentrating on economic decisions, and it would dispute the Europeans only on matters relating to the use of American aid. The British could nationalize industry or do anything else with their economy, and it was their business alone. However, if the British succeeded only in damaging their economy as a result of these adventures, they would threaten the usefulness of American aid, and it was at least legitimate at that point to consider the case for reducing American grants. Implicitly, it would not be an issue of intervention anymore, but something closer to a salvage operation for American resources.

But did Hoffman and his colleagues really believe in this distinction, and did they act upon it? It so happened that the annual Senate hearings furnished one of the most precise and thorough tests on this point, thanks in large measure to the persistence of Senator Fulbright. When the legislation was first considered in 1948, Fulbright maintained that the goal of economic integration was insufficient; political integration was the key to peace and the prerequisite to an integrated economic market. Fulbright continued to believe, for that reason, that the Marshall Plan would fail in its objectives so long as the ECA refused to push for political federation in Europe. Moreover, his challenge did not end in 1948 with the passage of the legislation. He used the hearings in the succeeding years to pick away at the performance of the ECA as a method of advancing his thesis. An important part of that argument over the years was to point out to Hoffman and his assistants that their decisions carried important political implications. If the top executives in the ECA could have been made to admit that they were involved in politics after all, then they might have been convinced to go all the way and seek a political solution. But interestingly enough, as doggedly as Fulbright would press the point, the ECA people would continue to resist; and they consistently failed to be persuaded.

When Fulbright asked Hoffman in 1949 why the ECA did not promote political integration instead of merely encouraging the movement of goods, Hoffman replied, "I am an ECA administrator, sir."

> SENATOR FULBRIGHT. Do you feel that because there was nothing in the authorization of the ERP regarding political matters that therefore your jurisdiction is limited to economics? That it would not be within the contemplation of the law that you have anything to do at all with the political pattern in Europe?
> MR. HOFFMAN. I think the Congress was very wise in limiting ECA to the economic field. I think that the State Department has an agency set up to deal with the political field. I think that we can do our job with the economic field, because we are an independent agency, perhaps better than could be done as part of a regular Government department. . . . I am certain we do not belong in the political field.[20]

Fulbright found the same resistance as he confronted one after another of the prominent officials in the ECA. At the time of the hearings there were reports in the press about the efforts to form a Council of Europe as a step toward the building of common political institutions. Fulbright was astonished then when Averell Harriman, as the Special Ambassador in Europe, professed to know nothing more about the development than what he read in the press. "I am not involved in the political aspect," Harriman explained, "I am very much involved in the development of cooperation in OEEC." [21]

As Deputy Chief of the ECA mission in Germany, N. H. Collison once withheld American aid until the directors of the German national railways agreed to balance their budget. But since that was obviously an "economic" problem, he too had little reason to suppose that he ever involved himself in politics. "My contacts," he told the Senate committee, "have been on economic matters rather than political matters. I do not recognize that I have any mandate or any responsibility politically under that law. I do have economic responsibility." [22]

On one revealing occasion in the hearings, Fulbright's hammering at the ECA finally moved Chairman Connally to step in:

> May I intervene right there? I want to suggest that under this bill, *which deals only with economics,* I would feel disposed to take disciplinary action against anybody in the ECA who exceeded his authority and began to meddle with the political situation in Europe. It is not the purpose of this bill to deal with the politics of Europe, either for a union or against a union or halfway between them.[23]

Coming as it did from one of the key Senate leaders who guided the original bill through Congress, this support for the peculiar approach of the ECA seemed particularly authoritative.

Was it fair to say, then, that the ECA people denied the presence of political overtones in their decisions, or that in some naïve way they were determined to make economics out of politics? The record would show, on the contrary, that they were not so simpleminded. It would demonstrate, rather, that their understanding followed the sense of our hypothetical operating rules. Hoffman never contended that there was a complete separation between politics and economics. He warned the Senate committee once that "life cannot be neatly divided into economic, political, social, and military compartments. Europe's problem cannot be attacked simply in terms of economics nor solved by our handing over a carefully computed number of dollars. . . ." [24] And after he had time for further reflection, he was able to respond to Fulbright in language that conveyed the essence of our operating rule:

> I do not think I have ever felt there is any real difference between yourself and myself on what should transpire in Europe. We have both agreed, I think, that there must be a greater unity among the free nations of western Europe. *The whole difference is a question of method,* and I felt quite certain that *as far as ECA was concerned, the Congress intended us to deal on the economic front* and intended us also *to so restrict our efforts* with the clear understanding that you cannot operate in an airtight compartment. What we do has political repercussions and vice versa.[25]

What made this distinction practicable was that the idiom of economics was entirely sufficient to the needs of the ECA. Political judgments were so naturally entangled with the economic, that there was enough to do simply in arguing about these so-called "economic" decisions. The ECA might believe, for example, that British competitiveness was undermined by labor practices that raised costs and retarded modernization. It could feel that the Labour Government was taking too soft a view toward labor, that its acceptance of overly full employment was inhibiting the reforms that were needed for a thorough recovery. But at the very least the British deserved to have that critique documented, for even some of the more articulate critics of the government could not subscribe to that thesis. The government could argue, in return, that the British problems were rooted in the structural changes brought about in the international economy by the war. It could point to the liabilities involved in managing sterling, and it could cite a pattern of neglect for capital investment that started early in the twentieth century. Surely there was enough to argue about in all these issues without flying to the conclusion that the British and American governments were divided on fundamental grounds of principle.

There was actually a coincidence of interests here. Both a decent respect for the British government and a concern for making the wise substantive decision would have suggested the propriety of exploring the factual matter at greater length before the disagreement was brought to the political level. At times, the mere challenging of a decision was enough, because it faced the recipient government with the burden of making a more coherent justification. If the government in question could cite some reasonable economic grounds for the decision, then that was as much as the ECA could legitimately expect, and as far as the Marshall Plan agency was concerned, that was enough in itself to make the decision considerably better. If there was still room for the play of political criteria, then that was the business of the local government; the ECA had done all it could on behalf of its own criteria. Was there something suspect in the location of two steel plants in France that were built with ECA funds? Then that was the concern of the French government, and it was better not to inquire too deeply into certain things. For was the steel not being produced, and was the production not contributing to the overall plan that measured European recovery?

By following these rules on the use of political criteria, the administrators not only made their own actions more consistent with the pluralist ethic conveyed by Marshall in his address at Harvard; they also contributed something that would last far beyond the life of their own agency: They prevented their own intrusions, which were occasioned by crisis conditions, from achieving the level of principle. The nonintervention doctrine would emerge from the Marshall Plan substantially intact. And thus, Donald Stone, who served throughout the program as the ECA Director of Administration, would consistently refer to the American operation in Greece as a "special case."

Few people were as intimately involved in the administration of the Marshall Plan as Stone was, and yet he never saw intervention as the typical form of ECA practice. It was always a matter of some importance to him to maintain the consciousness of the Greek venture as a noticeable exception to a general pattern of conduct.

If the operating presumptions in favor of economic criteria had not been held sincerely, it would be hard to account for the process by which the Marshall Plan was generalized from a limited European assistance effort to a permanent foreign aid program with universal application. In 1951 the Marshall Plan had been converted into an economic support program for the European rearmament effort. For many in the ECA the change was not merely one of emphasis, but an alteration that destroyed the very meaning of the Marshall Plan. Two months before the ECA was scheduled to close itself out, Donald Stone entered his own dissent in an almost emotional memorandum (he admitted in the preface that he was "all steamed up" when he wrote it). Stone objected to the new concept of aid, which subordinated economic assistance to military production. He still believed in the organizational decision of 1948—that the Marshall Plan was an autonomous program, with its own distinctive ends. Those ends, he declared, were in making a better life for the citizens of the recipient countries, to show them that democracy was an effective and worthwhile alternative to communism. It was a humanitarian program that demonstrated to the people of Europe that the United States was concerned with them as individuals and wanted to see them improve their lives. But this new program, according to Stone, would hold up a different meaning to the world. It would tell the Asians, for example, that the United States was "not really interested in improving conditions of life, that we are interested only in *their help* for *our defense* against communism." (Stone's emphasis.) What the new program was doing was throwing overboard what Stone saw as the theory of postwar foreign policy since 1947, "that security, peace, and in fact victory in our contest with communism, must be built upon sound economic foundations. . . ." There was a connection in Stone's mind between the goal of world peace and the commitment to economic welfare programs. Peace would come "only when enough government leaders and other important people . . . reflect in their personal lives those moral values which produce stable and democratic institutions." In turn, those values were acquired "when a sense of individual and national responsibility begins to be felt for human misery wherever it may be found. . . ." [26]

That same year, Paul Hoffman (now retired as Administrator of the ECA) published his own book, *Peace Can Be Won*. In it, Hoffman had the chance to give an account of his own work in the Marshall Plan and express his own understanding of the foreign aid program. Characteristically, he fell back on the old liberal cliché of commerce as a great healer. The Marshall Plan raised production, diffused prosperity, and in this way helped to prevent totalitarian revolutions in Europe.[27] In one of those strange conversions that occurs in public life, the practical man of affairs had become very much a man of theory. For the difference between a practical and a theoretical man must surely lie in a certain sensitivity to the detail and texture of particular cases, and to the circumstances that make some situations truly separate. And yet what practical man of affairs, having administered the Marshall Plan, would write as Hoffman did in 1951, that "We have learned in Europe what to do in Asia"? For where, after all, were the similarities, and what had Hoffman learned?

> While in Europe we concentrated on turbines and tractors, in Asia we are primarily concerned with vaccines and fertilizers. But the political principle remains the same. Only the deeds of democracy can enable the peoples still undecided between the lures of despotism and the life of freedom to make an honest choice.[28]

The principle, apparently, was that democracy got the goods to the people in time. When the minimal needs of the people were taken care of, when desperation was removed, then the people were able to sit back and make a rational choice among the competing political systems. This was the voice of Hoffman, the former used car salesman; it was all, in the final analysis, a matter of consumer's choice.

Yet, what was there in the program these two men administered that led them to such an understanding of the Marshall Plan? To say that the program improved the lives of the people by raising production or serving the "general good" is surely too broad and vague. If these characterizations by Stone and Hoffman meant anything, they had to mean something very close to the picture drawn by Hoffman of an active competition for the favor of the populace. That is, the Marshall Plan would have demonstrated the effectiveness of democracy by bringing dramatic improvement to the standard of living for the vast majority of Europeans. It would have been a form of Tory socialism that lured the workers away from the appeals of radical ideologies, and it would have done it by bribing the people, as it were, with a more egalitarian distribution of material goods. But it would require a wide stretching of the facts to make the record of the Marshall Plan fit this theory. As we have already seen, one of the most basic operating tests used by the ECA was to keep per capita consumption approximately at 1938 levels. The object was to allow additions to consumption only where that was necessary to check a potential inflation. Otherwise resources were to be directed toward investment, and manufactured goods were to be diverted from the domestic economy into the export market.

Hoffman himself admitted in 1950 that the ECA had taken no interest in promoting wage increases or a better standard of living for workers. At this same time he expressed his hope that the policy of transferring resources from consumption to investment "will, *after we have pulled out,* enable them to increase their standard of living considerably." [29] Improvements in the standard of living were to be deferred until *after* the Marshall Plan.

Real wages did in fact rise during this period. But that was not due to any increased assertiveness on the part of labor in demanding a larger share of the national wealth. The general pattern in wages was one of restraint. With the exception of the Netherlands, there was no direct control on wages, but there were some very successful programs of voluntary restraint, which held up until the wage-pull pressures of the post-Korean period, when there was a scarcity of labor. Labor governments were in an especially advantageous position to cajole the unions into restraint, and they backed up their own part of the bargain by a vigorous policy of taxing excess profits. At one point in the Netherlands the unions even accepted a cut in real wages as a contribution to a deflationary policy. [30] Here, as elsewhere in Europe, unions gave their support to austerity programs. As in Italy, workers came to appreciate the fact that their future consumption might depend on a stiff deflationary policy, which could make saving meaningful again. But the benefits in these cases were all in the long run; labor was not bribed into support for the political system with immediate payoffs. In fact, labor acceptance of these arrangements made sense only because the union members were already integrated into their political communities. If the situation was as Hoffman described it, with the population waiting to be sold on entering the political system, it might well have been irrational for the workers to have accepted these sacrifices. Deferring short-term advantages for long-term gains would have made far less sense if the working classes were still without leverage in their respective political systems; for they would have had far less assurance in that case that benefits were really being deferred, and that their governments would indeed make good on their promises later. What made this renunciation of self-interest possible was the fact that the workers were not outside their political communities, but thoroughly committed. One could not account for the behavior of European labor in this period, then, in the familiar terms of a consumers' politics. Instead, the analysis would require some rather traditional and unrevolutionary concepts like party loyalty, enlightened self-interest, or even civic obligation.

Finally, the ECA was bound to a conceptual apparatus that blocked it off from an active interventionist policy. The balance of payments analysis was a rather gross analytical tool, but for an agency that was equipped to do little more than pump goods into Europe, it was good enough. It was sufficient for dealing with advanced industrial nations, when the ECA had to do little more than authorize the procurement of goods. There was practically no need to provide facilities for unloading the materials or distributing them inside the country. It was unnecessary to teach the recipients what to do with the raw materials or how to market them when they were turned into finished goods. Thus, there was really no need for the ECA to inject itself in the production decisions of specific industries, even if it had the capacity to become involved. For this particular program, then, and for this particular set of nations, the balance of payments offered a fairly comfortable analysis. Moreover, the balance of payments had relevance for some of the more sophisticated problems facing these nations in the form of trade imbalances; and besides that, it seemed to do no special harm.

But the limits of the theory became evident in 1951, when an effort was made to mesh the operations of the ECA with the military aid program. In developing estimates for Fiscal 1952, it was found that the ECA was still using a modified balance of payments analysis. What the military required, however, was a very detailed model covering the entire production system. It was essential to have specific information on the total resources available in the participating countries for meeting targets of military production.[31] However, as long as the ECA was operating with the balance of payments analysis, it was incapable of dealing with specific production issues. It was virtually predictable, then, that when a new foreign aid agency moved into the underdeveloped areas and took up the responsibility for an assistance program in Southeast Asia, the balance of payments theory would have to be abandoned. Almost all of these countries had surpluses in dollars or other hard currencies as a result of selling raw materials to the West. Here, instead of providing a rough but useful index of a real economic problem, the theory worked to obscure a fundamental need for development.[32]

Nothing seems more fanciful, therefore, than the notion that an agency like the ECA, operating from afar with the bluntest of tools, could possibly regulate the distribution policies of the ERP countries and direct them toward egalitarian ends. The ECA did nothing to credit some of the early fears among conservatives that the Marshall

Plan would project the New Deal abroad. If, in retrospect, Hoffman and Stone tried to generalize the Marshall Plan as a program of welfare economics, they were misleading themselves.[33] But these were intelligent men, who were in the center of operations. There must have been something in the Marshall Plan that gave even that erroneous explanation some grounding in fact. And what that basis seemed to be was the sense of distinctiveness for the Marshall Plan as an autonomous program with a concentration on economic policy. Stone had difficulty in articulating the philosophy of the Marshall Plan, but there was no doubt in his mind that it was fundamentally different from the military program. From that persuasion it was a shorter step to the view that the Marshall Plan also had its own distinctive ends, which had to be related to the autonomy of its peculiar criteria. But was that not the essential content of Vandenberg's thinking in 1948, when he moved to separate the ECA from the State Department? Yes, but it was dependent also on several other strands of thought in the Marshall Plan, which combined in support of some concrete working rules. It was not simply that the people at ECA *perceived* themselves as separated from the State Department, but that the character of their agency actually made them different in their day-to-day work. Thus, to know how the Marshall Plan came to be generalized after 1951 one would have to account for that unshakable assurance with which Hoffman seemed to understand the exact character and place of his agency—how he could admit so blithely that the decisions of ECA were surrounded with political implications, and yet maintain through it all that in "ERP, however, our attention is focused on economic problems."

Notes

1. Senate Foreign Relations Committee, *Hearings on Extension of ERP,* 1949, p. 78.
2. See, for example, Howard Bruce in *ibid.,* p. 332; Hoffman in Senate Foreign Relations Committee, *Hearings on Extension of ERP,* 1950, p. 23 (and in almost every hearing at which he testified before the foreign relations committees), and Richard Bissell in Senate Committees on Foreign Relations and Armed Services, *Hearing on Mutual Security Act of 1951* (1951), p. 157.
3. Senate Committee on Appropriations, *Hearings on Foreign Aid Appropriations for 1951* (1950), pp. 172, 241.
4. ECA, *Recovery Progress and United States Aid,* 1949, p. 61.
5. Senate Foreign Relations Committee, *Hearings on Extension of ERP,* 1949, pp. 498 (Finletter) and 499 (Hoffman).

6. Senate Appropriations Committee, *Hearings on Foreign Aid Appropriations for 1951* (1950), p. 172.

7. Howard S. Ellis, *The Economics of Freedom* (New York: Harper and Brothers, 1950), pp. 530–31.

8. ECA, *Recovery Progress and United States Aid,* p. 62. Emphasis added.

9. *Ibid.,* p. 70. Emphasis added.

10. Senate Committee on Foreign Relations and Armed Forces, *Hearings of Mutual Security Act of 1951,* p. 180.

11. Senate Foreign Relations Committee, *Hearings on Extension of ERP,* 1949, p. 61.

12. See Senate Committee on Appropriations, *Hearings on Foreign Aid Appropriation for Fiscal 1951,* pp. 266–67.

13. *Ibid.,* p. 267.

14. See William Foster's testimony in House Subcommittee on Appropriations, *Hearings on Foreign Aid for Fiscal 1951* (1950), pp. 416–17.

15. Senate Foreign Relations Committee, *Hearings on Extension of ERP,* 1949, pp. 48, 59–61, 430.

16. *Ibid.,* p. 61.

17. Senate Foreign Relations Committee, *Hearings on Extension of ERP,* 1949, pp. 502, 507.

18. See the testimony of Thomas Finletter and the accompanying charts in *ibid.,* pp. 160–61.

19. ECA, *Recovery Progress and United States Aid,* p. 2.

20. Senate Foreign Relations Committee, *Hearings on Extension of ERP,* 1949, pp. 85–86.

21. *Ibid.,* p. 147; and see also, pp. 139–40.

22. *Ibid.,* p. 310.

23. Senate Foreign Relations Committee, *Hearings on Extension of ERP,* 1949, p. 198, and see also p. 309. Emphasis added.

24. *Ibid.,* p. 13.

25. *Ibid.,* p. 525. Emphasis added.

26. Donald Stone to F. J. Lawton, "Implications of Mutual Security Act and Requirements for Action," October 6, 1951, Bureau of the Budget, Series 39.27.

27. Paul G. Hoffman, *Peace Can Be Won* (Garden City, New York: Doubleday and Company, Inc., 1951), p. 20.

28. *Ibid.,* pp. 130–31.

29. Senate Committee on Appropriations, *Hearings on Foreign Aid Appropriation for Fiscal 1951* (1950), p. 241. Emphasis added.

30. See UN, *Economic Survey of Europe Since the War,* p. 72.

31. See Bureau of the Budget, *Survey of the ECA,* September 1951, p. 63. Series 39.32.

32. See *ibid.,* pp. 35–36.

33. For some reason there is a tendency to overlook the fact that the ECA subordinated the principle of "need" in 1949 when it decided to take the existing allocations as a base and make proportionate cuts with each

successive year. The matter turned in part on the question of incentives. If aid was reduced when a country's deficit contracted, it would have penalized improvement. Instead, the ECA determined to shift its incentives to reward success, even if it meant that aid might not go where it was most vitally needed. If there was any allocating principle more removed from the premises of a welfare orientation, it would have been hard to imagine. See Ellis, *op. cit.*, pp. 531–32.

7

Lutz Niethammer

Structural Reform and a Compact for Growth: Conditions for a United Labor Union Movement in Western Europe after the Collapse of Fascism

*Most studies of Cold War politics focus on nation-states, but in the
following essay Professor Niethammer of the University of Essen
analyzes comparatively the labor movement after World War II.
Organized labor had been a major victim of fascism and German
occupation: its cadres smashed, its leaders killed, imprisoned, or driven
into exile or underground. With the liberation of Italy and France in
1944 and the defeat of Germany in 1945, labor leaders looked toward
reconstruction of their prefascist unions. Since they felt that their
earlier divisions between communists, socialists, and Christian trade
unionists had prevented labor from organizing effective resistance to
fascist trends, there was a strong pressure for trade-union unity. Such
unity, however, proved precarious, and by 1947–48, the Western
European labor movements had fractured once again.*

*Niethammer examines this brief period of unity and the conditions
that enabled it to function. The unified labor movements pressed for
nationalization, welfare measures, and sometimes worker control of the
plants. But they could not survive earlier bitter differences and the
pressures of the Cold War. As the Soviet-American split overshadowed
Europe—as the East European regimes were molded into satellite states
and the communists were maneuvered out of the party coalitions in
the West, as too the United States announced the Marshall Plan and
the Soviet Union decided it could not participate—the labor movement
was caught in the cross fire. It proved impossible for communists and
the non-communist components to work together; indeed American
labor observers, such as the AFL and reluctantly the CIO, actively
urged the non-communists to secede and form their own unions. In*

Italy and France, the communists retained control of the federations in being, for they had gained strength and mass support during the resistance to fascism. In Germany because of the East-West split, communism remained dominant in the Soviet zone. Whatever adherents communism enjoyed in the western zones were rapidly thrust to the margin of politics. In all of Europe the schism became a major feature of the sociopolitical polarization that marked Cold War public life. While partially bridged over since the late 1960s, the split still effectively divides the West European labor movements.

Professor Niethammer's essay is written from a perspective on the Left that is critical of both the American and communist roles. My own feeling is that the euphemistic slogans of the Left (which often sought to monopolize such terms as "antifascist" or "democratic" for procommunists) are sometimes pressed into service too uncritically, whereas the rhetoric of liberalism is fully unmasked. Perhaps, too, the comparability of British developments with those on the Continent is overdrawn. Nonetheless, this is a highly sophisticated review of the massive literature on the unions, and the author valuably brings out all the inherent difficulties that stood in the way of radical renovation after the war.

A note on translation: Although it is cumbersome, I have used the term "political united union" for Niethammer's politische Einheitsgewerkschaft. *By political, the author wished to stress that the post-1945 labor organizations were intended to work in tandem with the affiliated parties of the Left for political and social as well as narrowly economic reform. To this idea he contrasts the idea of the "industrial union," charged with the advocacy of economic interests alone (e.g., wages, perhaps plant organization). The term "industrial union" is not intended here to suggest the American contrast of "industrial" versus "craft" unions (e.g., CIO vs. AFL).*

For this collection I have omitted a few pages at the beginning and end of the whole essay that address the Germans' own debate on the history and proper role for their own trade union federation (DGB). In these pages the author explains that his comparative approach is designed to rescue the history of the German union federation from too one-sided an analysis in terms of its national background alone; and in his conclusion he assesses both the achievements and the limits of the DGB. Footnotes have been made consistent with the text selections, which has entailed some rearrangement. When Niethammer has used French or English-language works in German translation, I have kept his citation for the sake of simplicity. Miss Rebecca Boehling lent some assistance with the translation. The author has made a few small revisions for this version of his article.

*The essay has been translated and reprinted with the permission of
the author and the publisher, Bund-Verlag of Cologne, from a
collection of essays edited by Heinz Oscar Vetter to commemorate the
post-1945 German labor leader, Hans Böckler:* Vom Sozialistengesetz
zur Mitbestimmung. Zum 100. Geburtstag von Hans Böckler [*From
the Law suppressing the Social Democratic Party (1878) to
Co-Determination (1950 and after). For the 100th Birthday of Hans
Böckler*], *Cologne, 1975. Professor Niethammer is also the author of,
among other works,* Entnazifierung in Bayern. Säuberung und
Rehabilitation unter amerikanischer Besatzung [*Denazification in
Bavaria: Purge and Rehabilitation under American Occupation*],
*Frankfurt/Main, S. Fischer, 1972. With Ulrich Borsdorf and Peter
Brandt he has coedited* Arbeiterinitiative 1945. Antifaschistische
Ausschüsse und Reorganisation der Arbeiterbewegung in Deutschland
[*Worker Initiatives 1945: Antifascist Committees and the
Reorganization of the Labor Movement in Germany*] *(Wuppertal: 1976).*

Typology of the Political United Labor Union

The first phase of the international history of the trade unions in
the postwar era was characterized by the formation and the collapse
of the World Federation of Trade Unions (WFTU).[1] This phase lasted
from 1945 to 1947, although in certain countries forerunners of the
united union emerged as early as 1943; and later the international
schism that resulted from the collapse of the movement went on into
1948–49. The WFTU phase was dominated by the effort to form the
most united organization possible, or at least an operational alliance
of unions on the national and international level. The attempt sought
also to go beyond the various party affiliations of the individual
unions; leaders wanted the unions to attain a pivotal position within
society as a whole. This task required participation in the antifascist
purges. It also meant helping to start up and to increase production
so as to overcome the postwar economic crisis by means of rapid
growth. It meant institutionalizing a working-class role in economic
management by means of state planning and control of monopolies
—e.g., by nationalizing heavy industries and establishing factory councils or other forms of worker participation in individual firms or at the
industry-wide level. As the concept of a united labor union was worked
out, each country's particular background and conditions led to different organizational forms. But the concentration of craft unions into
industrial federations and their political consolidation as forms of
pressure groups were unmistakable everywhere.

The political core of the united trade unions in the WFTU phase consisted of the effort to form to the greatest degree possible a mass union movement by integrating the prewar unions with the communists, who had greatly expanded in the European resistance against German fascism. In the former fascist countries, especially, where independent unions had been totally shattered and replaced by corporative organs designed to integrate workers and employers, the emerging Christian labor unions, which had also failed to survive as an independent movement, could be worked into a united organization. This new unity was made possible essentially because ever since Stalin had adopted a policy of seeking allies [against Hitler], the communists had accepted a reformist program. This reformist platform included different mixes for each country of partial nationalization, workers' participation, and economic planning. But it remained generally compatible with the concept of "Economic Democracy" that had been advanced by the German Social Democratic trade unions in 1928.* At the same time, giving the unions a broader political assignment—which all the differing labor groups agreed upon as a means of reconstruction and antifascist reform—also would allow more scope for the communist concept. They saw the union as an instrument for mobilizing and educating the proletarian masses, i.e., for extending the influence of the communist leadership. In tactical terms the united trade union enabled the communist cadres to apply the policy of a United Front "from above and from below" [i.e., at the union leadership and plant levels simultaneously]. This was attractive both for the communists in the West who wanted to anchor themselves in powerful positions in the state and economy and for the communists in the East who wanted to eliminate the organized opposition. Simultaneously it appealed to reformist leaders. They wanted not only to strengthen the power of the labor movement by avoiding conflict within the proletariat, but also sought to protect themselves from the possibility that their earlier rivalry with the communists might resume. Renewed rivalry could assume threatening proportions, given the popularity of the Eastern Ally in the lands freed from German occupation or the strength of the communists in the national movements of liberation. The discrediting of the European Right along with the widely held view that socialism was the next item on the agenda of history and was necessary for reconstruction; the confidence in the durability of the coalition against Hitler; and the socialists' par-

* Ed. note: Economic Democracy was a platform that called not for the abolition, but the progressive reform of capitalism—predominantly by increasing involvement of the unions in economic planning and control alongside managers in industry-wide councils.

ticipation in almost all European governments—all produced that optimism with which the united trade union experiment was undertaken in the WFTU phase. The tradition of Economic Democracy thus became the most suitable compromise platform for the united trade union. For the socialists its continuity with prewar *ideology* prevented dwelling on the [ineffective] prewar *practice* of the reformist unions. For the communists, as a partial objective it was compatible with the "antifascist-democratic" transitional strategy of Stalinism. At the same time both partners thought they could rely on the practical efficacy of their own party organizations to hold their own.

Economic Conditions

The goals of Economic Democracy were appropriate ones not only in view of the paralysis of the European economies, but also as surrogate objectives for the trade unions. For in this period of early social reconstruction, the rapid progress made in organizing the unions contrasted with the restricted role that the unions could play as participants in the struggle over income distribution. In view of this discrepancy the great influx of members into the unions in all the postwar European countries requires explanation; previous research has considered it insufficiently. It obviously drew most generally upon the spontaneous loyalty of the workers to their own organizations—those most identified with the working-class—which fascist and fascist-occupied regimes had deprived of rights. At the same time the unions represented the hope for some sort of socialist alternative for the future. First, however, they had to face more concrete problems.

All the European economic systems were afflicted by negative growth on account of the war:[3] disproportionally developed productive capacities, massive destruction of currencies and capital, plundering, death, the deportation or drafting of a large part of the labor force, collapse of the infrastructure, and extreme limits on international exchange. The postliberation economies were in acute crisis. They required extensive reconversion, and in heavily destroyed areas above all, reconstruction of the infrastructure (e.g., transportation facilities and public utilities). Despite the great losses of human life from war and terror, the Continent faced a growing surplus of labor—some of it overqualified. With few plants functioning, the economies had to absorb expellees, displaced persons, forced labor, and prisoners of war. The need for goods of all sorts vastly exceeded the productive capacity of the system. Thus the crisis had to be overcome by comprehensive reconstruction and by increasing productive capacity (with special urgency in heavy industry and mining, coal mining above all), if sufficient jobs were to be created and the most elementary needs of the population satisfied. In contrast to cyclical economic crises, the problem did not lie in underconsumption or overproduction—except perhaps for armaments, as was the case in part for Germany and the United States—but rather in enlarging and restructuring the productive apparatus. If the unions saw themselves not merely as spokesmen for one of the groups in the productive process, but as advocates of the laboring (or jobseeking) masses, then in order to create jobs and accelerate the flow of goods they had to concentrate their entire energies in the crisis on promoting growth—on increasing production, ensuring labor discipline, avoiding strikes, influencing systematic control of the productive and distributive apparatus. At the same time they had to watch out that reconversion was not carried out at the expense of the workers by mass layoffs in armaments factories, as in the United States and, at first, in Germany. To get production going once again and to increase it, they had to reabsorb all the professions that were indispensable, at least for the time being, to the economic system, especially technically skilled lower-level managers, engineering personnel, and independent small businessmen. These tasks represented, so to speak, an objective economic necessity even though they deviated from the traditional union struggle to reduce the exploitation of labor. And it was precisely these tasks that the united labor unions—including the cadres from each political party—carried out in all European countries, East and West, between 1944 and 1947. Their function of disciplining the labor force for the sake of the reconstruction of society as a whole made them so indispensable that they could demand a lot, especially in the way of structural reforms, from national leaders and from other social groups.

Alternatives?

Was there a basic alternative? In order to justify the fact that at the end of the war their party and union leaders did not press for an immediate transition to socialism (except in prevailingly agricultural Yugoslavia), communist literature has often argued that the workers' class consciousness had been overwhelmed by fascism and apparently even by the antifascist struggle.[4] But this argument obscures the real reasons. An immediate transition to socialism would have made the economic difficulties sketched above even more acute by setting additional impediments to production: lack of experts, losses of working time, bourgeois sabotage, further crippling of the infrastructure. Just to satisfy the most immediate needs of the working masses forced renunciation of an early revolution. Secondly, Western Europe was filled with American troops instructed to intervene in case of "disease and unrest." Revolution would thus have meant further war, especially if the Soviet Union, herself afflicted by the same acute shortages, had been forced to intervene in so completely uncertain a situation. But since in view of her own crisis she was unwilling to be dragged into any such adventure, she tolerated no such enterprises in her own sphere of influence and discouraged equivalent Communist Party initiatives in western and southern Europe. She favored instead a step-by-step policy, fitted to each country and permitting delay and halts.[5] But even leaving aside the military stabilization of the existing systems by the Americans, it is difficult to ascribe the failure of revolution in a highly industrialized system undergoing wartime collapse solely to a lack of will. To be sure there was a potential force of revolutionary activists, but they were fragmented into regional partisan bands and local committees and were politically uncoordinated. Granted that from the economic viewpoint most European countries still had a large enough stock of capital and a sufficiently skilled labor force to assure a high rate of growth during the reconstruction period, even after socialization of the means of production. The crisis of transition [to socialism] would still have entailed too high a cost. It might have caused food supplies to collapse completely and would not have been able to raise the level of production quickly. Even a revolution needs supplies if it is not to sacrifice its goals out of hunger and terror.

The other alternative, that of immediately liberalizing [i.e., deregulating] the capitalist system by ending the planning apparatus of the war economies can be even more quickly dismissed. This would have shoved the costs of the crisis exclusively onto the shoulders of the workers. Massive state intervention would then have been needed to recover from the postwar economic collapse. In turn it would have meant backing up economic deregulation with a right-wing political dictatorship for which no basis existed in the liberated countries. The workers' movements would have reacted with the support of armed partisans. In no way could this alternative have provided a suitable union strategy.

Thus the question remains: what concrete possibilities remained in the concept of Economic Democracy (to use this as a shorthand for the program of reconstruction); above all, were there any outcomes likely other than failure? To determine any such possibilities more precisely, several variables must be introduced and the constellation of national factors in the most important countries must be compared.

A United Trade Union and Limited Structural Reform: Italy. Italian conditions are especially useful to point up the special development of the trade unions in occupied Germany. Certainly Italy had undertaken an opportunistic switch to the Allied side in 1943–44, as one can see from the actions of the Badoglio government [Marshall Badoglio, royal appointee to succeed Mussolini in July 1943] and the country's elite. However, months before the Allied landing in Sicily, the Italian working class had demonstrated its own independent antifascist strength by means of largely spontaneous strikes in the industrial centers of the North. Such political and economic mass strikes were applied repeatedly and with increasingly organization over the next two years against the German occupiers in Northern Italy. They provided an essential backbone for building an armed partisan resistance. They led in the final stage of the war not only to local uprisings and efforts at liberation in the cities and the so-called partisan republics, but also to establishment of worker power in many factories through committees of liberation and agitation. While this struggle resembled that of other liberation movements fighting for national and social objectives in German-occupied Europe, Italy was distinguished by the fact that autonomous mass action arose under conditions of a homegrown fascist regime during the war.[6]

Those Italian experiences most comparable to Germany's, however (at least before the Germans occupied northern Italy), did not so much involve the independent activity of the working class as the political and trade-union organizations. Even the transitional regime of Marshal Badoglio can be compared with the conservative resistance of the 20th of July 1944 [the German conspiracy against Hitler]. As in Germany, the organized resistance of the unions and parties—in contrast to the spontaneous mass action in the final phase of the war—remained weak, isolated, and ineffective. The collapse of the regime led, however, to a rapid reconstitution of the prefascist organizational leadership as major party and union functionaries returned from exile or "inner emigration." As German resistance leaders also planned to proceed, union reorganization under Badoglio began with the assignment of top labor union officials from different parties as commissioners to high positions in the fascist corporative organizations. As in the case of the German Labor Front the Italian corporative bodies were organized by industry. To be sure, the rank and file resisted making use of the fascist organizational forms. But the period between the dismissal of Mussolini and the German occupation [i.e., July 25 to

September 8, 1943] proved too short to see how this emerging dispute over organization would turn out. Nevertheless, even in this brief interval working-class leaders did manage to reach an agreement with industrialists for the election of factory councils. This preempted wild-cat strikes in the factories and was supposed to provide an enduring basis for worker representation in the plants. Even these early initiatives revealed how willing the union leadership was to cooperate with the industrialists, if thereby they could immediately secure an extensive trade-union-like organization with a monopoly on labor representation. The same interest marked the 1943–44 concepts of German resistance labor leaders, Leuschner and Tarnow, for a transformation of the German Labor Front into a broad union with compulsory membership.[7]

With the German occupation of Northern Italy and the flight of the Badoglio government from Rome to the Allied-occupied South [September 1943], conditions for rebuilding the unions were transformed. Plans for converting fascist corporativism from the top down into a united union had the ground cut from under them by both the politically inspired resistance units in the North and the Allied powers in the South, who demanded a reconstruction of free trade unions.[8] As a consequence, a dualist system of political and economic working-class organization emerged in Italy. It could be roughly described as a relatively autonomous trade-union structure, organized to exert power at the national level in the South and on the factory level in the North. After liberation it was to prove a national two-tier system of long-term importance. The authority of the trade-union leadership derived from their political role in the antifascist parties; this was quite different from the Western zones of Germany and most comparable to the [Communist] Free German Union Federation [FDGB] in the Soviet zone of occupation. In the South of Italy politically oriented unions were the first to form—one a combined socialist-communist federation, one nonpartisan, and one Catholic. After negotiations between the union representatives of the national party executives, these were consolidated by the Pact of Rome on June 3, 1944, into a united union, the General Italian Confederation of Labor (CGIL). The CGIL aimed at a combined horizontal and vertical structure, whose regional and local components would have the power to overcome opposition from the industrialists' associations—not least because the proportional representation agreed to for local and regional elections would assure the parallel strength of the working-class political parties. In any case, the autonomous local and regional groups who held power in the North during the liberation might be expected to exert considerable influence. As General Secretaries of the united union, a socialist, a communist, and a Catholic each shared equal prerogatives. During the following years, however, the communist element rose to clear predominance because of the contingencies of personnel at the top and the Party's skillful organizational politics.[9]

These successes for communist organizational politics in the CGIL proved of decisive importance for political and economic reconstruction once they were extended to the liberated North. In an extremely flexible policy—Togliatti even entered the Soviet-recognized Badoglio government—the communists set the unions on a firm "antifascist-democratic" course. This included supporting an all-party government to establish a parliamentary republic as well as ideological and personnel purges. It also involved helping to advance economic reconversion and higher production by cooperation with management, by promotion of labor discipline, and by wage restraint. In working out the constitution, extensive planning powers were ceded to the state and apparently made politically secure by virtue of the workers' parties' role in the government. At the same time, provision was made for future enlargement of the nationalized sector of banks, energy concerns, and transformation industries, which Mussolini had already initiated. With its takeover of many state- and local-government positions, the working-class movement appeared to have become an integral part of the system. With the establishment of Chambers of Labor and the formation of joint labor-management committees to oversee many northern industries, the working class won the capacity for codetermination of economic and social issues. These committees had generally arisen during the struggle for liberation and represented the interest that managers as well as plant workers had in protecting industrial plants against destruction by the Germans. In view of the fact that the fascist regime had already greatly expanded the public sector of the economy, this structure of working-class achievements added up to what the program of Economic Democracy envisaged, even if the Italian reforms rested more on *de facto* victories than on statutory enactments. The communist leadership supported the constitution, participated in the cabinets, and despite the shift to the right in 1947 that led to its own dismissal, still sought to return to the government. The PCI could rightfully take pride in its role in sharply curbing national strikes or in limiting them to short, local conflicts.[10]

In fact, this policy failed on all levels. As was the case in Germany, contemporaries sharply overestimated the destruction of Italian productive capacity [and therefore of capitalist vitality]. Once the continuity of private property was recognized in principle, the position of the bourgeoisie grew stronger and stronger. The real problem lay [not in destruction], but in acute aggravation of Italy's chronic underemployment, which decisively weakened the economic position of the working class. Against this background, the division of functions in the government also played a role. Socialists and communists generally took over the administrative apparatus for labor and social welfare, but they left decisive positions over economic and financial policy to the bourgeois parties, in part because they just lacked ideas and experts. These posts were largely taken over by a group of old-laissez-faire economists who effectively intervened with measures to stabilize the middle classes and to continue deregulation of the economic system. At the same time, they used the new planning machinery only to get out of the postwar crisis, and by fiscal measures (lowering progressive taxation, deflating without redistributing the resulting losses or without protecting jobs) made capital accumulation easier.[11]

The CGIL leadership was not able to bridge the gap that separated it from its own rank and file. Because of its stress upon the needs of the economy as a whole and its agreement on reconstruction, the leadership exerted restraint on wages. It also inhibited any protests against the suppression of local resistance organizations by central administrative and parliamentary institutions. Besides the divergence in trade-union development between South and North during the dual occupation that was cited above, different political perspectives and economic conditions were also responsible for the cleavage between leaders and rank and file. Toward the end of the national liberation struggle, socialist and communist partisans made repeated attempts to push the local resistance movements in the direction of a socialist revolution. But the communists' "antifascist-democratic" strategy for Europe, which seemed so compelling while Anglo-American troops were in Italy, actually contributed to the leadership's undercutting all such revolutionary efforts. One example was the Sicilian city of Ragusa, where an attempted communist revolt was suppressed with the approval of the national Party leadership.

During the years 1945–46, the rank and file staunchly worked to preserve the organs created in the liberation struggle, while the strengthened business community sought to undermine the joint manager-employee committees and the state administration won out over the competing committees of liberation. The unions' policy of wage stabilization proved even more constraining since it meant that the postwar inflation and the reconversion of armaments plants cut into the workers' standard of living and reduced employment. While the national leadership of the working-class movement was concerned with avoiding strikes, the country was overtaken by waves of spontaneous or locally organized work stoppages, short in duration and in the nature of social protest.[12] The inability of the leadership to discipline the workers in general, or just to bring their own organizations into line, cost their policy of collaboration with the bourgeoisie its credibilty. On the other hand, the very emphasis the labor leaders placed on this policy underlined their limited capacity to integrate their own workers. In turn, this made popular-front unity fragile indeed. After 1946 anti-communism would serve increasingly as a way to weaken the labor movement.

The pressure for a united front between communists and socialists had already led to social-democratic splinter movements and had raised tension within the united labor unions. Dismissal of the communists from the government and the absolute majority won by the Christian Democrats, who campaigned in 1948 as an anticommunist bulwark against the Communist-Socialist People's Bloc, also split the CGIL. In autumn 1948 a Catholic union emerged, friendly to the government and concerned only with issues of salaries and wages (the LCGIL); later on, segments of liberal and socialist unions followed. The communists' emphasis on the concept of a political union catalyzed the schism. In light of the economic difficulties and the Americans' requirement for a cooperative stance in return for credits, the other union groups backed away, to revert to representation just of their adherents' immediate economic interests. The economic power that the workers had enjoyed in 1945–46 had not been effectively used by the communist-dominated unions to shape durable institutions suitable for political and social struggle. Hence, while the masses might still respond in 1947–48 to the call for a political strike against the Marshall Plan and the assassination attempt against Togliatti, these actions only hastened the collapse of their organization, and they were soon exhausted.[13] Reconstruction of the liberal economic order by continuing low wages and underemployment (and also by the institution of a powerful police apparatus) had melted away the potential for an enduring struggle. Political protest and attainable economic demands increasingly diverged. With the reestablishment of an economic system in which emigration served as ersatz cure for the chronic unemployment that was starkly revealed once again, the united trade union lost its strategic position.

A Limited United Union and Structural Reform: France. The development of the united trade-union movement in France deviated from that in Italy—and from that in Germany—because of the essentially different historical conditions that shaped it. The continuity and autonomy of the French parties and unions was not wholly destroyed by a home-grown fascism, nor was their post-liberation course of development supervised at the outset by a British-American occupation. Both these factors exerted only an indirect influence. Nonetheless, there were many similarities with Italy, attributable above all to the parallel behavior of the communists.

In France, too, the communists were the driving force behind the unification of the trade unions and won a predominant role in the union organization by virtue of their tactical superiority. In addition, they were able to credit to their account a massive influx of members as a result of the prestige acquired as a result of their dynamic Resistance combat in the second half of the war. France, too, revealed the split between a leadership pursuing coalition policies and the local, autonomous Resistance groups, especially those in the South, who frequently pushed for a revolutionary restructuring but were repressed by the central institutions of the administration, the parliament, and the interest groups. In France, too, the leaders of the PCF returned from exile in Moscow as the champions within the Left of a return to normalcy. They actively advocated a bourgeois-proletarian pact among the three mass parties (Communists, Socialists, Catholic M.R.P.) on behalf of reconstruction, and they invoked their prestige against local strikes protesting hunger and against other economically motivated, spontaneously ignited labor struggles. As in Italy, even after their dismissal from the government in the spring of 1947, the communists sought to return to the party coalition and for several months continued their policy of cooperation—until the dispute over the Marshall Plan.[14]

Nonetheless, the united trade union experiment encountered resistance from the outset even in the labor movement. Labor's traditions had remained compelling from the Third Republic through the Phony War, Vichy, the Resistance, and de Gaulle's government in exile. Except for Spain, socialists and communists had tried the experiment of a popular front government only in France. At first this experience reinforced the mutual opposition of the two parties, and with the Hitler-Stalin Pact of 1939, the communists were expelled from the General Confederation of Labor (CGT). Here their originally small communist union organization, which had merged during the preparations for the Popular Front, had already won increasing influence during the course of the Blum government to which they gave passive support. The Christian Unions' CFTC—then still merely an insignificant clerical movement—had remained on the sidelines and recruited opponents of the Popular Front.[15] Like the communists, who had adopted a policy of "revolutionary defeatism" during the period of the Hitler-Stalin Pact, some of the socialists who had collaborated with the Vichy regime were heavily compromised in the view of de Gaulle's exile government and the Resistance. Vichy prohibited both the CGT and the CFTC and replaced them with corporative organizations. Both federations, however, preserved considerable cohesiveness while illegal: witness the major strike among miners in Northern France in May 1941. An alliance between the CFTC and the noncollaborationist segments of the CGT thus seemed natural. They united on a common manifesto that attributed responsibility for the defeat of France to capitalism. The political functions of the state were to be separated from the economic ones of the unions, and production was to be directed by compulsory planning.[16] Once the Communist Party was freed from the Hitler-Stalin Pact [through the German attack on Russia] and could bring its own dynamic organization into the Resistance, it sought a rapprochement with the old CGT leadership. This bore fruit with the Perreux agreements of April 17, 1943, which provided for admitting three communists to the eight-man clandestine union leadership. Within the industry-wide as well as locally based unions, the political relationships that had existed before the schism of 1939 were to be restored.[17] In the National Council of the Resistance (CNR), the united CGT was represented by a nonparty member who was close to the communists. The CNR worked out a program whose central economic demands —nationalization of monopolies, of mineral deposits and banks, and state planning for economic reconstruction—reflected the interwar socialist program. The communists demanded only the expropriation of collaborators, a point that was disputed, however, among the Resistance organizations because it lacked precision. Although the communists pressed especially hard, no fusion of the reunited CGT took place with the CFTC. The Christian unions certainly joined the resistance struggle and agreed to a pact for unity of action with the CGT on socioeconomic issues; but they feared that in the case of a merger they could not successfully maintain their religious, educational, and cultural policies in the wake of the CGT, while on matters of organization they would be dragged along by the communists. In contrast to the Church hierarchy, the Christian unions comprised an active component of the Resistance, and they participated in the unions' struggle against the German occupation by means of strikes and sabotage. The agreement for united action proved its worth by the extensive resistance measures during the period of liberation, especially in the general strike called on August 18, 1944, which provided the basis within the city for the liberation of Paris.[18]

After liberation both unions grew mightily. The CGT regained its highest membership figures of the 1936 Popular Front with about 5.5 million adherents; the CFTC attained an absolute peak with three-quarters of a million. Since the CFTC insisted on keeping its own independence as an organization, the movement toward a united union was limited to a pact between socialists and communists. This turned out less cohesive than in Italy, for the French socialists had at least in part preserved their continuity and could resume a more successful and solid tradition. In contrast to the left-wing majority of the Italian socialists, the SFIO kept its distance as an organization from the PCF, and by cooperation in the cabinet with the MRP—then a prevailingly progressive mass party of Catholics—it created a counterbalance to the communist influence. In the long run the united trade union could not overcome the gap continuing between the parties, for the trade union federation served less as an economic interest group in the postwar crisis than as an instrument of political order. The distance between the two currents showed up as early as 1946, as the socialists within the CGT increasingly opposed communist organizational policies and their transformation of the united trade union into a mass political federation. The socialists paid for their ambivalent alliance policies with declining union membership as well as considerable losses at the polls and internal party revolts.[19]

On the other hand, it was the merit of the tripartite governments and of their alliance with the two major unions to transform into reality during 1945–46 a good part of the structural reforms that the National Council of the Resistance had envisioned: nationalization of mineral deposits, of large transportation enterprises, of the largest banks and insurance companies, the expropriation of collaborationists (especially of the Renault works), the establishment of the state's economic planning instruments, the participation of unions and consumer cooperatives in the supervision of nationalized industries, legal protection for factory councils, and extension of social security. Even if the achievement fell short of socialist demands, of all similar efforts to democratize the economies of the West, this came closest to realization.[20]

Structural reforms, however, could not solve the economic and financial problems of reconstruction. Instead, because an effective social redistribution of the costs of the war was avoided and the economy was progressively deregulated, a dichotomy resulted, similar to what had marked the Italian economy with far less pervasive structural reform. On the one hand, there was reconsolidation of the bourgeoisie, and on the other, undernourishment and underemployment of the working class. Even the CPF leaders could not durably resist the pressure from its rank and file—most notably a major strike for higher wages in the nationalized coal mines; and finally the leadership reluctantly had to take over the direction of a spontaneous strike in its own labor stronghold at Renault.[21] The socialist prime minister, who was then negotiating with the United States for economic assistance, took the occasion to dismiss the communists from the government. Although thrust into opposition, the communist leadership still behaved throughout the early summer months of 1947 as if it were a government party. On the other hand, as the American [Marshall Plan] initiative in Europe took shape, French government policies shifted to the Right. The new trend decisively increased the factionalism within the CGT and ended with the secession of the Socialist Force Ouvrière (CGT/FO) once the communists employed the CGT to unleash a political strike against the Marshall Plan, a tactic familiar from Italy. Still, as in Italy the preeminent participation of the French Communist Party in the Resistance and then in the postwar coalitions meant that although the socialist union leaders might secede from the CGT, there was to be no proportional loss of rank-and-file membership. The CGT remained the dominant economic and political interest group representing the French workers, while the FO remained a relatively insignificant faction, even in comparison to the Catholic CFTC.[22]

A United Movement Without a Unified Organization. Structural Reform Without Codetermination in England. The English case demonstrates that the movement toward united unions in the early postwar years was perhaps inconceivable without socialist-communist cooperation, but was nonetheless no mere consequence of communist preponderance (as might have been presumed from events in the Latin countries). Admittedly the British Communist Party had emerged from its sectarian isolation after its turn to the Popular Front and especially after 1941, and during the war it achieved control of a group of union locals and some regional federations. However, the disputes over accepting the CP as a corporate member of the Labour Party revealed that the communists and their supporters in 1943 had only a bit over one-third, and in 1946 not even a fifth of the votes at the union-dominated Labour Party conferences; and even of these the actual communist members were only a small minority.[23] Admittedly the communist position in the Trade Unions Congress was stronger, especially since the divisions separating them from other left-wingers were fluid. Nonetheless, communist representation was not the only, or even the immediate, cause for the TUC's major initiative to overcome the schism in the international trade-union movement. This derived instead from the situation of 1941 when only the Soviet Union and Great Britain stood as besieged military adversaries of German fascism and the TUC took the occasion to initiate an Anglo-Soviet trade-union committee. In the following years this first step was extended with the result that a united World Federation of Trade

Unions was formed on May 30, 1945, bringing together communist, independent, and united unions with the exception of the American Federation of Labor.[24] Without the political influence of the left wing of the TUC, which extended far beyond the communists, the great social-welfare progress of the wartime coalition government in Great Britain and of the [post-1945] Labour government would likewise have been brought about only with the greatest difficulty. On the other hand, even these epoch-making reforms in the areas of social insurance, national health service, educational reform, and urban reconstruction were more the products of liberal and technocratic innovation than of socialist or Marxist theory.[25]

Besides the initiative for trade-union unification and the gains for social welfare, few trends attributable to the Left connected the British with the Continental program for the united trade union. What was noteworthy in Britain was the great organizational progress of the TUC, which more than recovered the setbacks of the interwar period. The returning flood of old members into the unions and the additional recruitment was not distributed equally among all regional or factory locals of the fragmented English union movement, but redounded above all to the benefit of the large unions, once again those in the TUC. The average size of the TUC unions was about twice as large in 1945 as in 1930, but the number of unions was down about 10 percent to 192. Their total membership nearly doubled to about six and a half million, of which over half were concentrated in six large unions. The proportion of all union members whose federations belonged to the TUC attained what was to be a high point of 84.7 percent. Even in the five postwar years the concentration in favor of the large unions continued, although the TUC could not extend its own monopolistic percentage share of union members until the mid-1960s. At the end of the Second World War the number of independent unions was half the number of those at the end of the First World War, even if with 780 it remained very high. It is nonetheless clear that given extraordinarily difficult and fragmented conditions, the war and the immediate postwar period brought considerable growth of membership together with decisive progress toward large industrial unions and consolidation of a national union. Thus, along with the wartime "opening to the Left," the political and economic outlines of a united labor union were discernible even under specifically British conditions.[26]

Such progress would not have been thinkable without unified policies. Although spontaneous wage strikes took place more frequently toward the end of the war, ever since 1941 the leadership of the TUC, the Labour Party, and the Communist Party continued to support the efforts of Churchill's government to raise production and stabilize wages. As Minister of Labour, Ernest Bevin, the most prominent union representative in the cabinet, was even able to have organized strikes declared illegal, a ruling that the Labour government extended until 1951.[27] Pressure for increased production, wage stabilization, and avoidance of strikes under conditions of full employment were, however, to become points of conflict between the Labour government and the TUC, also between Right and Left, and between leadership and rank and file in the deepening postwar financial and balance-of-payments crises.[28] The record of workdays lost in the more or less spontaneous strikes that were not organized by the unions is eloquent: 1944, 3.7 million; 1945, 2.8 million; 1946, 2.1 million; 1947, 2.4 million. During the wage freeze of 1948 the number sank below the 2-million mark, to exceed it again only in 1952.[29]

The TUC's attitude toward structural reforms was also characteristic of the tendency to focus the broad united labor movement upon specific trade-union objectives. Great Britain not only developed its state-planning instruments during the reconstruction period, but the Labour government, decisively supported by the TUC, carried out a series of spectacular nationalizations. The government began with the Bank of England, the transportation industries, and other infrastructural key activities such as health and gas and electricity, then moved to strengthen control over public planning and eminent domain for the establishment of new cities, and finally nationalized the coal and steel industries. Certainly these measures did not come to pass because of any communist pressure; they corresponded far more to the technocratic tradition of the intellectual Fabian socialists—indeed it has been questioned whether such partial socialization is really in the interest of the working class.[30] The Labour government's nationalizations, nonetheless, were more extensive than those of any other Western country of the era (even if they were only a way in part of making up for prior backwardness). They exceeded even the short-term goals of the West German labor movement.

But quite in contrast to labor on the Continent, the English union leadership did not want to help direct the nationalized industries unless it was through party and state supervisory agencies. Traditionally the British saw codetermination, on the one hand, as an expression of left-wing syndicalism, much as represented by the shop-steward movement, guild socialism, and workers' control that had arisen to challenge union authority in the factories after World War I. On the other hand, British labor perceived a threat to the unions' capacity for resistance in that consultative committees in the plants might prove friendly to management. Even in the nationalized sector union leaders did not wish to infringe upon the principle of free collective bargaining. In accordance with English democratic tradition they interpreted industrial democracy as an application of the parliamentary conflict between government and opposition to the adversary relationship over salary and working conditions between the worker and management, even the management of the nationalized industries. Union participation in plant management would encourage ambivalent responsibilities, which, in view of the extensive autonomy of the rank and file in the British labor movement, could only produce a crisis of legitimacy for the union leadership. The TUC thus supported nationalization to achieve higher rationality for the national economy, but rejected any participation in the leadership or control of the factories. As a compromise, though, a group of the most important union leaders were summoned to the management boards of the nationalized sectors. In fact, they thus sacrificed their trade-union roles. They were certainly unable to avoid the reproach that they had merely won plums for the union elite, a charge that was levelled as soon as it became clear that wages and working conditions had not really changed by virtue of nationalization of the factories.[31]

A Flawed United Union and Postponed Structural Reforms in West Germany. Developments in organization and function certainly allow the united trade union in occupied Germany, especially in the Western zones, to be compared with those in the other large European industrial nations. But the contradiction between the especially restricted political sphere of action and the all-encompassing programmatic expectations of a democratic economic utopia remained characteristically German. The existing scholarly literature runs the risk of assuming that this vision, coupled with the constraints imposed on the rank and file at the time the unions were reorganized, added up to a dynamic socialist potential. Against this potential the repressive occupation powers are posited as a purely exogenous factor. But unless one answers the question why the French and Americans above all were in a position to prevent the rapid reconstitution of a united trade union in Germany as well as partially to prohibit, partially to postpone, its basic programmatic demands, one misconceives the problematic contrast between theory and practice.

Both the opportunities for, as well as the major impediment to, a united trade-union movement in Germany arose from the fact that the working-class movement had been so thoroughly defeated by fascism that it simply disappeared as an organization. The collapse of democratic counterweights—liberal institutions and an organized labor force —was what initially made possible the self-destructive running amok that capitalist society embarked upon in Germany in 1933 under National Socialist leadership. In this respect the loss of national sovereignty at the end of the war, which made the development of parties and unions directly dependent upon the respective interests of the victors, really goes back to the particular and the collective failures of the non-Nazi organizations during the world depression. The self-imposed isolation of the communist union organization and the nonresistance and compliance (*"Gleichschaltung von innen"*) [32] with which socialist and Christian union leaders hoped to preserve their organizations in the Third Reich had precluded their unity and any mobilization of their strength. Deprived of a common combat experience, the working class could not achieve a common effective resistance.[33] Fascist persecution of trade-union and political cadres forced the leadership, if not to imprisonment or death, into the atomization of foreign or "inner" emigration.

Still, the class basis of the union organizations (in contrast to the integrative nature of parliamentary parties) meant that whatever organizational unification of the working-class movement during the transitional period of resistance and emigration was achieved was most successful in the trade-union sphere. The common trend toward organizational and political unification did not mean, however, that the same format and programs were followed everywhere. The initiatives of those German trade-union groups in exile unmistakably reflected the trends in their lands of asylum. Similarly within Germany trade union leaders in the resistance often took the Nazi DAF (German Labor Front) as a starting point for a future democratic union evolution. Three major organizational forms can be distinguished: socialist and Christian labor leaders in the Resistance and in the Swedish emigration wanted a process of democratic transformation that would divest the DAF of its corporative characteristics.[34] The communists advocated a so-called *Eintopf*-[goulasch] union, a united political union borrowed from their experience in the Latin countries in which the political authorities at the local, regional, and national levels were to possess the upper hand over the economic interests of the factory- or industry-wide locals.[35] Finally, the union émigrés in England, influenced by the concept for the World Trade Union Federation, developed a model that laid less stress on central organization. With its emphasis on party neutrality it can be seen more in terms of an invitation to the Christian unions than as a unification of social democrats and communists.[36]

All three models proliferated widely among the groups seeking to found local unions once the Allies occupied Germany. In addition, local variants sprang up, such as shop-steward movements. Former union leaders who were reinstated in their old work resumed their old organization by industry. What proved decisive for implanting these models in the locals that were taking shape, but a factor that scholarly literature has hitherto understressed, was the return of numerous union leaders from abroad with the first Allied troops. The Communist Party groups attached to the Red Army are widely known; in the West, too, there were many delegates of the National Free Germany Committee for the West," who flowed from France, Switzerland, and Belgium into western and southern Germany especially. [The Free Germany Committee had been organized originally among German prisoners of war in the Soviet Union and was thus sympathetic to Russian objectives; the one for the West presumably united sympathizers from the other countries.—Ed.] Finally, there was a group of social democrats from the English emigration who were placed in the most important German cities as collaborators of the American intelligence service, the OSS. Although officially enjoying only an advisory function, they still provided significant help with programs and organization by virtue of their knowledge and connections.[37]

In contrast to this indirect assistance, the Allies also intervened directly in trade-union autonomy. The Soviets advanced the *Eintopf-* union model in their zone, seeking so far as possible an all-German federation with a centralized Party-nominated leadership. In the western zones, as well as in the East, it included a strong communist component and generally took the name Free German Trade Union Federation (FDGB). All the occupation authorities vetoed any effort to convert the DAF into a union, a goal that was sought, for example, by Hans Böckler in Cologne or Markus Schleicher in Stuttgart. The Americans favored organizing unions industry by industry as economic interest groups. The British and Americans imposed a step-by-step plan for organizational reconstruction from the local and factory level up and thus hindered any rapid buildup of trade-union power at the higher leadership levels of the Weimar era, while the French permitted federation at the state (*Land*) level but tenaciously resisted any consolidation of national unions.[38] Besides the influence of the emigration and the military governments, foreign unions also played a role, as they sought —sometimes in cooperation with the occupying power—to win over German colleagues for their own union format and programs. The AFL committed its efforts for the longest period, rejecting the gradualist pattern of union reconstitution that the American military government desired because it feared that this procedure would result in a larger communist influence. Instead, the AFL advocated building up economically oriented industrial unions in the western zones with strong participation on the part of the prewar reformist union leadership. A TUC delegation also played an important role when it made clear to the union leaders of the British zone that the English would never agree to any form of centralized united union whether derived from the DAF or the communist model.[39]

Thus preliminary decisions on organizational questions tended to set the pattern for a highly diverse structure of unions, which in fact tended initially to stagnate at the regional or zonal level. From the outset two paths diverged. The first was the political, centralized united union of the Soviet sphere, which was also represented among those western locals that had a particularly strong communist rank and file. The second included the diverse variants of the already elastic model from the English emigration—now watered down even further—that prevailed in the western zones. The western Allies could look with all the more favor on regional organizational levels retaining their predominance, because this would avoid any repetition of the split between local groups striving for autonomy and the national summit of the labor movement, such as had occurred in Italy under American impetus.[40]

The second basic problem of organization concerned the extent, the interests, and the spontaneity of the potential unions. Reorganization began immediately after the occupation. It was regarded by all participants as more important than the building of political parties, and quickly became a wide-ranging effort.[41] Independent of their immediate interests and their political affiliations, many workers and employees saw joining the new unions as the most natural and direct response to their earlier suppression in the Third Reich, no matter what sort of form they might be taking in their own particular locality. The unions were founded on two different bases at the same time: on the one hand, built around the usual old leaders organized by region; on the other, organized at the plant level.[42] In contrast to Italy, however, neither sort of organization won much power. Regional fragmentation weakened the leadership groups, while the rank and file lacked the experience of conflict and the militance of the national movements of liberation. Without the self-consciousness imbued by a successful resistance, diminished by the large numbers of workers drafted for war service, and demoralized by their own split from the reserve army of forced labor the Nazis had imported, German workers had relatively little spontaneous capacity for political action, especially for carrying out any purge. On the other hand, they demonstrated intense interest in cooperative self-help and union representation in order to resume production, to secure jobs, and to reach a minimal level of welfare. This working class was far readier than, say, the partisans in southern Europe to accept union wage restraint within an overall partnership for growth in order to overcome the postwar crisis. Certainly there were cases in Germany, as elsewhere, of the divergence between union cooperation on behalf of recovery for society as a whole and the immediate interests of the rank and file. Comparatively speaking, however, these discrepancies were mere nuances. The dismantling of Antifa [Antifascist groups that were organized by workers at the time of surrender] and factory committees, then later of factory councils as unions and administrative agencies were reestablished, ran an undramatic course. The same activists frequently just took over a new function. This certainly contributed to democratizing the regional leadership of the emerging union organizations, but at the same time meant subordination to new responsibility and discipline.[43]

Besides labor's own weakness, direct Allied rule and the more serious postwar economic and infrastructure crisis in Germany also contributed to the restraint on "class struggles in the western zones." [44] These conditions diminished the clout and influence of the unions. In a situation where planning and wage freezes were not the work of a national government that needed the support of union leaders, but were instead decreed directly by the military authorities in the different zones, military power replaced the strength of the labor unions in integrating workers into the process of reorganizing and increasing production. To the degree, however, that the unions in Germany were unnecessary for the economic system, they failed to win the positions that would have let them exact social and economic structural reforms or essential social welfare gains as the price of their cooperation. On the other hand, insofar as the bargaining position of the unions was already weak at the start of the occupation, there was less conflict than in other countries with the rank and file, which was itself less active than elsewhere. (The relative position of the grass roots in the unions did benefit, however, from the fact that all social interaction tended to be reduced to the local level during the economic crisis.) Instead the leaders and rank and file both concentrated on the effort just to build a united trade union in the face of Allied restrictions. Thus the early postwar years were dominated by the question of organization. And the unifying tradition that a common resistance against fascism provided elsewhere was replaced by a united resistance to the limitations on union development that the Allies imposed as well as against their industrial dismantling policies.

The situation changed when the occupying powers abandoned efforts to increase coal production by coercive measures. But the new incentives to extract higher output promptly precipitated in 1947 familiar short-term reactions: a campaign for increased output, strikes protesting malnutrition, progress toward codetermination and nationalization.[45] Although the occupying powers prevented the German unions from taking advantage of the general socioeconomic function served by the West European united unions until 1947, and even, in part, through 1949, the unions still sought to play the equivalent social role as elsewhere. They aligned themselves as auxiliaries in the Allied-directed process of reconstruction. For many union leaders believed along with Hans Böckler that the capitalist order at home had been critically weakened with the collapse of Germany's economic potential.[46] This meant that they felt labor could first fulfill its social responsibilities and help with reconstruction, then later could always push through nationalization and other structural reforms. The very social democrats who in 1945 frequently viewed socialism as the task of the hour were now willing to postpone it according to Kurt Schumacher's maxim: *Primum vivere, deinde philosophari* [The first thing is to live; philosophy comes later].[47] In practice this meant following the communist tactic of seeking strength for a future socialist transformation by undergoing a period of testing in the pragmatic work of reconstruction.

Resuming the program of Economic Democracy[48] in the 1945 situation also seemed to mean at first inheriting its greatest disadvantage, namely, the lack of any strategy to compel nationalization, planning, and codetermination. Many advocates believed that these concepts should no longer be fought for, but merely introduced into a receptive economic order by recourse to the ballot. This would supposedly have let the unions inherit a pivotal social role as organizer of a communal economic order. The unions themselves would then become the instrument of social bargaining and compromise while they could downplay their old role, still retained in England, of championing the particularistic interests of the working class in labor struggles. By virtue of the extensive list of nationalizations and the demand for an equal union voice in management, German objectives likewise transcended French goals, even though the CGT occupied a far more favorable strategic position vis-à-vis the reformist political coalition than did the fragmented German unions in respect to the occupying powers. The majority of German union leaders thus faced an unresolved contradiction between an overambitious socialist utopia and their actual partnership for economic reconstruction with the military governments and with the firms and state agencies that had survived and whose very recovery made realization of the union program ever more unlikely. This contradiction resulted from a flawed perception of the international interests in contention, but it also derived from an abstract union plan for reconstruction that failed to relate the unions' organization and envisaged function either to each other or to the tactical situation, but only to the expectation of some future socialist order.

The special role of the communists in the postwar unions still requires explanation. Just as the communists in the Russian zone of occupation sought to establish their own form of the united union by means of negotiations among the organizational elites in the FDGB,[49] they similarly cooperated in the unions of the western zones and in their practical behavior were distinguishable only in nuance. Still, it is inaccurate to claim, as is frequently said about 1945–46, that political differences played no role in reconstructing the unions. Sufficient examples can be cited in which former socialist and Christian trade unionists perceived the growing number of communists in the unions and especially in the factory councils as a threat and sought to cut them back.[50] The communists, however, wanted to use union discipline and concerted action to achieve unity and establish themselves. Tilman Fichter has argued that this method of taking root and mobilizing a mass base was more realistic than urging socialism as the task of the day, but that the communists were politically inconsistent in 1947. At that time spontaneous strikes broke out in the Ruhr, as in France, against a union-supported campaign for increased output even while food shortages continued. In Fichter's view the communists failed to develop the socialist mass base that had become, as it were, capable of action. Instead they domesticated the class struggle and proved unable to mobilize an equivalent potential with their subsequent political struggle against the Marshall Plan.[51] Since a more accurate analysis of the motives and course of these 1947 strikes still remains to be written, any estimate of their potential must remain uncertain. In any case the critique completely fails to take into account the limiting conditions on communist policy of the day. If we bear in mind the French events of the spring of 1947 as well as the continuing FDGB efforts at interzonal conferences to achieve a united union throughout Germany (granted, one that would follow their own pattern as far as possible) [52] there is no doubt that the communists insisted on a united union from higher considerations quite independent of the interests of specific workers. In particular, they wanted to keep developments in each country during the "antifascist-democratic" transitional phase parallel and coordinated, and not let themselves become isolated in terms of Europe as a whole by letting the class struggle break out prematurely in different locations.

The Schism

The united union movement broke off during 1948 in the West European countries. In France, the socialists, and in Italy, Catholics, liberals, and a segment of the socialists split from the united unions, which thereupon became entirely communist mass organizations. In England a campaign against communist union officials was begun and the TUC withdrew its membership in the WFTU. Anti-communism and adherence to the new International Confederation of Free Trade Unions (ICFTU), which arose out of the WFTU schism, also characterized developments in the West German zones once efforts failed to found an all-German union organization (which alone could have produced a political united union in Germany). These last sections of the article should reveal what factors led to the political split in the unions and what consequences resulted for the changing functions of the rump unions, especially for the German Trade Union Federation (DGB) that was constituted only at this time.

Some reasons for the end of the WFTU have already been given. As worked out in recent research they contrast with accounts of the time that presented the union schism as an expression of a democratic struggle for self-determination against communist subversion.[53] Causes now adduced include the large-scale political and economic initiatives of the United States' European policy after 1947 and AFL support for the European opponents of the united unions.[54] These external factors certainly require closer illumination. On the other hand, external influences could never have proved effective if within the political united unions, and in the relationship of their policies to actual social conditions, the explosive material was not already at hand for American policy to ignite. It is worth analyzing here again the internal problems of the political united union so as to counteract the superficial thesis that manipulation alone was at bottom—as if the vital currents of the European working-class movement could be held back by virtue of diplomatic trickery and a bit of bribery.[55]

Organizational Reasons. We have tried to demonstrate here that the typical political united union basically rested on an alliance between social democrats and communists. In the case of the postfascist countries, this was an alliance in which Catholic unions could also participate because once all unions had been shattered and compulsory corporative bodies established, a wider solution had become possible. For the communists the united unions were a means for establishing themselves politically and for carrying out their gradualist "antifascist-democratic" strategy of transition. For the social democrats, the united unions offered a means to integrate the labor movement and then by virtue of its united mass to push through structural reforms along the lines of the Economic Democracy program. The unions would thus become an instrument of rational planning and of compromise among interests for the sake of society as a whole. For both points of departure the national political economy took priority over the traditional function of representing particularistic worker interests, especially in view of the postwar economic crisis, shortages, and the need for growth. On the other hand, the noncommunist labor leaders had been trained precisely in the old unions that had always focused on wage issues. They hardly felt that the goals of Economic Democracy, as they had been worked out in the 1920s by social democratic intellectuals, were their primary task.

Conflict was thus in the offing between a policy on wages and social issues geared to the interests of the membership and a policy of united union cooperation on issues of wage stabilization, growth, and structural reform for the sake of the economy as a whole. Throughout 1945–46 it smouldered in the tensions between local and plant organizations and the top leadership. Only in Western Germany did this conflict fail to produce a clear confrontation because there, reconstruction of the unions was delayed. Even in the other countries it did not initially shatter the organization because in the crisis at the end of the war, cooperation was more important than wage-and-price issues, the future seemed open, and the labor movement was granted, as it were, a vote of confidence in advance. The more the economic system recovered, however, the more important the pay issue became, and the more difficult it grew to secure union cooperation in the campaign for higher production. After the difficult winter of 1946–47, when throughout large areas of Europe energy and food supplies fell to their lowest point, the latent conflict came to a head with massive strikes. The centrist union elites were put under pressure from both the left and right of the working-class movement to reorient the political united union toward more direct advocacy of the workers' immediate economic interests. In France, for example, the AFL delegation found a willing ear among the [noncommunist] opposition with their argument that worker interests should take precedence over political unity and were best represented by industrial unions, even if they had to secede.[56]

On another level, however, the conflict broke out even earlier in Germany. The primacy of industrial unions over political united organizations was not merely wrested from the union leadership by the military government and the TUC. From the outset it found support—

most clearly in Hamburg [57]—among the old industrial union leadership of the Weimar era who feared that a centralized united union would replace the old labor functionaries with communist politicians and neglect wage contracts in order to pursue political tasks with murky goals. Had the Anglo-American influence not found a willing reservoir of experienced trade-union organizers, the Allies' injunctions against the centralized political union could have been treated as mere formalism and easily circumvented. In fact, they amounted to deciding between two German groups, one of which might call for unity from the base up [58] while the other—the noncommunist—was able to build largely independent industrial unions with a quiet efficiency. In France and Italy, on the other hand, the noncommunist secessionists lamented their lack of organization because the syndicalist tradition and the extreme breadth of the postwar unions worked against the German pattern.

Party disputes partially strengthened, partially overshadowed this conflict. In the united union organization social democratic or Catholic officials competed directly with communists in terms of tactical and propaganda skills and dynamism. Until 1947 the communists made rapid progress in this competition everywhere that the occupying powers did not exert counterpressure; nor could anyone demonstrate their disloyalty. This was the case not only within the CGT, the CGIL, and the TUC—leading to a clear communist preponderance in the first two—but also in Germany, for example, in the FDGB of Greater Berlin or the industrial unions (for example, the mine workers) in the British zone.[59] At the same time communist gains were also clear within the executive organs of the World Federation of Trade Unions.[60]

Yet after the experience of Stalinist reversals on the question of unity, competitors still suspected that the communists' tactical adroitness far outstripped their credibility. The forced unification of communists and social democrats in the Soviet zone of Germany certainly strengthened this conviction. Yet to help those who had been outmaneuvered reconquer their mass base and their majorities required the effective public-relations tactic of exposing the communist advance as one of subversion carried out with sordid methods such as electoral fraud, organized tricks, political disloyalty (e.g., contrivance of "spontaneous" strikes), or as a misappropriation of the workers' interest groups for partisan ends. Events that could be interpreted in this sense were not lacking, and between 1946 and 1948, especially in the communist-dominated organizations, they were exposed with increasing propagandistic effectiveness (made possible in part through AFL assistance). In Germany the formation of the Berlin Independent Union

Opposition (UGO) against the FDGB was the most spectacular expression of this widespread trend.[61]

Reasons in International Politics. What proved finally decisive in triggering the potential for conflict within the united union was the social crisis of 1947, which took place in most of those European countries where the working class governed in alliance with bourgeois forces. For the bourgeois and some of the socialist representatives in these governments reacted overwhelmingly to the economic collapse of the winter and spring of 1947 with a desire for foreign economic aid.

The calculation of the liberal [i.e., laissez-faire] economists who directed economic and financial policy (including the West German Bizone * since mid-1947) looked toward the reestablishment of capitalist relations of production by replacing the political pact for growth with market mechanisms.[62] Economic stabilization was expected from elimination of the excess money supply left from the war and deregulation of the economy. This would raise the value of landed and industrial property, compel rationalization [i.e., higher efficiency and concentration of enterprises], lower the price of labor and bring the concealed unemployed into the labor force, attract investment, and draw goods to market. Capital assistance from abroad could thus help to prevent the collapse of state revenues and of the balance of payments, and the additional investment might provide a spur to growth that could at least partially limit the expected decline in wages and increased unemployment.

Given the fact that the Marshall Plan, whose capital grants made possible these [neo-liberal] reforms, divided the parties in the unions, it must be noted that American capital assistance was an economic prerequisite only within the framework of this program for liberalization. In most respects the collapse of early 1947 could be attributed to an infrastructural crisis of growth and of distribution within and between the European countries—for example, a breakdown of transportation in the Bizone at the end of 1946.[63] In this respect the collapse could also have been overcome by greater reliance on, and coordination of state control mechanisms—especially if coupled with an easing of restrictions on German production and foreign trade on the part of the occupying powers—along lines of elaborating the structural reforms already introduced.

---

* Ed. Note: The Bizone referred to the 1947 joining of the British and American zones into a common economic and administrative unit. Once French resistance was overcome a year later, this became the basis for a West German state.

The agreement of the West German unions to United States credits was a key decision because the food problem of the Bizone was the immediate spur to the American project and because the communists in many other united unions campaigned against American assistance. So far as we can tell, the German union leaders felt themselves under duress, given the need to finance food imports under the discriminatory foreign-trade constraints imposed by the Allied powers. Nonetheless they recognized the dangers of accelerating the division of Germany and of increasing the American influence hostile to structural reforms, especially to nationalization in the Ruhr. But since a direct conflict with the occupying power seemed hopeless, they could only attempt to at least hold open the option for structural reforms while advocating the credits. Hans Böckler coined the effective public slogan: If necessary it was better to postpone socialization than to starve.[64]

The Americans, who were obviously interested in the productive employment of their European aid, seized their opportunity. Their capital exports gave them a strategic position in the affected European economies, and at the same time allowed them to integrate these economies into a political order.[65] Even in the preliminary phase of the Marshall Plan they made it clear, not only by military government interventions in Germany but through loan negotiations with France and Italy as well, that as complementary measures they expected security against any revolutionary reaction by the labor movement, including containment of its influence and of anticapitalist structural reforms. Dissolving the ties with the communists in the governments and the unions thus had fundamental importance. The dismissal of the communists from the French government and the secession of a Christian union in Italy created the preconditions for economic aid.[66]

In Western Germany the Americans could be active in their own right once the British had conceded the American leadership role in Germany as a consequence of their own credits from the United States. They could delay decartelization, suspend nationalization in Hessia and North Rhine Westphalia, break the social democratic majority in the Bizone by setting up a second level of institutions, favor the Berlin noncommunist unions, keep in force a wage freeze and a prohibition on strikes, and undertake their own currency reform.[67] Military government looked on approvingly as the communists left the state governments and as the interzonal trade-union conferences ran into increasing difficulty and finally ended. Clay also recommended to union leaders that they give up structural reforms and tend more to the immediate interests of their members (although he interpreted even these interests very narrowly, in accordance with a preconception of class collaboration).[68] Not without reason, the Soviet Union saw the

Marshall Plan as an effort to undercut the economic and political basis of the communist strategy of an "antifascist-democratic" transition to socialism. This was to have been directed after all by means of communist participation in the European governments and mass organizations, especially the united unions. From the second half of 1947 the Communist parties of Western Europe thus threw their entire weight into demonstrations against the U.S. initiative. But just this focusing of an economic into a political crisis had to end up serving American purposes. For the middle-class Left and the social democratic doubters who saw the Marshall Plan as essentially a welcome injection of capital could only recognize that the communists were seeking to make the unions the transmission belt of their political defensive and were dropping their moderation in this conflict with their previous government partners. The Soviet trade-union newspaper [*Trud*] demanded that the reformist advocates of the Marshall Plan be expelled from the leadership of the WFTU. The TUC responded with the counterthrust that ended with the schism of the WFTU.[69]

Secondly, the Soviet Union saw the Marshall Plan as an attack on the integrity of its Eastern European sphere of influence. The desire of the Czech government to receive Marshall Plan funds was an index that American containment policy already possessed implications of "rollback." But as an unoccupied country, Czechoslovakia was the classic model of an "antifascist-democratic" transition to socialism in the garb of a bourgeois republic. Were she to vote for the U.S. credits the issue would immediately arise whether to repress similar desires in other peoples' democracies by military force or to accept political reversals as a consequence of American capital exports. For that reason the communists had to act preemptively in the Czechoslovak Republic. First the Czech government was threatened into withdrawing its assent to the Marshall Plan conference, which also blocked in advance any similar inclinations elsewhere, as, for example, in Poland. Developments in Czechoslovakia were then forced apace, especially by means of the communist-dominated factory groups and unions; the coalition was ended by the thoroughly organized Prague coup, and finally a Stalinist dictatorship was instituted.[70]

The Prague coup, for which the ground at least was prepared by a hysterically defensive reaction on the part of the Soviet Union, was a political folly of the first order insofar as Western Europe was concerned. Comparable to the foundation of the Socialist Unity Party two years earlier [which forced East German social democrats into a communist-dominated structure] and to the later Berlin blockade, the Prague coup became a psychologically pivotal event that led to the far-reaching isolation of the communists in Western Europe and destroyed all their postwar labors. More effectively than any American propaganda or pressure, the Prague coup cost the communists their credibility among their trade-union allies. The communist reaction to the announcement of the Marshall Plan made the noncommunist working class's adjustment to the political order entailed by American policies of economic restoration far easier. The reorientation began with the hitherto contained conflicts in the WFTU finally coming to a head and ending in schism. Then, according to the different balance of political forces from place to place, came the secession of the noncommunist unions (in France, Italy, Berlin) or the imposition of clear anti-communist limits by the predominantly social-democratic unions (in England and West Germany).[71]

The AFL, which had remained distant from the international union movement even in 1945 because of its uncompromising hostility to communism, abetted this process of secession by sending several missions to Europe with moral and material support. After early successes these initiatives for isolating the communists in the European unions—which complemented those of the Marshall Plan—won CIA support.[72] In France they certainly created the preconditions for the secession of the social-democratic Force Ouvrière but could hardly prevail upon the mass working-class base to switch loyalties. Nonetheless, the inner dynamic of the CGT was broken, especially since industrialists further sabotaged the union in the area of wage contracts. Even the proposal that businessmen negotiate with the noncommunist unions and thus leave the communists economically functionless corresponded to an American suggestion. What was left of the CGT, however, was too strong simply to be circumvented. The upshot of the tactics followed after the breakup of the united union was simply to weaken the entire French labor movement for more than a decade.[73]

In Western Germany the AFL was not content merely with strengthening a sympathetic union potential by sending CARE packages to tried-and-true officials, providing newsprint and money for anti-communist propaganda (e.g., for the Berlin UGO), and exerting influence on behalf of independent bread-and-butter unions. Above all the AFL was able to exert pressure on the American government so that it would no longer impede the reconstruction of union organizations at the bizonal or trizonal levels. For delay only weakened the position of the old union leadership vis-à-vis the integrated organization of the FDGB.[74]

This meant that major union officials faced an especially painful decision in view of the whole labor movement's (CDU members included) post-1945 commitment to all-German goals. Either they could discontinue organizing the unions at the new [West

German] levels of political decision-making; or, in cooperation with the occupying authorities, they have to accept the political order implicit in the move toward a West German state. With the collapse of the interzonal trade union conference over the issue of the Berlin UGO in mid-1948, priority would be given to developing a cartel of industrial unions in the three western zones rather than to the long-term goal of political, all-German organizational unity. Nonetheless, this meant more than just retaining the bird in the hand. Admittedly the provisional character of the Basic Law [the constitutional instrument of the Bonn Republic] made it easier to agree to a Western state and to renounce a constitutional framework that would have established the structural reforms inherent in the basic union demands. Nevertheless, the fact that the same concepts of Economic Democracy still shaped the DGB's platform of 1949 [75] demonstrated that despite all the constraints and defeats of the occupation period, union leaders still believed they could yet bring about the program of the united union. For now the unions were organized at the highest levels of the political order, and labor's claims could no longer be countered by military demands.

After the international union schism, the labor movement in most European countries went on the defensive for a good decade. In the period of Cold War reaction the collapse of the political united union made it possible not only for businessmen to play off the unions against each other, but also led to a smouldering crisis of function and identity among the competing unions, especially in France and Italy. The structural reforms of the postwar years were partially reversed (e.g., some of the British nationalizations), or completely changed their social function under conditions of capitalist restoration—as in the case, perhaps, of planning and control of investment in France. For most unions the given way to overcome this identity crisis was to resume an aggressive wage policy, whether with longer-term objectives of class conflict or social partnership, and this generally led to a relatively high level of pay within limited national rates of economic growth. (Where bourgeois monetary reform redisclosed structural unemployment as in Italy, even wage possibilities remained very limited.) At the same time, though, wide circles of workers and especially white-collar employees assimilated the values of efficient performance and consumption that characterized capitalist society. . . .

Notes

1. Horst Lademacher, *et al.,* will be publishing a long essay on the WFTU

in the 1978 *Archiv für Sozialgeschichte*. For now, see Julius Braunthal, *Geschichte der Internationale*, vol. 3 (Hanover, 1971), pp. 23ff., Hans Gottfurcht, *Die internationale Gewerkschaftsbewegung im Weltgeschehen* (Cologne, 1962), pp. 169ff.; W. Z. Foster, *Abriss der Geschichte der Weltgewerkschaftsbewegung von den Anfängen bis 1955* (Eâst Berlin, 1960), pp. 524ff., 593ff. Some important documentation in FDGB (Freier Deutscher Gewerkschaftsbund), ed., *Zwanzig Jahre Weltgewerkschaftsbund*, vol. I (East Berlin), 1965. For the Communist Party concept of the "antifascist-democratic" stage in Europe, cf. the survey in M. Einaudi, J.-M. Domenach, A. Garosci, *Communism in Western Europe* (Ithaca, N.Y., 1951); F. Claudin, *La crise du mouvement communiste*, vol. 2 (Paris, 1972), pp. 361ff.; F. Fejtö, *Geschichte der Volksdemokratien*, vol. 1 (Graz, 1972); E. Seeber, "Die volksdemokratischen Staaten Mittel- und Sudeuropas in der interationlen Klassenauseinandersetzung zwischen Imperialismus und Sozialismus (1944–1947)" in *Jahrbuch für Geschichte der sozialistischen Länder Europas*, vol. 16, 2 (1972), pp. 39ff.; W. Diepenthal, *Drei Volksdemokratien* (on Poland, Czechoslovakia, and East Germany, 1944–48), Cologne, 1974; and for country studies especially A. J. Rieber, *Stalin and the French Communist Party 1941–1947* (New York, 1962); A. Sywottek, *Deutsche Volksdemokratie* (Düsseldorf, 1971). Of documentary value for the German case: G. Mannschatz, J. Seider, *Zum Kampf der KPD im Ruhrgebiet für die Einigung der Arbeiterklasse und die Entmachtung der Monopolherren 1945–1947* (East Berlin, 1962); H. Laschitz, *Kämpferische Demokratie gegen Faschismus* (East Berlin, 1969).

2. On the results of structural reform, cf. the stock-taking in W. Weber, ed., *Gemeinwirtschaft in Westeuropa* (Göttingen, 1962); R. Krisam, *Die Beteiligung der Arbeitnehmer an der öffentlichen Gewalt* (Leiden, 1963); G. Leminsky, *Der Arbeitnehmereinfluss in englischen und französischen Unternehmen* (Cologne, 1965).

3. The economic history of the immediate postwar phase is still largely unresearched, and just reconstructing the statistical basis for this period of great fluctuations presents special difficulties. For a survey see M. M. Postan, *An Economic History of Western Europe 1945–1964* (London, 1967); for an American estimate of the political economy of Western Europe in 1945–46, Gabriel and Joyce Kolko, *The Limits of Power* (New York, 1972), pp. 146ff. For a basic model of reconstruction, F Jánossy, *Das Ende der Wirtschaftswunder* (Frankfurt, n.d. [1969]), and for the period at the end of the phase see the comparative analysis of labor force potential in Charles P. Kindleberger, *Europe's Postwar Growth* (Cambridge, Mass., 1967). The economic crisis at the end of the war concealed a largely preserved stock of industrial capital and a still highly qualified labor force, which could quickly bring high growth rates to all European countries. In the German case the expansion of the war economy, which exceeded the toll of destruction, was balanced out by the postwar immigration. The economic upswing was delayed because of a longer aftereffect of the postwar crisis (e.g., collapse of raw materials and intermediate product supplies, effects of the occupation regime); but it did not begin merely because of

liberalization and the Marshall Plan. Cf. W. Abelshauser, *Die Wachstums-bedingungen im britisch-amerikanischen Besatzungsgebiet 1945–1948* (Stuttgart, 1975); M. Manz, *Stagnation und Aufschwung in der französischen Besatzungszone von 1945 bis 1948* (Dissertation: Mannheim, 1968).

4. In this respect little has changed since Walter Ulbricht informed German Communist Party functionaries in East Berlin on June 25, 1945, that the "ideological devastation . . . has penetrated deep into the ranks of the working class." Walter Ulbricht, *Zur Geschichte der deutschen Arbeiterbewegung*, vol. 2 (East Berlin, 1963), p. 437. Justification of the coalition policy despite a "revolutionary wave in all of Europe," in Institut für Marxismus-Leninismus beim Zentralkommittee der Sozialistische Einheits Partei, ed., *Geschichte der deutschen Arbeiterbewegung*, (East Berlin, 1968), chap. 12, pp. 28ff.; Jean Duclos, et. al., *Histoire du Parti Communiste Francais (Manuel)* (Paris, 1964), pp. 439ff.

5. The policy of the U.S. armed forces in respect to the civilian population in the liberated areas is documented by H. L. Coles and A. K. Weinberg, *Civil Affairs: Soldiers Become Governors* (Washington, 1964). For contemporaries the British intervention in Greece had special impact. See Heinz Richter, *Griechenland zwischen Revolution und Konterrevolution (1936–1946)* (Frankfurt, 1973), pp. 495ff. On the American attitude to the European Left, Gabriel Kolko, *The Politics of War* (New York, 1970), pp. 31ff., 428ff. Even in 1946, the U.S. wanted to intervene militarily in France and Italy in case of a communist electoral victory or attempted coup: see J. and G. Kolko, *Limits of Power*, pp. 149f., 156f.

6. On union development in postwar Italy, B. Salvati, "The Rebirth of Italian Trade Unionism, 1943–1954," in S. J. Woolf, *The Rebirth of Italy, 1943–1950* (London, 1972), pp. 181ff.; D. Albers, "Von der Einheit zum Kampf um die Einheit," in *Das Argument* AS 2 (1974), pp. 120ff.; D. L. Horowitz, *The Italian Labor Movement* (Cambridge, Mass., 1963), pp. 181ff.; on the political connections the essays by Quazza and Catalano in Woolf, *Rebirth*, pp. 1ff., 57ff.; Braunthal, *Internationale*, vol. 3, pp. 69ff.; Federico Chabod, *Die Entstehung des neuen Italien* (Reinbek, 1965). On the resistance movement and the strikes of March 1943 in North Italy, R. Battaglia and G. Garritano, *Der italienische Widerstandskampf 1943 bis 1945* (East Berlin, 1970), pp. 16f.; Charles F. Delzell, *Mussolini's Enemies* (Princeton, 1961), pp. 207ff. On self-government in the liberated area there is only one pioneering study in German: H. Bergwitz, *Die Partisanenrepublik Ossola* (Hanover, 1972), pp. 64–66 on its unions.

7. E. Rosen, "Victor Emanuel III und die Innenpolitik des ersten Kabinetts Badoglio im Sommer 1943," in *Vierteljahrshefte für Zeitgeschichte* 12 (1964), pp. 44ff., especially 81ff. Text of the Buozzi-Mazzini agreement on factory councils in M. F. Neufeld, *Labor Unions and National Politics in Italian Industrial Plants* (Ithaca, N.Y., 1954), appendix A. For the German parallel, Fritz Tarnow, "Labor and Trade Unions in Germany," in *The Annals*, 260 (1948), pp. 90ff.: "Great eagerness to arrange a May 2nd in reverse and to take over the German Labor Front." (p. 92).

8. For the developments under German occupation in the North, see

Salvati, in Woolf, *Rebirth*, pp. 189ff.; for the Allied attitude in the South, C. R. S. Harris, *Allied Military Administration of Italy 1943–1945* (London, 1957), pp. 445ff.

9. Salvati, in Woolf, *Rebirth*, pp. 185ff.; Horowitz, *Italian Labor Movement*, pp. 186ff.; M. F. Neufeld, *Italy: School for Awakening Nations* (New York, 1961), pp. 451ff.

10. On Togliatti's *"svolta"* (his change from antifascist opposition to Badoglio to joining the royal government), cf. Delzell, *Mussolini's Enemies*, pp. 336ff.; Claudin, *La crise*, vol. 2, pp. 403ff. For the CP influence on the CGIL and the affiliated socialists, Braunthal, *Internationale*, pp. 79ff., and in detail in Horowitz, *Italian Labor Movement*, pp. 202ff., 244ff. Nationalization in Italy did not derive from communist influence, but rather was initiated by Mussolini, then De Gasperi, to protect the private economy by taking over firms threatened by the depression. Cf. R. Jochimsen, "Die öffentlichen bzw. öffentlich beherrschten Wirtschaftsunternehmen im Italian," in Weber, ed., *Gemeinwirtschaft*, pp. 229ff., esp. 245; and M. Einaudi et al., *Nationalization in France and Italy* (Ithaca, N.Y., 1955), pp. 196ff.

11. Marcello De Cecco, "Economic Policy in the Reconstruction Period, 1945–1951," in Woolf, *Rebirth of Italy*, pp. 156ff.

12. Salvati, in Woolf, *Rebirth*, pp. 189, 195ff. Admittedly agreement was reached on wage escalator clauses (Albers, in *Das Argument*, pp. 128ff.), and mass dismissals were prevented at first. Nonetheless, the pay level had barely reached the austere prewar levels when prices had already doubled.

13. Albers, in *Das Argument*, pp. 132ff.; Horowitz, *Italian Labor Movement*, pp. 208ff.

14. See note 1; also W. Goldschmidt, "Ökonomische und politische Aspekte des gewerkschaftlichen Kampfes in Frankreich seit dem Zweiten Weltkrieg," in *Das Argument*, AS 2 (1974); Val R. Lorwin, *The French Labor Movement* (Cambridge, Mass., 1966), pp. 99ff.; Georges Lefranc, *Le mouvement syndical de la libération aux événements de mai-juin 1968* (Paris, 1969), pp. 11–40; J. Bruhat, M. Piolot, *Aus der Geschichte der CGT* (East Berlin, 1961), pp. 169ff.; A. Barjonet, *La C.G.T.* (Paris, 1968). For communist policy, R. Tiersky, *Le mouvement communiste en France (1920–1972)* (Paris, 1973), pp. 94ff.; J. Fauvet, *Histoire du Parti Communiste Français*, vol. 2 (Paris, 1965), pp. 139ff., 159ff., and local studies such as P. Guiral, *Libération de Marseille* (Paris, 1974), pp. 111ff.; Etienne Dejonghe and D. Laurent, *Libération du Nord et du Pas de Calais* (Paris, 1974), pp. 157ff., 217ff. For the communist stance on purging the CGT of collaborationist socialists see Rieber, *Stalin and the French Communist Party*, pp. 177ff.; Peter Novick, *The Resistance versus Vichy* (New York, 1968), pp. 131ff.

15. Henry W. Ehrmann, *French Labor from Popular Front to Liberation* (New York, 1947); anon. *La C.F.D.T.* (Paris, 1971), pp. 32ff.; G. Adam, *La C.F.T.C. 1940–1958* (Paris, 1964), pp. 37ff.

16. Text in Lorwin, *French Labor Movement*, pp. 315ff.

17. Ehrmann, *French Labor*, pp. 262ff.

18. Program of the CNR and CGT proposals for it, in Henri Michel

and B. Mirkine-Guetzevitch, eds., *Les idées politiques et sociales de la Résistance* (Paris, 1954), pp. 199ff., 215ff. To the CGT proposal were appended communist and socialist amendments that indicated that the communists sought the renewal of the Popular Front's social legislation while the socialists wanted a large sphere of uncompensated nationalizations. On the CFTC attitude, Adam, *La C.F.T.C.*, pp. 93ff.; Lefranc, *Le mouvement syndical*, pp. 16ff. In addition, the CGT (like the German Federation) was impaired by the foundation of employee unions, especially the Confédération des Cadres. See H. Lange, *Wissenschaftlich-technische Intelligenz—Neue Bourgeoisie oder neue Arbeiterklasse?* (Cologne, 1972), pp. 113ff.

19. B. D. Graham, *The French Socialists and Tripartisme 1944–1947* (London, 1965), pp. 184ff.

20. On the nationalizations, H. Raidl, "Unternehmen und Institutionen der öffentlichen Wirtschaft in Frankreich," in Weber, ed., *Gemeinwirtschaft*, pp. 97ff.; M. Byé, "Nationalization in France," in Einaudi, ed., *Nationalization*, pp. 238ff.; a comparison with England in W. A. Robson, ed., *Problems of Nationalized Industry* (London, 1952), pp. 238ff. On participation, Leminsky, *Arbeitnehmereinfluss*, pp. 70ff.; P. Durand, *Die Beteiligung der Arbeitnehmer an der Gestaltung des wirtschaftlichen und sozialen Lebens in Frankreich* (Luxembourg, 1962). On planning and its transformation, P. Bauchet, *La planification française* (Paris, 1966).

21. On the PCF's campaign for production and on the strikes up to its dismissal from the government, Lefranc, *Le mouvement syndical*, pp. 29ff., 42ff.; Braunthal, *Internationale*, vol. 3, pp. 61–65; Lorwin, *The French Labor Movement*, pp. 105ff. Graham, *French Socialists*, pp. 252ff.; Rieber, *Stalin and the French Communist Party*, pp. 310ff., 347ff.; Duclos, *Parti Communiste (manuel)*, pp. 469ff.

22. On the schism and the preceding so-called Molotov strike, Lefranc, *Le mouvement syndical*, pp. 52ff.; Lorwin, *French Labor Movement*, pp. 119ff.; Barjonet, *C.G.T.*, pp. 49ff., who emphasizes CIA involvement in the formation of FO. From a syndicalist viewpoint, P. Monatte, *Trois Scissions syndicales* (Paris, 1958), pp. 176ff.; communist viewpoint in Duclos, *Manuel*, pp. 507ff.; and especially Bruhat and Piolot, *Geschichte der CGT*, pp. 193ff:; FO viewpoint itself in G. Vidalenc, *Die französische Gewerkschaftsbewegung* (Cologne, 1953), pp. 60ff.; A. Bergeron, *F.O.* (2nd ed.: Paris, 1972), pp. 24ff.

23. Braunthal, *Internationale*, vol. 3, pp. 24ff.; Henry Pelling, *The British Communist Party* (London, 1958).

24. See note 1 above.

25. On the influence of the labor movement on the government, H. Pelling, *A History of British Trade Unionism* (2nd ed.: Harmondsworth, 1971), pp. 210ff.; P. Oehlke, "Grundzüge der Entwicklung der britischen Gewerkschaftsbewegung," in *Das Argument* AS 2 (1974), pp. 65ff., esp. 91ff.; E. Bandholz, *Die englischen Gewerkschaften* (Cologne, 1961), pp. 41ff.; and on the two most important union leaders, W. Citrine, *Two Careers* (London, 1967), and Alan Bullock, *The Life and Times of Ernest Bevin*, vol. 2 (London, 1967).

26. P. E. P., ed., *British Trade Unionism* (London, 1948), pp. 5ff.; Tables also in Pelling, *Trade Unionism*, pp. 280ff.; cf. A. Villiger, *Aufbau und Verfassung der britischen und amerikanischen Gewerkschaften* (West Berlin, 1966), pp. 76ff., 105ff.

27. To avoid a wage freeze or similar government controls Bevin instituted compulsory arbitration for wage negotiations and prohibited strikes and lockouts with his Order 1305 of June 10, 1940. J. Lovell and B. C. Roberts, *A Short History of the T.U.C.* (London, 1968), pp. 146ff. On the institutions, P. E. P., *Trade Unionism*, pp. 35ff.; on resistance to the restraint policies of the government, Pelling, *Trade Unionism*, pp. 216f., 224ff.; Oehlke, "Grundzüge," p. 92.

28. For the government attempts to ease the balance of payments crisis, which led to a wage-freeze agreement with the TUC from 1948 to 1951, see G. A. Dorfman, *Wage Politics in Britain, 1945–1967* (London, 1974), esp. pp. 51ff.; criticism from the communist perspective in Oehlke, "Grundzüge," pp. 97ff.

29. Pelling, *Trade Unionism*, pp. 282f.

30. Among the discussions of British nationalization see: E. F. Schumacher, "Die Sozialisierung in Grossbritannien," in Weber, *Gemeinwirtschaft;* the survey in W. A. Robsen, ed., *Problems;* B. W. Lewis, *British Planning and Nationalization* (New York and London, 1952); D. Goldschmidt, *Stahl und Staat* (Stuttgart and Düsseldorf, 1956)—which also treats denationalization; and for a critique of the mixed economy from a Marxist perspective, B. A. Glynn and B. Sutcliffe, *British Capitalism, Workers and the Profits Squeeze* (Harmondsworth, 1972), pp. 162ff.

31. H. A. Clegg, *Industrial Democracy and Nationalization* (Oxford, 1955); for the opposition from within the unions, the opposed treatment of K. Coates and T. Topham, *The New Unionism—The Case for Workers' Control* (London, 1972), pp. 109ff.; Rudolf Kuda, *Arbeiterkontrolle in Grossbritannien* (Frankfurt, 1970), esp. pp. 139ff. Cf. Leminsky, *Arbeitnehmereinfluss*, pp. 21ff.; W. W. Haynes, *Nationalization in Practice: The British Coal Industry* (London, 1953), chap. 9ff.

32. G. Beier, "Einheitsgewerkschaft," in *Archiv für Sozialgeschichte*, 13 (1973), p. 230.

33. Admittedly many trade union leaders were politically persecuted by the Nazis, and one can demonstrate their general effort to keep in touch with each other, discussions about reconstruction plans for after fascism, and even individual acts of heroism. But neither an active mass resistance nor efforts at organizing a coup emanated from the labor movement. H. G. Schumann, *Nationalsozialismus und Gerwerkschaftsbewegung* (Hanover, 1958); H. Bednareck, *Gewerkschafter im Kampf gegen die Todfeinde der Arbeiterklasse und des deutschen Volkes 1933–1945* (East Berlin, 1966); H. Esters and H. Pelger, *Gewerkschafter im Widerstand* (Hanover, 1967); L. Reichhold, *Arbeiterbewegung jenseits des totalen Staates—Die Gewerkschaften und der 20. Juli 1944* (Cologne, Stuttgart, and Vienna, 1965).

34. Cf. Ulrich Borsdorf, "Der Weg zur Einheitsgewerkschaft," in J. Reulecke, ed., *Arbeiterbewegung an Rhein und Ruhr* (Wuppertal, 1974),

pp. 394ff., which also considers the temporary communist tactic of trying to penetrate the German Labor Front. Cf. note 7 and the essay by Hans Mommsen in the Reulecke volume.

35. On the foundation of the Berlin FDGB, J. Klein, *Vereint sind sie alles?* (Hamburg, 1972); Werner Conze, *Jakob Kaiser. Politiker zwischen Ost und West* (Stuttgart, 1969), pp. 11ff.; also K. Blank, *Beiträge zum innerdeutschen Gewerkschaftsdialog* (Bonn, 1971), vol. 1, pp. 15ff.; G. Griep and Ch. Steinbrecher, *Die Herausbildung des Freien Deutschen Gewerkschaftsbundes* (East Berlin, 1968); K. Fugger, *Geschichte der deutschen Gewerkschaftsbewegung* (East Berlin, 1949; reprinted West Berlin, 1971), pp. 251ff. The significance of the CGT in the formation of the Comintern and for the German Communist Party concept of the trade unions is stressed by H. Bednareck, *Die Gewerkschaftspolitik der KPD 1935–1939* (East Berlin, 1969), pp. 121ff.; experiences of the other Communist parties (especially the Italian) after 1943 as they influenced the Central Committee of the KPD in Laschitza, *Kämpferische Demokratie*, p. 125. Cf. note 37.

36. Klein, *Vereint sind sie alles?*, pp. 108ff.; Borsdorf, "Weg zur Einheitsgewerkschaft," p. 398.

37. On the National Committee for a Free Germany in the West and on the German-language groups in the CGT, see Klein, pp. 11ff,; K. Pech, *An der Seite der Résistance* (Frankfurt, 1974), pp. 263ff.; H. Duhnke, *Die KPD von 1933 bis 1945* (Cologne, 1972), pp. 407ff.; on the cooperation of the OSS Labor Desk in London with the International Federation of Trade Unions (IGB), see P. H. Smith, *OSS* (Berkeley, 1972), pp. 204ff.

38. On the formation of the unions within the limits set by the occupying powers, see the Beier, Klein, Conze, Borsdorf titles above and: B. A. Enderle and B. Heise, *Die Einheitsgewerkschaften,* 3 vols., mimeographed (but not edited) by the DGB (Düsseldorf, 1959); Eberhard Schmidt, *Die verhinderte Neuordnung 1945–1952* (Frankfurt, 1970); U. Schmidt and T. Fichter, *Der erzwungene Kapitalismus* (West Berlin, 1971); J. Kolb, *Metallgewerkschaften in der Nachkriegszeit* (Frankfurt, 1970), and regional studies such as F. Hartmann, *Geschichte der Gewerkschaftsbewegung nach 1945 in Niedersachsen* (Hanover, 1972); P. Brandt, "Antifaschistische Einheitsbewegung. Parteien und Gewerkschaften," (dissertation, Berlin, 1972) and now published as *Antifaschismus und Arbeiterbewegung* (Hamburg: Christians, 1976); H. Christier, *Die Hamburger Arbeiterbewegung 1945–1949* (dissertation, Hamburg, 1974); and such union accounts as I. G. Metall, eds., *75 Jahre Industriegewerkschaft 1891–1966* (Frankfurt, 1966); K. Anders, *Stein für Stein* (Frankfurt, 1969); Hans Mommsen et al., *Bergarbeiter* (exhibit catalogue, Bochum, 1969), pp. 32ff.; DGB Landesbezirk Berlin, ed., *Berliner Gewerkschaftsgeschichte von 1945–1950* (Berlin, 1971). Not generally realized is that the French government—supported at home by communists and socialists—began its policy of obstructing all-German union development in the ninth session of the Allied Control Council on October 20, 1945, in opposition to the wishes of the other three powers. See *Foreign Relations of the United States*, 1945, III, 846–852.

39. G. Beier, *Probleme der Gründung und des Aufbaus westdeutscher Gewerkschaften unter dem Primat der Aussenpolitik* (Kronberg, 1972); also R. Radosh, *American Labor and United States Foreign Policy* (New York, 1969), pp. 325ff., and G. S. Wheeler, *Die amerikanische Deutschlandspolitik* (East Berlin, 1958), part 2. For the relations of the WFTU to Germany see the survey from the FDGB perspective in A. Behrendt, *Der Weltgewerkschaftsbund und die deutschen Gewerkschaften* (East Berlin, n.d. [1965]), chaps. 2–6.

40. Cf. th. R. Fisher, "Allied Military Government in Italy," in *The Annals*, 267 (1950), pp. 114ff., especially 117ff.

41. A few exceptions such as Kurt Schumacher aside, most of the activity of the labor movement in the days after liberation or surrender consisted of forming non-party Action Committees and unions, or preliminary factory councils and shop-steward movements, since unity in these areas seemed undisputed. (See notes 43 and 58.) Furthermore the American military government attitude, which allowed union but not political activity, made union work all the more significant. On union policies see Klein, *Vereint sind sie alles?*, pp. 135ff.; and for the licensing of political activity, Lutz Niethammer, *Entnazifierung in Bayern* (Frankfurt/M., 1972), pp. 126ff., 198ff.

42. Many examples of this in Brandt, *Antifaschismus;* Hartmann, *Gewerkschaftsbewegung;* Klein, *Vereint sind sie alles?;* and E. Schmidt, *Verhinderte Neuordnung.*

43. On the Action Committees, Niethammer, *Entnazifierung,* pp. 124ff.; Brandt, *Antifaschismus;* Hartmann, *Gewerkschaftsbewegung;* and Walter L. Dorn, *Inspektionsreisen in der U.S.-Zone,* L. Niethammer, tran. (Stuttgart, 1973), pp. 34ff. The difference from the radicalism of many partisan movements is perhaps clearest by comparison with the Greeks: see D. Eudes, *Les Kapitanios* (Paris, 1970). See also the documentary collection of Borsdorf, Brandt, Niethammer, *Arbeiterinitiative 1945* (Wuppertal, 1976).

44. U. Schmidt and Fichter used this subtitle (for *Der erzwungene Kapitalismus*) to suggest a radical potential. On the unions, G. Beier, "Zum Einfluss der Gewerkschaften," p. 40, I believe, also errs in overemphasizing the unions as "the strongest power in the interregnum."

45. On this combination in Ruhr in 1947 see E. Potthoff, *Der Kampf um die Montanmitbestimmung* (Cologne, 1957), pp. 34ff.; E. Schmidt, *Verhinderte Neuordnung,* pp. 75ff., 134ff.; Schmidt and Fichter, *Der erzwungene Kapitalismus,* pp. 23ff.; F. Deppe et al., *Kritik der Mitbestimmung* (Frankfurt, 1969), pp. 58ff.; Mommsen et al., *Bergarbeiter,* chap. 36ff.; Peter Hüttenberger, *Nordrhein-Westfalen und die Entstehung seiner parlamentarischen Demokratie* (Siegburg, 1973), pp. 410ff.; John Gimbel, *Amerikanische Besatzungspolitik in Deutschland 1945–1949* (Frankfurt, 1971), pp. 159ff., 225ff.; Mannschatz and Seider, *Zum Kampf der KPD,* pp. 195ff.; R. Badstübner, *Restauration in Westdeutschland 1945–1949* (East Berlin, 1965), pp. 233ff.

46. "Capitalism is at its last gasp," Hans Böckler, for example, declared in 1946 (E. Schmidt, *Verhinderte Neuordnung,* p. 68).

47. Said at the Nuremberg Party Congress of the SPD in 1947 (Beier, *Probleme der Gründung,* p. 43): the expression referred most immediately to acceptance of the Marshall Plan but still describes prior party practice.

48. On the further development of the tradition of Economic Democracy among the unions and the SPD see E. Schmidt, *Verhinderte Neuordnung,* pp. 61ff.; H. P. Ehni, "Sozialistische Neubauforderung und Proklamation des 'Dritten Wegs,' " in *Archiv für Sozialgeschichte,* 13 (1973), pp. 131ff.; R. Blum, *Soziale Marktwirtschaft* (Tübingen, 1969), pp. 13ff.; W. Weddingen, ed., *Untersuchungen zur sozialen Gestaltung der Wirtschaftsordnung* (West Berlin, 1950).

49. Cf. note 35. Like the CGIL and the united CGT, the FDGB was constructed from a central executive for the entire Soviet zone of occupation. West German union leaders were forced to renounce this model and work on the regional level by their occupation authorities.

50. E. Schmidt, *Verhinderte Neuordnung,* pp. 120ff.; Mommsen et al., *Bergarbeiter,* chaps. 35 and 38.

51. T. Fichter and E. Eberle, *Kampf um Bosch* (West Berlin, 1974), pp. 26ff. Similiar dissident communist criticism is found in U. Schmidt and Fichter, *Der erzwungene Kapitalismus,* pp. 43ff.; E. U. Huster et al., *Determinanten der westdeutschen Restauration 1945–1949* (Frankfurt, 1972), pp. 175ff. Since this chapter was written a new book on these strikes has appeared: Christoph Klessmann and Peter Friedemann, *Streiks und Hungermarsche im Ruhrgebiet 1946–1948* (Frankfurt and New York, 1977).

52. Only two polemically edited documentary collections are now available on this matter: A. Behrendt, *Die Interzonenkonferenzen der deutschen Gewerkschaften* (East Berlin, 2nd ed., 1960); DGB-Bundesvorstand, ed., Versprochen-gebrochen. *Die Interzonenkonferenz der deutschen Gewerkschaften von 1946–1948* (Düsseldorf, n.d. [1961]). Communist willingness to compromise was expressed in the willingness to keep the Marshall Plan issue out of the WFTU.

53. TUC, ed., *Die unabhängigen Gewerkschaften verlassen den Weltgewerkschaftsbund* (London, 1949).

54. J. and G. Kolko, *Limits of Power,* chap. 12; for the unions see also note 39.

55. This is suggested by G. S. Wheeler, *Politik mit dem Dollar* (East Berlin, 1958), an edition of parts I and II of Wheeler, *Amerikanische Politik,* published by the FDGB.

56. Radosh, *American Labor and U.S. Foreign Policy,* pp. 316ff.

57. Klein, *Vereint sind sie alles?,* pp. 192ff.; Christier, *Hamburger Arbeiterbewegung,* pp. 103ff.

58. This willingness for unity is often interpreted one-sidedly as an innovation of a new class consciousness without its authoritarian and traditional elements being taken into account. Cf. F. Moraw, *Die Parole der 'Einheit' und die Sozialdemokratie* (Bonn, 1973), pp. 60ff.

59. See note 10 and 50; Lorwin, *French Labor Movement,* pp. 107ff.

60. See note 53; Gottfurcht, *Die internationale Gewerkschaftsbewegung,* pp. 185ff.

61. Radosh, *American Labor and U.S. Foreign Policy*, pp. 310ff., esp. 331ff.; J. Fijalkowski et al., *Berlin—Hauptstadtanspruch und Westintegration* (Cologne and Opladen, 1967), pp. 41ff.

62. The Italian example of this position is analyzed by De Cecco, "Economic Policy in the Reconstruction Period," in Woolf, *Rebirth,* pp. 160ff.; for the German western zones see Blum, *Soziale Marktwirtschaft*, pp. 38ff., 207ff., where the currency reform is seen as the high point of American liberalizing intervention. For the European complex of events, J. and G. Kolko, *Limits of Power*, pp. 428ff.

63. *Ibid.*, pp. 346ff.; for the Bizone, Abelshauser, *Die Wachstumsbedingungen*, pp. 212ff.

64. On Böckler's stance see Ulrich Borsdorff, "Hans Böckler—Repräsentant eines Jahrhunderts gewerkschaftlicher Politik," in H. O. Vetter, ed., *Vom Sozialistengesetz zur Mitbestimmung. Zum 100. Geburtstag von Hans Böckler* (Cologne, 1975). In general on the union stance, Beier, *Probleme der Gründung*, pp. 42ff,; E. Schmidt, *Verhinderte Neuordnung*, pp. 114ff.; Theodor Pirker, *Die blinde Macht* (2 vols.: Munich, 1960); V. Schmidt and Fichter, *Der erzwungene Kapitalismus*, pp. 37ff. That the political and economic problems of the western zones of Germany were the immediate spur to the Marshall Plan—and that the Americans developed the institutional models for carrying it out in Germany (JEIA, GARIOA)—is undisputed in the literature. See J. and G. Kolko, *Limits of Power*, pp. 349ff.; Gimbel, *Amerikanische Besatzungspolitik*, pp. 196ff., 216ff.; Hadley Arkes, *Bureaucracy, the Marshall Plan, and the National Interest* (Princeton, 1972), pp. 19ff.; J. H. Backer, *Priming the German Economy* (Durham, N.C., 1971), pp. 157ff.; A. Piettre, *L'économie allemande contemporaine* (Paris, n.d. [1952]), pp. 469ff. The most specific such argument is now in John Gimbel, *The Origins of the Marshall Plan* (Stanford, 1976).

65. That U.S. and West European economic stabilization was a motive is shown (besides by Kolko and Gimbel) by J. M. Jones, *The Fifteen Weeks* (New York, 1953), p. 205; H. B. Price, *The Marshall Plan and its Meaning* (Ithaca, 1955), pp. 29ff.; E.-O. Czempiel, *Das amerikanische Sicherheitssystem 1945–1949* (Berlin, 1966), part 3; Arkes, *Bureaucracy*, pp. 43ff., 153ff. In contrast, the anticommunist containment ideology, which grew more intense during the preparation of the aid program, both inside and outside the U.S., was geared more toward creating the public atmosphere and willingness to approve the funds. On this see, R. M. Freeland, *The Truman Doctrine and the Origins of McCarthyism* (New York, 1972).

66. Cf. note 71.

67. The best survey is in Gimbel, *Amerikanische Besatzungspolitik*, passim; for the economic aspect, Blum, *Marktwirtschaft*, pp. 182ff.; H.-H. Hartwich, *Sozialstaatspostulat und gesellschaftlicher status quo* (Cologne and Opladen, 1970), pp. 61ff.

68. Beier, *Probleme der Gründung*, pp. 33ff., 46ff.; also Beier, *"Gründung,"* pp. 47f. for specially clear examples. Documentary material also in Wheeler, *Politik mit dem Dollar*, passim.

69. For an overview, J. and G. Kolko, *Limits of Power*, pp. 361ff.; Her-

bert Feis, *From Trust to Terror* (New York, 1970), pp. 260ff.; Foster, *Abriss*, pp. 606ff.; Gottfurcht, *Die internationale Gewerkschaftsbewegung*, pp. 189ff.

70. Braunthal, *Internationale*, vol. 3, pp. 179ff.; J. and G. Kolko, *Limits of Power*, pp. 384ff.; Claudin, *La crise*, vol. 2, pp. 525ff. for surveys. For the end of the Czech coalition as connected to the collapse of the "third way" in France as a result of the Marshall Plan: R. Künstlinger, *Parteidiktatur oder demokratischer Sozialismus* (Starnberg, 1972), pp. 78ff.; also J. K. Hoensch, *Geschichte der Tschechoslovakischen Republik* (Stuttgart, 1966), pp. 136ff; as a purely internal revolution in the Czech people's own self-conception: Gewerkschaften Prace, ed., *Menschen, Arbeit, Gewerkschaften in der Tschechoslovakei* (Prague, 1959), pp. 55ff.; on the role of the unions, Diepenthal, *Drei Volksdemokratien*, pp. 122ff.

71. For the Italian schism, Salvati, in Woolf, *Rebirth*, pp. 201ff.; Horowitz, *Italian Labor Movement*, pp. 215ff.; in France, Lorwin, *French Labor Movement*, pp. 125ff.; Lefranc, *Le mouvement syndical*, pp. 65ff.; for Berlin, see note 61; for the collapse of the planned Interzonal Congress in Germany, E. Schmidt, *Verhinderte Neuordnung*, p. 118; Behrend, *Interzonenkonferenzen*, pp. 172ff.; cf. note 50. On the anticommunist campaign in the TUC, which was particularly disturbed by the communist agitation against its wage-freeze agreement, see Pelling, *Communist Party*, pp. 153ff.

72. Barjonet, *C.G.T.*, p. 51; Radosh, *American Labor and U.S. Foreign Policy*, p. 323.

73. Goldschmidt, "Ökonomische und politische Aspekte," pp. 22ff., Lefranc, *Le mouvement syndical*, pp. 77ff.

74. Besides Beier, "Probleme der Gründung," pp. 33ff., see the documentation of the Free Trade Union Committee of the AFL, ed., *Die A.F. of L. und die deutsche Arbeiterbewegung* (New York, 1950), and the contemporary critique of Viktor Agartz, *Gewerkschaft und Arbeiterklasse* (2nd ed.: Munich, 1973), pp. 97ff. ("Der Gewerkschaftliche Marshallplan").

75. For union leaders such as Böckler the connection between the Marshall Plan and the division of Germany was clear, but there is no treatment of the union stance during 1947–48 comparable to Hans Peter Schwarz, *Von Reich zur Bundesrepublik* (Neuwied and Berlin, 1966), pp. 299ff. and 483ff., who has analyzed Jakob Kaiser and Kurt Schumacher as representatives of the national labor movement forced into a decision between Marshall Plan and the communists. On the union policy in the constitutional debate see Beier, *Gründung*, pp. 53ff.; W. Sörgel, *Konsensus und Interessen* (Stuttgart, 1969), pp. 201–213.

Bibliographical Note

English-language publications have generally been cited in the Introduction to this volume, in my own essay reprinted here as chapter 1, and in the brief prefaces to the various selections. A few more works also merit citation: John W. Wheeler-Bennett and Anthony Nicholls, *The Semblance of Peace* (New York: St. Martin's Press, 1972); Lisle A. Rose, *Dubious Victory: The United States and the End of World War II,* vol. I of *The Coming of the American Age, 1945–1946* (Kent, Ohio: Kent State University Press, 1973); on historiography: Robert W. Tucker, *The Radical Left and American Foreign Policy* (Baltimore: Johns Hopkins Press, 1971). Robert James Maddox, *The New Left and the Origins of the Cold War* (Princeton: Princeton University Press, 1973) is in my opinion a flawed critique. On the uses made of history during the Cold War see Ernest May, *"Lessons" of the Past* (New York: Oxford University Press, 1973).

Special country studies could be cited at great length. I have not included a selection on Greece, where President Truman claimed to see a direct Soviet challenge but more likely misinterpreted a native communist uprising, provoked in part by British policies in 1944–45 and later encouraged by the Yugoslavs. The interested reader can turn to John Iatrides, *Revolt in Athens: The Greek Communist "Second-Round," 1944–1945* (Princeton: Princeton University Press, 1972). Iatrides is now carrying forward his research into the civil war of the 1946–48 period. Among the foreign-language studies of European countries in the Cold War period, students should be aware of Hans-Peter Schwarz, *Vom Reich zur Bundesrepublik. Deutschland im Widerstreit der aussenpolitischen Konzeptionen in den Jahren der Besatzungsherrschaft 1945–1949* (Neuwied and Berlin: Luchterhand, 1966), an authoritative effort to describe the revival of West German political life within the options left by great-power rivalry. Ernst Nolte's equally massive, *Deutschland und der Kalte Krieg* (Munich: Piper, 1974) is almost a philosophical reflection, provocative but idiosyncratic and taking its departure point more from the student revolt in the German Federal Republic than from the Cold War itself. Some Italian studies have already been cited; for a synthesis from the perspective of the Left see Franco Catalano, *Europa e Stati Uniti negli anni della guerra fredda. Economia e politica* (Milan, 1972). On the general conditions of Europe see Richard Mayne, *The Recovery of Europe 1945–73* (rev. ed., New York: Anchor Books, 1973).

I have not included a selection on the problem of nuclear weapon rivalry, but the student who wishes to explore this important area can well begin with Martin J. Sherwin, *A World Destroyed: The Atomic Bomb and the Grand Alliance* (New York: Knopf, 1975), and Barton J. Bernstein, "The Question for Security: American Foreign Policy and International Control of Atomic Energy, 1942–1946," *Journal of American History*, LX, 4 (March 1974), 1003–1044, or his "Roosevelt, Truman and the Atomic Bomb: A Reinterpretation," *Political Science Quarterly*, 90 (1975–76), 23–69.

References to social and economic issues in the Cold War era are available in the Niethammer piece above, Thomas Paterson's *Soviet-American Confrontation* (Baltimore, Md.: Johns Hopkins, 1973), and my own essay "The Politics of Productivity: Foundations of American International Economic Policy after World War II," *International Organization*, vol. XXXI (Fall 1977), published also as: Peter Katzenstein, ed., *Between Power and Plenty* (Madison: University of Wisconsin Press, 1978). Labor history for the period has become a specialty in itself and the student can best keep up with literature and documentation for this and earlier periods by following two journals: *Le Mouvement Social* and the IWK (*Internationale Wissenschaftliche Korrespondenz zur Geschichte der deutschen Arbeiterbewegung*). *Le Mouvement Social* has featured discussions of the great strikes and workers' protests of 1947–48. See also the annual *Archiv für Sozialgeschichte*, published by the Friedrich-Ebert Stiftung.

Other major journals that specialize in the contemporary era and the Cold War years include: *Revue d'Histoire de la Deuxième Guerre Mondiale* (with themes that spill over into the eary postwar years); *Revue d'Histoire Moderne et Contemporaine*, and *Rélations Internationales* (both covering a broad period); the *Journal of Contemporary History* (London); *Italia Contemporanea* (formerly *Il Movimento di Liberazione in Italia*)—see, especially, "Il secondo dopoguerra in Italia: orientamenti della storiografia," no. 116 (July–Sept. 1974), 3–96; and *Storia Contemporanea*—with occasional important contributions to the period in *Il Mulino* and *Studi Storici*. The Munich Institut für Zeitgeschichte, which specializes in German history and documentation for the era since 1933, publishes the important *Vierteljahrshefte für Zeitgeschichte*. For ongoing United States contributions and bibliography check the *Journal of American History* and also *Diplomatic History* (along with the *Newsletter* of the Society for Historians of American Foreign Relations).

Primary Source Material: While archival investigation is essential for publishable work, students have the opportunity for exciting and genuinely fruitful research in published documentation. The United States Department of

State's *Foreign Relations of the United States* is edited at a stately pace and volumes presently extend up to 1949 and 1950. Those who have worked with both the printed *FRUS* and the State Department files on which they are based testify to the fairness and cogency of the selections made for publication. The underlying files are ordinarily closed for research until the corresponding volumes are published, hence the *FRUS* material is new; and even the volumes of earlier years offer much that has not been systematically thought about and written on. Within each year's issue of documentation, the first volume or two takes up U.N. or security issues and is followed by regional and country collections. For the period during and after World War II, materials on the major international conferences and the postwar Council of Foreign Ministers have been assembled in special volumes. After the publication of upcoming volumes, the State Department will switch to a three-year format so that documents of the 1950's will be selected and published in triennial units. This may diminish coverage and slow up release of the files for the years involved.

No other country currently offers an equivalent series for the post-1945 era, although the British, French, or Russians occasionally publish special collections of documentation relating to treaties and other international matters. As noted above, British cabinet papers, including summaries of cabinet meetings and special papers or studies made for cabinet consideration, are opened up through the last calendar year less thirty. French Foreign Office archives (the Quai d'Orsay) appear to be generally inaccessible for the post-1945 era, but some of the other ministerial collections may slowly be opening up for advanced students. The West German archives for the period of the Occupation reveal the faltering rebirth of political debate within very circumscribed limits. The various files collected at the Federal Archive in Koblenz require permission from the later ministries of the Federal Republic that inherited their functions. The student interested in the German situation in the Cold War can valuably consult the continuing series: *Akten zur Vorgeschichte der Bundesrepublik Deutschland 1945–1949,* issued by the Bundesarchiv and the Institut für Zeitgeschichte and published by R. Oldenbourg in Munich.

Legislative debate can often be frustratingly wordy and imprecise. Still, the student can find important rationales for policy in the U.S. *Congressional Record* and *Hansard's Parliamentary Debates.* The then-important Senate Foreign Relations Committee has also published a Historical Series (1973) of *Hearings Held in Executive Session* on important bills: *Foreign Relief Aid: 1947. Hearings . . . on S. 1774.* 80th Congress, 1st Sess., 1947; *Foreign Relief Assistance Act of 1948. Hearings . . .* 80th Congress, 2nd Sess., 1948; *Legislative Origins of the Truman Doctrine. Hearings . . . on S. 938.* 80th Congress, 1st Sess., 1947; *The Vandenburg Resolution and the North Atlantic Treaty. Hearings . . . on S. Res. 239 and on Executive L.* 80th Congress, 2nd Sess., 1948 and 81st Congress, 1st Sess., 1949.

Major repositories in the United States for unpublished collections include: the National Archives in Washington (with the State Department papers up through the publication date of FRUS) and the Modern Military

Records; the Federal Records Center in Suitlands, Md. (contiguous to Washington) with embassy files and the massive OMGUS papers; the Library of Congress; the Franklin D. Roosevelt Presidential Library at Hyde Park, N.Y.; the Harry S. Truman Presidential Library in Independence, Mo., all with important personal Manuscript collections, and in the case of the Presidential Libraries with the diverse official White House files as well. Princeton University houses the massive James Forrestal diary and papers as well as the John Foster Dulles papers and the partially accessible George Kennan collection.

Published memoirs abound but must, of course, be used with caution. As a beginning, students might consult the following: Dean Acheson, *Present at the Creation. My Years in the State Department* (New York: Norton, 1970)—superbly styled and self-assured and, in a way, representative of two whole Yale University generations of believers in beneficent American power; Konrad Adenauer, *Memoirs 1945–1953*. Beata Ruhm von Oppen, trans. (Chicago: Henry Regnery, 1965); James F. Byrnes, *Speaking Frankly* (New York: Harper & Row, 1947); Lucius D. Clay, *Decision in Germany* (Garden City: Doubleday, 1950)—see the note to the papers below: Milovan Djilas, *Conversations with Stalin,* Michael Petrovich, trans. (London: Pelican Books, 1969); W. Averell Harriman and Elie Abel, *Special Envoy to Churchill and Stalin, 1941–1946* (New York: Random House, 1975); George Kennan, *Memoirs 1925–50* and *Memoirs 1950–63* (Boston: Little, Brown, 1967, 1972); Paul-Henri Spaak, *The Continuing Battle: Memoirs of a European,* Henry Fox, trans. (Boston: Little, Brown, 1972); Harry S. Truman, *Memoirs:* vol. I, *Year of Decisions,* and vol. II, *Years of Trial and Hope* (Garden City: Doubleday, 1955, 1956).

More rewarding than the memoirs are certain journals and diaries, especially John Morton Blum's edition *From the Morgenthau Diaries,* of which vol. III, *Years of War, 1941–1945* (Boston: Houghton Mifflin, 1967) introduces postwar problems; also Blum's edition, *The Price of Vision: The Dairy of Henry A. Wallace* (Boston: Houghton Mifflin, 1973); David Lilienthal's *Journals. The Atomic Energy Years 1945–50;* Jean Edward Smith's edition of *The Papers of General Lucius D. Clay: Germany, 1945–49,* 2 vols. (Bloomington: The Indiana University Press, 1974). Former French President Vincent Auriol's *Journal du Septennat 1947–1954,* Pierre Nora and Jacques Ozouf, eds., 7 vols. (Paris: Armand Colin, 1970–) has a wealth of material on French politics during the height of the Cold War in Europe.

Index

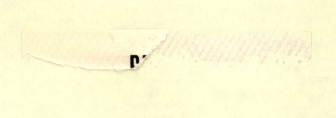